BEHAVIOR BELONGS IN THE BRAIN

NEUROBEHAVIORAL SYNDROMES

Edited by Pasquale J. Accardo,
Bruce K. Shapiro, and
Arnold J. Capute

YORK
PRESS Baltimore

This book was manufactured in the United States of America.
Typography by The Type Shoppe, Inc.
Printing and binding by BookCrafters
Cover design by Joseph Dieter, Jr.
Book design by Sheila Stoneham

Library of Congress Cataloging-In-Publication Data
Behavior belongs in the brain : neurobehavioral syndromes / edited by
    Pasquale J. Accardo, Bruce K. Shapiro, and Arnold J. Capute.
        p.   cm.
    Includes bibliographical references and index.
    ISBN 0-912752-41-6 (pbk.)
    1. Pediatric neuropsychiatry. 2. Neurobehavioral disorders.
3. Autism in children. 4. Prenatal influences. I. Accardo,
Pasquale J. II. Shapiro, Bruce K. III. Capute, Arnold J., 1923-

    [DNLM: 1. Child Behavior Disorders--etiology. 2. Brain-
-physiopathology. 3. Autism, Infantile. 4. Maternal-Fetal
Exchange. WS 350.6B4173   1997]
RJ486.5.B44   1997
618.92'89--dc21
DNLM/DLC   96-54476
For Library of Congress   CIP

Contents

Contributors

Pasquale Accardo, M.D.
Westchester Institute for
Human Development
Cedarwood Hall
New York Medical College
Valhalla, New York 10595

Margaret L. Bauman, M. D.
Harvard Medical School
Brookline, Massachusetts

Michael Bender, Ed.D.
Kennedy Krieger Institute
1750 East Fairmount Avenue
Baltimore, Maryland 21231

Ira J. Chasnoff, M.D.
National Association for
Families and Addiction
Research and Education
200 North Michigan Avenue
Suite 300
Chicago, Illinois 60601

Claudia A. Chiriboga, M.D., M. P. H.
Division of Pediatric Neurology
Department of Neurology
College of Physicians and
Surgeons
Columbia University
Neurological Institute
710 West 168th Street
New York, New York, 10032

Michelle Dunn, Ph. D.
Saul R. Korey Department of
Neurology and Rose F.
Kennedy Center for Research
in Mental Retardation and
Human Development
Albert Einstein College of
Medicine
Bronx, New York 10461

Nancy J. Minshew, M.D.
Western Psychiatric Institute
and Clinic
3811 O'Hara Street
Bellefield Towers, Suite 430
Pittsburgh, Pennsylvania 15213

Isabelle Rapin, M.D.
Saul R. Korey Department of
Neurology
Department of Pediatrics
Rose F. Kennedy Center for
Research in Mental
Retardation and Human
Development
Albert Einstein College of
Medicine
Kennedy Building 807
1410 Pelham Parkway South
Bronx, New York 10461

Peter B. Rosenberger, M.D.
Learning Disorders Unit
WHP 7-106
Massachusetts General Hospital
Boston, Massachusetts 02114

Renee C. Wachtel, M.D.
University of Maryland School
of Medicine
Walter P. Carter Center
630 West Fayette Street,
Room 5-866
Baltimore, Maryland 21201

Preface

When Dr. Arnold J. Capute selected the title *Behavior Belongs in the Brain* as the theme for the seventeenth annual Spectrum in Developmental Disabilities course held at the Johns Hopkins Medical Institutions in Baltimore, Maryland, March 27 through March 29, 1995, he did so with a certain degree of conceptual aggressiveness that, in fact, had the unfortunate results of alienating a number of the speakers who considered his emphasis misplacead, if not downright objectionable. The purpose of this preface is to clarify that misunderstanding.

In considering the title *Behavior Belongs in the Brain*, it would be well to analyze the separate components. Most professionals and lay people have a clear and adequate understanding of the *brain*. In those organisms whose level of complexity entails a hierarchical structure to their nervous systems, the brain represents the usually centrally located organ of executive function. The large and rapidly growing body of neuroscience literature contributes to the impression that we know a vast amount about how the brain works while the presence of significant gaps is often quietly glossed over. Nevertheless, for all practical purposes the brain is both defined and located.

If we are relatively familiar with the nature of the *brain*, this is not the case with *behavior*. Despite the fact that everyone knows what behavior is, there exists no generally accepted definition of behavior. Indeed, it remains doubtful that a scientifically acceptable definition for this nebulous concept will ever be achieved. The approach of behavioral psychology to consider only specific definable behaviors rather than "behavior" as a whole is a laudable but ultimately ineffective corrective to this intuitive deficiency.

If consideration of *behavior* has left us somewhat perplexed, *belongs* will only more thoroughly confuse the issue. Is behavior, however poorly defined, the possession of the brain? If not, then what can be meant by belongs?

Could Dr. Capute have intended to identify the brain as the sole source of behavior? This would be a rather simplistic notion. Certainly the brain is an absolute prerequisite for anything that we would call behavior in higher primates, so that its necessity can be assumed, but in what manner, other than as a required substrate, can the brain be said to determine behavior?

Some degree of clarification might be achieved if we consider the alternatives to the brain as an exclusive determinant to behavior. Further refinement of our focus will also be achieved if we narrow in on the more isolated case of the infant brain and infant behavior. Infant behavior must derive either from within the infant (with its executive organ, the brain), from outside the infant (the environment) or from the interaction between the two. For infants, the last two choices can be conveniently lumped together in the person of the individual who, for all practical purposes, is both the infant's environment and the principal source of all interactions—the mother. It should be readily apparent to the reader that we have here a reincarnation of the old nature/nurture debate, not necessarily in the form of genetics versus learned behavior, but in a more delimited form that attempts to discriminate those delays and deviations in behavior that stem from adverse influences on brain structure and chemistry from those that are interactionally mediated. The former are often, but not always, genetic in origin.

One of the greatest boons that neuroscience will be able to offer parents in the coming decades will be just such a clearer delineation of which behaviors are not the result of poor mothering. Problems that exist with the mother or with mother/child interactions are generally blamed on the mother, her psychological make up, if not her psychopathology, her family dynamics, or her inadequate education in and learning of appropriate child-rearing techniques. Parents today are bombarded with parenting advice and expectations that, quite simply, are beyond anyone's competence. The raising of children is depicted as a venture fraught with insurmountable dangers and generally beyond any individual family's abilities and resources without the support of an army of professionals, both medical and nonmedical.

Many of the behavioral conditions that are used as proof of parental, and especially maternal, incompetence represent neurobehavioral syndromes (O'Brien and Yule 1995). To best manage and understand such conditions, some professional support may very well be indicated, however, this support will be most effective when it is grafted onto a basic presumption of parental competence.

If the advances in neuroscience do not contribute to relieving the burden on families by eradicating many of the misconceptions in the literature on child rearing, then a golden opportunity will have been missed. It will be only too easy to interpret the evolving scientific data within the older paradigm that has as its major premise, "always blame the mother" (Eyer 1992). Such willful blinding has been successfully accomplished in scientific circles for at least the past half century.

As child neurology begins to merge with developmental pediatrics to produce the new field of neurodevelopmental disabilities in pediatrics and child neurology (Capute and Accardo 1992), a weakening, if not an eradication, of this pernicious doctrine would represent an excellent introduction into the next millennium. It would also go a long way toward justifying the vast research expenditure in this decade of the brain.

Pasquale Accardo, M.D.
Westchester Institute for Human Development
Valhalla, New York

Capute, A. J., and Accardo, P. J. 1992. Neurodevelopmental disabilities in pediatrics. *Journal of Child Neurology* 7:315–20.
Eyer, D. E. 1992. *Mother-Infant Bonding: A Scientific Fiction*. New Haven, CT: Yale University Press.
O'Brien, G., and Yule, W. 1995. *Behavioral Phenotypes, Clinics in Developmental Medicine*, Number 130. London: MacKeith Press.

Part • 1

Behavior and the Brain

Chapter • 1

The "Expanded" Strauss Syndrome

Pasquale Accardo

"Everything that arises from the brain must converge"
                                                        not Flannery O'Connor

Almost a quarter of a century ago, Paul Wender (1971) observed that the fact that minimal brain dysfunction (MBD) "occurs in conjunction with—and *possibly* as the basis of—*virtually* all nosological categories of childhood behavior disturbances is embarrassing but true" (p. 31). This peculiarly extensive MBD syndrome evolved from the earlier work of Alfred A. Strauss (1897–1957) on what he had referred to as the "brain-injured child syndrome." The road from the brain-injured child through minimal brain dysfunction (MBD) to attention deficit hyperactivity disorder and other entities has been long and complicated. Several years ago, Capute (1991) argued for a fundamentalist return to what he called an "expanded Strauss syndrome." In point of fact, there is no expanded Strauss syndrome: the original clinical description covers the entire spectrum of brain-damage symptoms in children. It was only the offshoot syndromes, the historical descendants, that attempted to narrow the focus and restricted the application of Strauss's original conceptualization. To better place this evolution in context, the present chapter will briefly review the life and work of Alfred A. Strauss (Cruickshank and Hallahan 1981).

EARLY CAREER

Strauss was born on May 29, 1897 in Karlsruhe, Germany. In 1922 at the age of 25 he obtained his medical degree from the University of Heidelberg. For the next five years he completed training there in neurology and psychiatry. In 1924 he served as an assistant to Dr. Kurt Goldstein at Frankfort. Goldstein had pioneered in the description of "traumatic dements" in his studies of soldiers who had suffered significant head injuries in World War I. The clinical behavioral picture of these brain-damaged adults included figure-background confusion, forced responsiveness to stimuli, meticulosity, perseveration, concrete behavior, and catastrophic behavior. While there existed more specific functional deficit patterns that could be attributed to the localized areas of brain that had been injured, the most "generalized disturbance" seen in these traumatic dements was interpreted as being independent of any specific localization for the brain-damage.

From 1927 to 1930 Strauss was a research associate at Heidelberg. From 1930 to 1933 he served as the head of the Neuropsychiatric Polyclinic in Heidelberg where he also worked in close collaboration with a variety of facilities for special children. From 1932 on he began to focus more exclusively on the area of rehabilitation in the field of mental retardation. Over the next decade he expressed an increasing frustration with the paucity of contributions from the field of neurology to the understanding of mental retardation. Developmental problems were organically invisible, and the neurological identification of the "organism" with the "adult organism" continued to be assumed. Then, as now, children quite simply got the short end of the stick.

With the rise of Adolf Hitler, Strauss fled Germany for Spain in 1933. There he became one of the founders of the child guidance movement in that country. In 1936 the outbreak of the Spanish Civil War forced him to again emigrate, first to Switzerland, then to England, and finally to the United States where in 1937 he took a position as chief research psychiatrist at the Wayne County State Training School in Northville, Michigan. He was soon joined there by another refugee from Hitler's Germany, the gestalt psychologist Heinz Werner (1890–1964). Throughout the next two decades this research pair collaborated in landmark attempts to delineate the quantitative and qualitative behavioral characteristics that distinguish brain-damage in children (Werner 1948). This combination of gestalt concepts with brain localization data later formed the basis for the modularity concept and the theory of multiple intelligences discussed by Rosenberger (Chapter 2, this volume).

The major additions that Strauss made to Goldstein's original listing of symptoms observed in adults with traumatic brain injury included hyperactivity, distractibility, disinhibition, and a tendency to make far-fetched, uncommon, and peculiar, if not fantastic, verbal and causal associations on object sorting tests. (These latter findings bear a striking resemblance to Rapin's [Chapter 6, this volume] semantic deficits in autism: atypical organization of the lexicon, unusual word choices, and chaining association by word sounds rather than by word meanings.) Children with this brain damage syndrome were understood to be "early traumatic dements." This was a direct recognition of Goldstein's seminal influence.

THE BRAIN-INJURED CHILD

Strauss was convinced that successful education, habilitation, and rehabilitation for brain-damaged children would be strongly dependent on distinguishing those children with a loss of intellectual capacity secondary to exogenous mental retardation, due to brain-damage, from those children with endogenous mental retardation secondary to a congenital lack of intellectual ability. He came to view a clearer understanding of the neurological substrate to selected cases of mental retardation as a necessary prerequisite to and an essential component of educational planning.

Strauss started from the clinical hypothesis that children with both mental retardation and cerebral palsy would generally be accepted as having a brain-damage etiology for their developmental diagnoses. He then attempted to separate those perceptual, cognitive, and behavioral characteristics that could not be directly attributed to either cognitive limitations associated with mental retardation or motor limitations associated with cerebral palsy. The resulting neurobehavioral syndrome would still occur in children with cerebral palsy and mental retardation but with several qualifications: (1) the motor involvement in cerebral palsy could be expected to mitigate the expression of any behavioral symptoms, and (2) in mental retardation the behavioral symptoms would be more prominent in that subgroup of children who had experienced brain-damage, while they would be less obvious to absent in that subgroup of mentally retarded children who were delayed on a genetic basis or who were otherwise assumed to be without any underlying brain-damage. (3) The neurobehavioral characteristics peculiar to brain-damage were also expected to be more prominent in children with severer degrees of mental retardation rather than in those cases with mild retardation.

In an interpretation well ahead of his time, Strauss also predicted that most of the symptoms of this brain-damage syndrome would be at their extreme in cases of infantile autism.

What came to be called the "Strauss syndrome" or the "brain-damaged child syndrome" included the following symptoms:

hyperactivity,
distractibility,
disinhibition,
verbal and causal associations that were far-fetched, peculiar
    and fantastic,
figure-ground confusion,
forced responsiveness to stimuli,
meticulosity,
perseveration,
concrete behavior, and
catastrophic behavior.

It is important to note that this syndrome combines behavioral pathology with both perceptual and conceptual difficulties. In modern terminology, it would be said to encompass both attention deficit hyperactivity disorder and learning disability as well as other associated central nervous system impairments along the spectrum of developmental disabilities. Strauss's analysis of the component symptoms helped to define much later understanding of these and related syndromes.

BEHAVIORAL SYMPTOMS OF DAMAGE

The brain-damaged child with disinhibition rushes in with responses that are not adequate to the situation, responses that a normal child readily inhibits because they are instantly recognized as inappropriate to the situation. Today we might refer to this "disinhibition" as impulsivity, or with Denckla (1995) as intention-inhibition disorder.

Distractibility secondary to brain-damage had two peculiar aspects for Strauss: (1) The associated forced responsiveness to stimuli could interact with the distractibility so that rather than not responding to a stimulus, the child with brain-damage would demonstrate undue fixation on some irrelevant stimulus detail. In other words, some distractibility would present as overfixation and a prolonged attentional focus. Thus long attention span as well as short attention span might equally well reflect the presence of brain-damage. (2) Children with distractibility can exhibit figure-ground perceptual discrimination problems; this again contributes further to their selecting the wrong stimulus detail on which to focus.

Strauss pioneered in the use of stimulus reduced environments to help educate the brain-injured child. Not only did he recommend cubicles with bare walls, but he went as far as to advise the classroom teachers to wear clothes with plain colors rather than distracting patterns and to avoid the use of jewelry and other decorative accessories. Bright colors and other means to set off the subject material to be learned were to be used as parts of a controlled multisensory approach to teaching the child with brain-damage. Despite his emphasis on structure, Strauss also warned against any early overreliance on rote memory.

In his development of individual educational intervention programs for children, Strauss placed himself squarely in the main line of historical development alongside those other physicians who contributed significantly to the development of the field of special education. He completed the list that began in the nineteenth century with Jean Marc Gaspard Itard (1775–1838), Edouard Onesimus Seguin (1812–1880), and Maria Montessori (1870–1952). In the introductory chapter to his first volume (Strauss and Lehtinen 1947) he specifically cited Itard, Seguin, Johann Jacob Guggenbuehl (1816–1863) and Samuel Gridley Howe (1801–1876) as his exemplars. Whereas his forerunners had generally recommended an increase in the amount of stimuli to be presented to the child with mental retardation and developmental delay, Strauss had discovered the benefits of reduced stimulus input for a significant subpopulation of children with disabilities.

Meticulosity is defined as extreme distress caused by any lack of orderliness of exactness in the environment. Perseveration is the persistent repetition or continuance of an activity once begun: the brain-damaged child is unable to break off a successful or at least a safe performance to begin a new task or respond to a different demand. Laughter persisting well beyond reasonable limits is characterized as silly; questions stereotypically repeated are judged as irritating. For Strauss there are two types of perseveration: repetitive and iterative. The repetitive type involves immediate repetition, while the iterative type consists of delayed repetition. Along with most of the other components of the brain-damaged child syndrome, these symptoms were noted to be especially prominent in early infantile autism.

Meticulosity, perseveration, and overfocused attention are interpreted as defensive strategies against a perceived chaos and incoherence in the child's perceptual environment. These traits are included in a larger perceptual style construct that is sometimes referred to as rigidity. In the presence of such rigidity, the child with brain-damage has difficulty in switching from one set to another. Rigidity entails behaviors such as pedantry, fixation, stereotypy, inelasticity, and concreteness. As an explanatory construct, rigidity is no longer accepted in the field of mental retardation research. As a clinical construct to place symptoms in a group and to suggest associations, it still retains some limited heuristic value.

Behavior needs to be objectively described before it can be interpreted. Frequently when parents and teachers are asked to describe a child's behavior, they begin to interpret and explain the behavior. The explanations given are most often moralistic and assume deliberate willfulness, if not outright maliciousness, on the child's part (Denckla's [1995] "incorrigibles"?). When they are instead encouraged to detail behavioral particulars, it often becomes apparent that much of the child's described behavior is actually quite incompatible with the proffered interpretations. Strauss quoted with approval Leo Kanner's concern that much that showed up at the child psychiatrist's door was colored by a "complaint factor" that reflected an adult dissatisfaction with a child's behavior that might represent a justified inability or unwillingness on the part of the child to conform to unreasonable adult demands.

An experimental diagnostic technique that Strauss used can still be quite helpful clinically. He administered a list of paired words descriptive of children's behavior to parents and teachers and requested them to choose which of the two words best describe the child's typical behavior. Selecting neither or both choices was allowed. With minor modifications, some of these word pairs included:

Expressive movements
graceful	clumsy
smooth	jerky
normal	peculiar
energetic	inactive
purposeful	aimless
certain	hesitant
awkward	skillful

Laughter
hearty	flat
explosive	soft
noisy	quiet

Personality
furious	restrained
erratic	stable
decisive	drifting
neat	sloppy
hit-or-miss	planning
clear-headed	muddled

Social behavior
dependable	undependable
lonesome	sociable
cooperative	uncooperative
misfit	belonging
acceptable	wallflower
popular	unpopular
leader	follower

annoying	undisturbing
attractive	repellent
critical	accepting
reliable	unreliable

One of the words that I have always found to be descriptively helpful, "woolgathering," is no longer understood by most parents under age 40.

FROM MENTAL RETARDATION TO LEARNING DISABILITIES

Something close to Strauss's use of behavioral patterns to distinguish different subtypes of mental retardation had actually been suggested earlier by Alfred Binet (1857–1911) and Theodore Simon (1873–1961) in their *Mentally Defective Children* (1914). In their work on the development of the first intelligence test, they had distinguished three subtypes of mental retardation: (1) cases of simple mental retardation in which the retarded children perform much like normal children who are chronologically several years younger; (2) children who are described as ill-balanced and undisciplined, and who exhibit cognitive and behavioral peculiarities that are not typically found in younger children; these cases were described variously as unruly, talkative, inattentive, and sometimes "wicked" (their clinical histories recall the older psychiatric and forensic descriptions of "moral insanity" and "moral imbecility" [Ray 1838]); and (3) a mixture of the first two subtypes.

Strauss's neurobehavioral syndrome of attentional deficits, impulsivity, distractibility, hyperactivity, and perceptual abnormalities, can be clinically identified as a syndrome that is secondary to organic brain dysfunction, in part overlapping with but not completely identical to such entities as minimal brain dysfunction and attention deficit disorder. While he allowed that his behavioral phenotype might be imitated in part by other emotional or environmentally mediated factors, he strongly concurred with the formulation expressed by Arnold Gesell and Catherine Amatruda in their classic *Developmental Diagnosis* (1958):

> The child with a selective injury is usually so obviously handicapped that sympathetic understanding of his difficulties is a natural consequence. The child with only a minimal injury needs the very same recognition and understanding, and he too needs more than ordinary protection from stress and competition. . . . In all these cases we are dealing with an extremely complicated interaction of developmental potentialities and dynamic forces. Even though the original motor injury was mild, the damages in the personality sphere may be considerable and more or less permanent. In the interpretation of the development of

these infants, psychiatric concepts are often less helpful than an understanding of developmental neurology.

The brain-damaged child syndrome with it perceptual, conceptual, and behavioral symptoms can exist both with and without the mental retardation and the cerebral palsy that were well recognized outcomes of more severe brain-damage. Mental retardation and cerebral palsy were thus not the only long-term effects of significant brain-damage. This leap toward a long-term outcome for prenatal, perinatal, and postnatal events mirrored the historic insight of William John Little (1810–1894) in his association of cerebral palsy with asphyxia neonatorum (1861–1862). It is similar to that classic observation also in that, although both researchers were correct to correlate the later motor and neurobehavioral symptomatology with earlier insults to the brain, the obstetrical complications once so notoriously blamed in the perinatal period as causing cerebral palsy, mental retardation, and minimal brain dysfunction, are now recognized as generally postdating the original injury to the central nervous system. The overwhelming majority of cases of brain-damage are increasingly considered as of genetic origin.

Much of the complexity involved in formulating this syndrome is reflected in the definition that was prefixed to Strauss's first volume on the subject. It was arrived at both late and carefully:

> A brain-injured child is a child who before, during, or after birth has received an injury to or suffered an infection to the brain. As a result of such organic impairment, defects of the neuromotor system may be present or absent; however, such a child may now show disturbances in perception, thinking, and emotional behavior, either separately or in combination. These disturbances can be demonstrated by specific tests. These disturbances prevent or impede a normal learning process. Special educational methods have been devised to remedy these specific handicaps. (Strauss and Lehtinen 1947, p. 4).

Some of the striking aspects of this "definition" are that it allows for the diagnosis of an organic neurological condition through the use of the qualitative as well as the quantitative aspects of psychological tests; a fairly wide spectrum of possible symptom combinations is allowed to determine the diagnosis; and the correlation of medical diagnosis with educational intervention is included as a necessary part of the definition. For Strauss the educational component did not come "at the tail end" (Bender Chapter 3, this volume) but at the very beginning. The marriage between special education and developmental pediatrics that thrived in Strauss's day has evolved beyond separation to divorce in the intervening years, much to the detriment of the management of children.

There is an implicit (and one that would later become explicit) extension of his findings in exogenous mental retardation to children who were cognitively normal.

MENTAL RETARDATION

Much of Strauss's work was aimed at distinguishing exogenous mental retardation (that secondary to brain-damage) from endogenous mental retardation (that associated with socio-cultural, familial or polygenetic factors). A major focus for this distinction involved the detection of striking individual differences in the learning profile of people with mental retardation secondary to brain-damage. It was because of this research into uneven cognitive profiles that Strauss was later recognized as a pioneer in the emerging field of learning disabilities.

Strauss argued that global IQ alone was insufficient to define mental retardation and specify the optimal educational remediation (Bender Chapter 3, this volume). Cases of exogenous mental retardation would regress when they received the same educational intervention that helped cases of endogenous mental retardation to make progress. In other words, some children with mental retardation were also learning disabled.

Strauss's work in the field of brain-damage did much to destroy the concept of mental retardation as a homogeneous entity. Global IQ was not an adequate measure of intellectual functioning in children; further and more detailed profile analysis of perceptual and cognitive strengths and weaknesses was needed before a comprehensive diagnosis could be made so that it could contribute to the formulation of an intervention plan. Such pattern analysis might be as much qualitative as it is quantitative, if not more. Strauss both imposed such a subscore analysis on the old Stanford Binet Intelligence Scale and devised tests of his own as more sensitive discriminants of processing deficits he felt were necessary to support the presence of brain-damage in children. In 1938 he identified finger agnosia as a sign of acalculia or mathematics disability in children who were mentally retarded. The combination of finger agnosia, dyscalculia, and dysgraphia as a disturbance in body image had previously been reported in adults by Gerstmann (1924) in a syndrome that bears his name.

While this distinction of exogenous mental retardation versus endogenous mental retardation has not held up very well (Zigler and Balla 1982), the functional and behavioral differences remain. Today it is well recognized that many different mental retardation syndromes with specific genetic etiologies (examples of his exogenous mental retardation such as Fragile X syndrome [Baumgardner and Reiss 1994; Reiss 1995]) may present with many of the symptoms of the Strauss syndrome. From the perspective of developmental pediatrics the mere presence of mental retardation can be considered a presumptive sign of brain-damage.

Strauss's insight was radical in its time: that brain-damage or brain involvement can be diagnosed on the basis of a specific functional clinical picture with or without localizing neuromotor findings and with or without significantly delayed psychometric test scores. That the manifestations of such minimal brain dysfunction could be almost invisible and yet so disabling was interpreted by the next generation as supporting a causative role for minimal obstetrical irregularities or perinatal distress. This now disproven hypothesis was considered possible, but was not strongly advocated by Strauss. While it would readily simplify treatment needs if improved obstetrical care really eradicated or significantly lessened the problem of brain-damage in children, experience has demonstrated this association to be false. The majority of cases of both exogenous as well as endogenous mental retardation now appear to be genetic in origin.

THE EMPHASIS ON PERCEPTION AND LANGUAGE

In 1939, Strauss collaborated with Werner in demonstrating the utility of the marble board test as a perceptual motor instrument to discriminate brain-damaged subjects from mental-age matched mentally retarded controls presumably without brain-damage. He also recommended the use of drawing tests on condition that close observation showed how the child approached the task rather than simply being used to evaluate the final graphomotor product. Oddities of perceptual organization represented an excellent first screening step for the neurologically oriented pediatrician to detect signs of brain involvement in children.

The emphasis throughout the first two decades of his work had been on perceptual motor, visual motor, and visual perceptual motor skill training. This continued to represent the primary focus developed later by his students and collaborators who included Laura E. Lehtinen, Newell C. Kephart, and William Cruickshank. Shortly before his health forced him to resign from his position at Wayne County State Training School in 1946, Strauss had begun to turn his attention to the similarities between exogenous mental retardation (brain-damage) and aphasia or what he referred to as oligophasia. His few published remarks on the subject of linguistics remain suggestive but incomplete. Taking the lead from then current professional wisdom, he discounted the significance of early infant vocalizations.

Again starting from a gestalt perspective, he interpreted early language as fundamentally perceptual. He had followed closely the work of his friend Jean Piaget but disagreed with the latter's interpretation of early language as animistic. He saw "why" questions as perceptual in nature: they were for all practical purposes equivalent to "what" questions. A child's naming of an object involves organizing all the perceptions relating to that object. Thus when a child asks, "Why is the sky blue?", the answer that would satisfy is not a detailed metereological explanation but rather a listing and description of all the things one thinks of when contemplating a blue sky. "What do you think of when you say blue sky?"

In 1947 Strauss founded the Cove Schools for Brain-Injured children in Racine, Wisconsin, as a residential training program. Alfred Strauss died on October 27, 1957, at the age of 60. His bibliography lists 57 papers, one chapter, and three books. The best summary of his work can be obtained from the books: the first volume of *Psychopathology and Education of the Brain-Injured Child* (Strauss and Lehtinen 1947) detailed his work with brain-injured children who were also mentally retarded. Almost two decades later, Clements (1966) noted that "few single volumes have been so influential in the production of fresh considerations in the areas of pathology, diagnosis, education, and investigation of children with learning and behavioral disabilities. It refocused attention on the neglected area of individual differences among children." The second volume in this series (Strauss and Kephart 1955) focused more on brain-injured children with normal intelligence.The third volume in the series, *The Other Child* (Lewis, Strauss, and Lehtinen 1951) remains one of the classic introductions for parents on how to understand and live with a chronically neurologically different child. The projected fourth volume on linguistics and aphasia was never completed.

HISTORICAL ASSESSMENT

We tend to read history through tinted spectacles. We unreflectively assume that millions and millions of people have lived and died just so that we could be right. We are quite ready to judge their lives and their ideas under the single criterion of agreement with our briefly ascendent perceptions of scientific truth. I have related the achievements of Alfred Strauss in such a way as to emphasize just those aspects of his work that would be positively received by a modern audience of professionals interested in developmental disabilities in children.

Many writers, however, would take Strauss to task for claiming an organic basis for a wide spectrum of developmental and behavioral symptoms. Despite the fact that his principal goals in researching the contribution of organicity were to improve approaches to remediation, to increase the success of habilitation efforts, and to discover intervention modes better fitted to the individual needs of each specific child, there nevertheless exists a modern presumption that the very notion of an organic basis to a developmental disability signals defeatism and conceals racist sentiments. Against this prejudice, even Strauss's flight from Hitler's Germany stands him in little stead.

Strauss's "brain damaged child syndrome" is often interpreted as an example of lumping, but in fact represents one of the first major occurrences of splitting in the field of mental retardation since the development of IQ ranges to discriminate the different levels of mental retardation. The later evolution of the Strauss syndrome took lumping and splitting in diverse and sometimes contradictory directions. Minimal brain dysfunction (MBD) placed all the neurobehavioral symptomatology from the Strauss syndrome as well as soft neurological signs under a single rubric (Clements 1966). This exercise in lumping collected together many of the signs and symptoms of specific learning disabilities, diverse incarnations of attention deficit disorders, language disorders, and minor motor dysfunction. This short lived offspring of the Strauss syndrome was soon replaced by any number of cognitive and behavioral fragments. The splitting of MBD proceeded to an extreme in the realm of clinical diagnosis as professionals searched for elusive and illusory single diagnostic markers with, for example, hyperactivity becoming pathognomonic for attentional deficits and letter reversals for dyslexia.

This is not to suggest that there may not be advantages to splitting up the components of the Strauss syndrome or minimal brain dysfunction. In the presence of an attention deficit disorder for example, the child is more likely to have a learning disability when hyperactivity is absent, and hyperactivity when a learning disability is absent. The presence of both soft neurological signs and elevated dysmorphology scores relate to the presence of both attentional deficits and learning disabilities: the exact patterns of these associations remain to be clarified. The varying correlations between diverse components of the Strauss syndrome can be utilized for both diagnosis and prognosis. If we were to apply Strauss's perspective to the autistic spectrum that now includes autistic disorder, Rett syndrome, childhood disintegrative disorder, Asperger syndrome, and pervasive developmental disorder not otherwise specified, then perhaps much more emphasis would need to be placed on the overlap with mental retardation (Minshew Chapter 4, this volume) and the interface with various non-verbal learning disability patterns (Denckla's [1955] "not quite autism").

Strauss would probably be surprised to see himself criticized as a lumper: he grouped together conceptual, perceptual, and behavioral symptoms into a single entity quite simply because they belonged together as distinct from the majority of cases of mental retardation. His revolutionary step was to attempt to split a subgroup from the homogeneous mass of children with mental retardation as part of a larger attempt to individualize educational treatment.

Today it must, at least occasionally, produce some modicum of embarrassment from the clinician to have to inform parents that their child has an attention deficit hyperactivity disorder, a specific learning disability with a left brain deficit pattern impacting on reading, a developmental disorder of expressive language, a written language disorder with dysgraphia, a phonological disorder, and an oppositional defiant disorder. These parents came to the professional asking what was wrong with their child, and they are rightly upset to be given a laundry list that expresses in long words exactly the same symptoms that they had previously expressed in their concerns. (Their "Why?" is the "Why" of an adult and not the "Why?" of the child.) Most children with a diagnostic profile such as is given in the above listing do have a unitary diagnosis: brain-damage, often idiopathic brain-damage, sometimes familial brain-damage, rarely perinatal brain-damage. That is the one thing wrong with their child, and it can explain almost all the rest. To avoid making that diagnosis is to give the parents a stone for bread. The almost pathological avoidance of etiology that characterizes DSM-IV makes puzzling any interpretation of that manual as too strongly influenced by the "medical model" (Riddle 1995).

Strauss's rich and colorful descriptions of the wide ranging manifestations of brain-damage in children reflect their firm grounding in clinical observation. Against a backdrop of diagnostic, nosological, and therapeutic fads, his work has achieved more than historical permanence.

REFERENCES

Baumgardner, T., and Reiss, A. L. 1994. Fragile X syndrome: A behavioral genetics' window into understanding social emotional learning disability. In *Learning Disability Spectrum: ADD, ADHD, & LD*, eds. A. J. Capute, P. J. Accardo, and B. K. Shapiro. Baltimore: York Press.

Binet, A., and Simon, T. 1914. *Mentally Defective Children*, translated by W. B. Drummond. London: Edward Arnold.

Capute, A. J. 1991. The "expanded" Strauss syndrome: MBD revisited. In *Attention Deficit Disorders and Hyperactivity in Children*, eds. P. J. Accardo, T. A. Blondis, and B. Y. Whitman. New York: Marcel Dekker.

Clements, S. D. 1966. *Minimal Brain Dysfunction in Children: Terminology and Identification*. Washington, DC: U.S. Department of Health, Education, and Welfare (DHEW Publication No. [NIH] 73–349).

Cruickshank, W. M., and Hallahan, D. P. 1981. Alfred A. Strauss: Pioneer in learning disabilities. In *Concepts in Special Education: Selected Writings*, W. M. Cruickshank. New York: Syracuse University Press.

Denckla, M. B. 1995. From brain to mind, paper presented at The Spectrum of Developmental Disabilities XVII: Behavior Belongs in the Brain, Johns Hopkins Medical Institutions, March 27–29, Baltimore, Maryland.

Gerstmann, J. 1924. Fingeragnosie: Eine unschreibene Storung der Orientierung am eigene Koerper. *Weiner Klinische Wochenschrift* 37:1010–12.

Gesell, A., and Amatruda, C. 1958. *Developmental Diagnosis: Normal and Abnormal Child Development: Clinical Methods and Pediatric Applications*. New York: Paul B. Hoeber.

Lewis, R. A., Strauss, A. A., and Lehtinen, L. A. 1951. *The Other Child: The Brain-Injured Child*. New York: Grune & Stratton.

Little, W. J. 1861–1862. On the influence of abnormal parturition, difficult labour, premature birth, and asphyxia neonatorum on the mental and physical condition of the child, especially in relation to deformities. *Transactions of the Obstetrical Society of London* 3:293–344.

Ray, I. 1838. *A Treatise on the Medical Jurisprudence of Insanity.* Boston: Charles C. Little and James Brown.

Reiss, A. L. 1995. Behavioral Dysfunction in Genetic Syndromes: Specific?, paper presented at The Spectrum of Developmental Disabilities XVII: Behavior Belongs in the Brain, Johns Hopkins Medical Institutions, March 27–29, Baltimore, Maryland.

Riddle, M. A. 1995. Shortcomings of DSM-IV, paper presented at The Spectrum of Developmental Disabilities XVII: Behavior Belongs in the Brain, Johns Hopkins Medical Institutions, March 27–29, Baltimore, Maryland.

Strauss, A. A., and Lehtinen, L. E. 1947. *Psychopathology and Education of the Brain-Injured Child I: Fundamentals and Treatment of Brain-Injured Children.* New York: Grune & Stratton.

Strauss, A. A., and Kephart, N. C. 1955. *Psychopathology and Education of the Brain-Injured Child II: Progress in Theory and Clinic.* New York: Grune & Stratton.

Wender, P. 1971. *Minimal Brain Dysfunction in Children.* New York: Wiley-Interscience.

Werner, H. 1948. *Comparative Psychology of Mental Development.* New York: International Universities Press.

Zigler, E., and Balla, D., eds. 1982. *Mental Retardation: The Developmental-Difference Controversy.* Hillsdale, NJ: Lawrence Erlbaum Associates.

Chapter • 2

Brain Disease and Learning Ability

Peter B. Rosenberger

THE BRAIN AND COGNITION

Basic Principles

Of all the aspects of behavior with which the developmental pediatrician deals, the one that seems most naturally to "belong in the brain" is cognition. Yet I am intuitively uncomfortable with the concept of the brain as isolated agent or "engine" of cognition. Such colloquialisms as "The nose knows" or "He has the skill in his fingers" speak to common experience of the body as an integrated whole in the process of knowing. It is thus appropriate in any discussion of the brain and behavior to consider evidence for the specific role of the central nervous system in cognition.

What is Learning?

Approaching the topic from a developmental perspective, we think of cognition largely in terms of learning. How, in this context, to define learning? Miller (1967) has identified what he calls "Grade A Certified Learning" as "a relatively permanent increase in response strength, which is dependent upon previous reinforcement and is stimulus-specific." A word about the qualifiers is instructive. "Relatively permanent" distinguishes learning from immediate retention and retrieval, yet makes allowance for forgetting. "Increase in response strength" removes from primary consideration all types of avoidance learning, which, while they may otherwise qualify, nevertheless have their own special psychology, physiology, and pharmacology. "Previous reinforcement" excludes the basic drive of the rat toward the smell of food, or the infant for the nipple; *experience* is the necessary ingredient. "Stimulus-specific" distinguishes learning from other processes, such as the acquisition of physical prowess during exercise, which might satisfy the first three criteria, but would not comfortably be included as forms of learning.

What is Learning Ability?

An essential distinction, often confused in the discussion of learning ability, is between aptitude or talent on the one hand and skill or achievement on the other. The proper definition of learning disability requires that "ability" in this context be used in the sense of aptitude, or *potential* for achievement, not unlike visual acuity or muscular strength.

For clinical purposes, learning ability is measured by standard tests of aptitude, the best known of which are the intelligence tests. What the physician needs to know about these tests has been reviewed in detail elsewhere (Rosenberger 1981). Several general points need to be kept in mind. First, whatever their intercorrelations, the abilities that make up intelligence as we understand it are diverse. It is frequently helpful to remind the learning-disabled patient that "there are many different kinds of smarts, and school smarts are only some of them." The standard intelligence tests define learning ability, more or less narrowly, as scholastic aptitude. They were designed to predict academic success, not life fulfillment or happiness, and this they do very well, so long as (a) measurements are made under the conditions under which the tests are standardized, and (b) results are interpreted in light of these conditions. In one sense, the special education enterprise could be conceived as the effort to change, for the student, the learning conditions under which the standard tests have predicted his/her failure.

Second, although intelligence is conceived as aptitude, it can only rarely be measured apart from achievement. The tests attempt to measure *capacity* by taxing achievement with increasingly difficult challenges until failure is reached. Much of the pursuit of "culture-fair" assessment of intelligence is in fact the attempt to measure aptitude independently of past achievement. Even though the college board admission tests ("SATs") are designated as aptitude tests, they are much more dependent on achievement than are standard intelligence tests. One may score well on an intelligence test without ever having attended school. One very common characteristic of specifically learning-disabled students is that their SAT scores do not compare favorably with their IQ scores.

Third, intelligence increases with age. As a person grows older, not only does learning occur, but capacity for learning increases. This increase is most dramatic during childhood, at least for those aptitudes most relevant to school achievement, and in fact was first brought to light as a largely serendipitous finding in the early studies of Binet. It probably continues to some extent throughout adult life however, and becomes inextricably interwoven with the converse process of dementia in aging.

Fourth, the concept of intelligence, as we employ it clinically, relates almost exclusively to the original etymology of the word ("read across into"), that is to say, capacity to understand or be effectively aware of external events. It thus ignores much of the creativity and spontaneity that we normally associate with being "bright."

Issues of Historical Importance

Although many of the important specific learning disabilities recognized today are clearly not the reflection of damaged brains, it has been recognized for centuries, and is no less true today, that acquired brain dysfunction in children frequently manifests itself in alterations of capacity for learning. A consideration of several threads of historical development will help bring the issue into perspective.

The Law of Mass Action

Pierre Paul Flourens (1794–1867) viewed the cerebral cortex as the organ of the mind, distinct from other central nervous system structures that subserve individual motor and sensory behaviors. As Tizard (1959) points out, Flourens' formulation was far from new; in its theoretical aspects, in fact, it differed little from classical concepts of brain function going back to antiquity. It was the localizationalist theory of Gall (1807) that was new, and the novelty of Flourens' refutation of Gall was that it was backed up by experimental evidence from his own studies. Flourens' description of progressive loss of visual function by the pigeon with extirpation of increasingly large sections of cerebral cortex formed the basis of two concepts that have come to be synonymous with his name. The first is that of *equipotentiality* of various areas of the brain (one could cut anywhere in the pigeon's brain and sight would suffer); the second is what Lashley (see below) would later explicitly formulate as the *law of mass action* (the more brain is removed, the more function is lost).

A more modern application of Flourens' concepts is found in the work of Karl Lashley, whose major work, *Brain Mechanisms and Intelligence* (Lashley 1929) exerted considerable influence on twentieth century psychology. Testing rats on different learning tasks before and after experimental lesions in different areas of the brain, Lashley found that for some tasks, such as visual brightness discrimination, location of lesion is relevant to task performance, while for others, such as maze learning, disruption is relatively independent of lesion location. For both types of task, extent of disruption of performance was shown to be a function of the amount of cerebral tissue lost in the lesion, the difference being that for the brightness discrimination, mass effect is restricted to the occipital third of the cortex. Lashley concluded therefrom that the principles of equipotentiality and mass action, while related, do not necessarily entail one another.

Tizard (1959) points out that Lashley's formulations were heavily influenced by Gestalt psychology, which viewed specific mental functions not simply as discharges from isolated brain centers, but rather as the result of interaction of "fields of force," rather like magnetic or electrical fields, which were to be viewed as "wholes" having characteristics not explicable as a simple sum of their parts. As applied for example to visual perception by Goldstein, these fields would distinguish figures from ground, and at a very simple level would allow "closure" of incomplete figures into "Gestalten." More recently these concepts have been applied to the study of perceptual deficits caused by traumatic brain injury (Bender and Teuber 1946). "Field theories" are generally regarded as anti-localizationalist, but may, in light of more recent developments, represent more of a synthesis between the two opposing views (see below).

Controversies Among Localizationalists

It is clear that one of the reasons field theories have not appealed to neurologists is that they are difficult to conceptualize in terms of concrete neural structures (Bender and Teuber 1946). The argument could be made that controversies among neurologists concerning localization are really arguments among localizationalists. This would certainly apply to Pierre Marie, a French neurologist of the late nineteenth century. Marie never maintained that frontal lobe lesions did not interrupt speech, only that the anarthria caused by purely frontal lobe dysfunction does not qualify as aphasia because it does not involve language. This concept of the frontal lobe as being not so much formulator as executor of propositional speech has had lasting appeal, and has found expression in modern aphasiology in the writings of Eberhard Bay (1962) and Henri Hecaen (1972). Mohr (1976) succeeded in showing that lesions strictly limited to the posterior part of the third frontal convolution, the association area for movements of the facial musculature (Broca's area), characteristically result in a transient global mutism followed by rapid and substantial recovery. The most static deficit known as Broca's aphasia, he claims, nearly always involves more widespread lesions of the peri-Sylvian cortex.

The most prominent apologist for localization in the present century was Norman Geschwind (1926–1984), who re-introduced localization concepts in terms acceptable to twentieth century psychology. His first paper to attract attention (Geschwind 1962) explained the impairment of left-handed writing in a patient with a frontal tumor in terms of interruption of fibers connecting association areas of the two frontal lobes through the corpus callosum, the great fiber bundle connecting the two cerebral hemispheres. A most comprehensive work, published in two parts (Geschwind 1965) presented essentially Geschwind's entire model of the neocortex in the form of discussion of multiple functional deficits as disconnections between primary association areas.

The IQ Controversy

An entirely different current of scientific development in the early twentieth century also comes to bear on the question of cerebral localization of intellectual function. This was the development of intelligence, or learning capability, as a measurable quantity. The history is well reviewed by Herrnstein (1971) among others. The earliest measurements were psychophysical in nature, and perforce involved a multiplicity of tests. The idea of intelligence as a single property or quantity probably arose from Binet's development of a test of child intelligence in response to a single commission, i.e., to predict school failure. Subsequent students of the subject tended to become polarized into two camps. The one, represented by the British statistician Charles Spearman, called attention to a single statistical variable, which they termed "g," which accounted for significant proportions of the variability in learning capability in the population. The other approach, exemplified by the American engineer L. L. Thurstone, viewed intelligence as a collection of more or less independent "primary mental abilities," initially derived by factor analysis of test scores, then identified by names familiar to us today—perceptual ability, verbal comprehension, numerical ability, and so forth. These factors were, of course, to some extent correlated, but the recognition that the correlation is not complete was the starting point for the notion that specific mental aptitudes might be geographically localizable during development as well as in the adult state.

Piaget

The next important development in the study of mental abilities was provided by the work of the Swiss psychologist, Jean Piaget. Although starting from the perspective of IQ measurement, Piaget quickly shifted interest to the *processes* by which children arrive at the answers to specific IQ test challenges, as well as the *strategies* employed. Although they did not lend themselves well to neuropsychological interpretation, Piaget's processes were arranged in hierarchical order, from the concrete and empirical to the abstract and rational, viewing the movement from one to the next as a maturational process. Probably their chief contribution to study of the nature of intelligence was that they allowed for attempts to understand forms of thinking that go beyond simple information processing.

THE MODULARITY CONCEPT

Historical Background

For nearly as long as scholars have been aware of a controversy between those who do and those who do not view mental processes as localized in specific areas of the cerebral cortex, there have been attempts at synthesis of the two opposing views. Geschwind (1965) pointed out that according to Wernicke's original treatise, it is not such complex functions as are recognized by the terms speech, reading, writing, etc. that are represented in various cortical locations, but rather the elemental behaviors or primary mental processes of which those functions are comprised. The pioneer localizationalist Bastian wrote in 1898, as quoted by Geschwind (1964):

> ... There must be certain sets of structurally related cell and fibre mechanisms in the cortex ... Such diffuse but functionally unified nervous networks may differ altogether from the common conception of a neatly defined "centre", and yet for the sake of brevity it is convenient to retain this word and refer to such networks as so many "centres" ...

As Geschwind points out, this is "little different from Head's definition of a schema!" (Geschwind 1964). While Geschwind's intent here is to show that the opponents of the localizationalists also subscribed to their theories, it is clear from the quotations themselves that localization theory quickly surpassed the naive connectionism of the phrenologists.

Current Studies

The most modern schema for understanding how mind and brain relate is still in the early stages of development. Known as the "modularity concept" (Fodor 1983; Gardner 1983), it draws heavily upon new developments in neuropsychology, neurophysiology, and developmental neuroanatomy, and in so doing allows once again for the notion of localization of function, albeit in close synthesis with the

Gestaltists' "fields of force." According to modularity theory, both the anatomic structure of the brain and the organizational structure of primary mental abilities may be viewed in terms of "modules" or "vertical columns," proceeding from the simple (sensory, concrete) to the complex (rational, abstract) with regard to a particular functional or pragmatic unit. The theory has been most explicitly discussed by Fodor (1983), who stresses the independence of these cognitive devices from one another, rejecting such horizontal concepts as perception and memory. Gardner (1983) argues that Fodor has not held consistently to his pluralist position, positing also the need for a central processor involved with problem solving and decision making. Important for our discussion, however, is the fact that the "modules" draw their identity from precisely those processes discussed by the localizationists for the past century.

Modules, or combinations of them, have been further characterized by Gardner (1983) as "multiple intelligences." In a discussion that very much recalls the controversy between the followers of Spearman and Thorndike (see above), Gardner describes five individual intelligences—linguistic, musical, logical-mathematical, spatial, and bodily-kinesthetic—as well as a category to which he refers as "personal intelligences," having to do with the peculiarly human attribute of "sense of self." He then suggests that the advancement of knowledge through group effort is facilitated by the "socialization" of individual human intelligences through the use of symbols. A somewhat unique feature of Gardner's theory is that he does not claim to have accounted for the whole of human mental activity—only that part whose physiology is currently available to us.

An ideal example of a module according to this formulation is the process of "phonemic awareness" described by Liberman and colleagues (Liberman and Mattingly 1989). Briefly, these workers have specified, in acoustic terms, the uniquely phonetic processes that allow perception of speech consonants and vowels, and have shown how these processes differ from other acoustic perception. Their experiments have been designed to demonstrate a unique role of the major temporal lobe of the brain in these processes, which "make possible a vocabulary comprising vastly more than the number of holistically different sounds that humans can efficiently produce and perceive" (Liberman and Mattingly 1989, p. 491). These studies have been followed and enlarged upon by other workers in actual clinical settings to characterize the phonologic deficit that underlies much disorder of written language in childhood. Recently, therapeutic exercises have been designed to improve phonemic awareness, and have been successfully tested on children with specific language deficits (Tallal et al. 1996).

BRAIN DISEASE AND COGNITIVE DEFICIT

What has been discussed thus far is largely by way of prologue to the principal task of this chapter, which is to convince the reader that, from the limited perspective of cognition at least, knowledge of the brain is helpful to the understanding of children's behavior. We now need to consider the evidence that various acquired encephalopathies do have specific effects on various aspects of cognition in children. We shall not attempt an exhaustive review, but rather call attention to important and illustrative cases in point. We shall divide our discussion according to facets of cognition rather than the disease processes involved.

Attention

As Colby (1991) has observed, attention is a process widely distributed in the brain. This fact probably accounts for frustrations encountered in attempts to assign a particular anatomic locus to attention deficit (AD). By the same token, as has long been recognized by clinicians, acquired brain damage in any one of many loci, or indeed diffuse damage with no particular locus, may have AD as a prominent clinical feature.

The Attention Deficit Syndrome

Some of the earliest descriptions of attention deficit in children are in relation to brain disease syndromes. English (1904) reviewed the after effects of traumatic brain injury in children, and suggested that the pervasiveness of the intellectual deficits may be related to the fact that a developing brain is injured. Strecker and Ebaugh (1924) measured distractibility in children with post-traumatic encephalopathy, and commented on how much they resembled children in post-encephalitic states. Kahn and Cohen (1934) coined the term "organic drivenness," and Strauss (1944) popularized the concept of a specific intellectual deficit profile, including deficits of selective attention, in the "brain-damaged" child. Subsequent studies have, of course, made it clear that recognizable structural brain pathology does not account for more than a small subset of the total population of children with attention deficits. However, recognition of its role has provided part of the impetus to continued anatomical, biochemical, neurophysiological, and functional imaging studies of the syndrome in the present day (see Rosenberger 1991 for review).

Diffuse Encephalopathy and Attention

Recently it has come to be recognized that attention deficit is an important feature of the cognitive aftermath of a number of syndromes of diffuse damage to the developing brain. Examples include diffuse trauma (Chadwick et al. 1981), hypoxia (O'Dougherty et al. 1985; Regard et al. 1989), lead intoxication (David et al. 1972; Landrigen et al. 1975), CNS leukemia and its treatments (Brouwers et al. 1984), maternal smoking during pregnancy (Nichols 1980), and maternal alcohol ingestion during pregnancy (Shaywitz et al. 1980).

A recent followup study of the school performance of children of very low birth weight (Hack et al. 1991) shows a correlation of head circumference at age eight months with IQ scores, basic skills achievement, and hyperactivity scores; further study may show that AD is an important factor in this group as well.

Finally, AD is an important side-effect of several medications commonly prescribed for children.These include anticonvulsants, most notably barbiturates (Reynolds 1975) and antihistamines, of which the phenothiazines (Sprague et al. 1970) are a special case.

Perception

Although the localizationists have classically thought of visual perception as primarily a minor hemisphere function, the long-term studies of Teuber and colleagues (Teuber 1963) on the sequelae of battlefield head injuries have made it clear that perceptual deficits may be found following trauma to the cerebral cortex in practically any location, being most common with parietal lobe injuries, and somewhat more prominent in fact with left hemisphere involvement. Detailed prospective studies (Chadwick et al. 1981) have confirmed that the performance deficits that persist longest after closed head injury in children are non-verbal, involving perceptual-motor tasks and manual dexterity. The prominence of perceptual deficits with diffuse brain insult has been confirmed in the case of hypoxia secondary to congenital heart disease (Newburger et al. 1973) and cranial irradiation (Silverman et al. 1984).

Language

Focal brain disease affects language processes in the child, as well as the adult, brain. However, it has long been recognized that, for the developing brain, the rules of localization are somewhat different. The child under age 10 who loses language already acquired because of disease in one cerebral hemisphere, either left or right, nearly always reacquires the lost skills to some extent within a year. Basser (1962) showed that when such children then undergo resection of the originally damaged hemisphere (usually because of intractable epilepsy), they do not lose their reacquired skills. Since such reacquisition must have been accomplished by the originally nondominant hemisphere, the conclusion was that in the developing brain the hemispheres are more or less equipotential for language, according to Flourens' law (see above).

The later studies of Woods and Teuber (1978), however, called this conventional wisdom into question, showing a definite difference in prevalence of language deficits following acquired cerebral lesions in children, according to whether the left or right hemisphere was primarily involved. Woods and Teuber further showed that when verbal and performance IQ are compared in such children at a later date, verbal scores are higher on the average whether the original lesion was in the left or right hemisphere, although the difference is greater for the right hemisphere lesions. This finding lent further credence to what Teuber had termed the "crowding hypothesis," which states that during the process of recovery by the intact hemisphere, verbal skills, being more essential to the organism's survival, tend to "crowd out" nonverbal skills.

Further evidence of the developmental nature of hemispheric specialization for language is found in the fact that the so-called "fluent" dysphasias are practically unheard of in children. The tendency of the child whose language skills are affected by brain disease is to become either mute or underproductive of speech rather than to speak with jargon or paraphasias. Because in the adult such errors tend to disappear during recovery as comprehension improves, the child's mutism may result from the fact that bilateral hemispheric representation of speech provides him with sufficient residual comprehension to preclude protracted output of nonsensical verbiage.

The one exception to the above scenario, also the one important exception to the rule that acquired brain disease in children is not manifested as language deficit, is the syndrome of acquired epileptic aphasia (Landau and Kleffner 1957). The syndrome is encountered in children, usually between ages 2 and 5, with a history of normal speech acquisition, who over the course of weeks become first dysphasic, then mute. The neurologic examination is usually normal except for language function. The electroencephalogram shows epileptic discharges, usually with shifting lateralization, sometimes localized in temporal regions. Frank seizures are not a common feature. Spontaneous recovery is highly variable, and usually features some degree of social withdrawal, sometimes sufficient for a diagnosis of autism. Analysis of the language deficit usually shows a profound receptive deficit, sometimes identifiable as a complete verbal auditory agnosia—not the usual case with developmental language deficit, but common among autistic children. The epileptic EEG activity is frequently sensitive to anticonvulsants, but the language response is disappointing in most cases. Little is known of the pathology of the lesion responsible (Cole et al. 1987). However, recent trials of therapy with corticosteroids have shown promising results, generating much enthusiasm among parents of autistic children.

Epilepsy and Learning

Seizure disorder is an important factor in learning disability, although numerically it does not figure in a large percentage of cases. Even in a hospital-based clinic such as the Learning Disorders Unit at the Massachusetts General Hospital where we see over 700 new cases yearly, in not more than one in ten does either history or examination justify ordering an electroencephalogram. Nevertheless, where the aim is to identify brain dysfunction as a pathophysiology of learning disorder, paroxysmal functional derangement can be an important clue.

The Nature of the Relationship

The relationship between epilepsy and learning dysfunction can be quite complex. The first, most obvious, and perhaps simplest connection is that the epilepsy and the learning disorder share an underlying disease in common. This relation is much easier to understand from the perspective of the modern realization that epilepsy is not a disease in itself, but rather a description of a class of functional deficits, much like fever, diarrhea, etc., which are the manifestations of underlying disease. What complicates the picture in the case of epilepsy is the fact that in so many cases we are unable to identify the disease process. We call those cases "idiopathic epilepsy," but sometimes lose sight of the fact that the term "idiopathic" is a declaration of diagnostic failure, not success. Nevertheless, in the case of tuberous sclerosis, for example, it is quite clear that the learning disorder and the seizures are essentially independently caused by the disease process, although for the most part they go hand in hand.

Secondly, epilepsy and learning disorder are related through the seizure itself. This event, in turn, can be divided into several parts. Probably the most important of these from the standpoint of cognition is the aura, or initial phase, lasting from minutes to days. It was well known to the ancients; in fact, the epileptic's frequent description of a feeling of discomfort beginning in the abdomen and rising to the head was probably the basis of the Hippocratic formulation of "pneuma" or "rising wind." Sensory symptoms may be present; these may take the form of distortions or hallucinations, or in the case of Jacksonian or Roandic epilepsy may be focal. Behavior is frequently deranged, attention span compromised, and capacity to form memories impaired, resulting in a degree of retrograde amnesia from the point of the seizure.

The ictus, in the case of "grand mal" or generalized tonic-clonic seizures, obviously interfere with learning ability, since the patient is usually unconscious. The situation is not so clear with "petit mal" or absence seizures. The momentary lapse of awareness during such a spell is frequently obvious. However, the condition of "petit mal status," in which mentality is dulled and behavior sometimes mildly deranged, can exist for days in the absence of frank seizure, and thus be a source of great frustration to parents and teachers. Finally, the post-ictal state may include not only aphasia, as Jackson has observed, but a more general mental dullness.

The third type of relation between seizure and learning disorder consists of cerebral dysrhythmia in the absence of frank seizure. This is a relatively recently recognized phenomenon, apparent only since the advent of the electroencephalogram. The distinction between this state and "petit mal status" may not be entirely sharp, particularly when the dysrhythmia in question is of the classical three-per-second type. It is this state that has occupied the attention of most recent research (see below).

Fourthly, we have the question of "epileptic dementia." This refers to the gradual deterioration of intellectual capability seen over the course of years in some individuals who suffer from frequent epileptic seizures. Although it has been a concept for centuries (see above), its status and precise nature are still matters of controversy. A classical concept of the mechanism of this phenomenon has derived from the observation that cells in the hippocampus, a structure known to participate in memory formations, are unusually sensitive to hypoxia, to which epileptics are often subjected in varying degrees during seizures. More recent studies of regional brain metabolism have promised to shed light on the concept of "exhaustion" first raised by Jackson.

Finally, and nearly always a factor, especially in difficult cases with prolonged therapy, are the anticonvulsant drugs. Their "quieting" effect on central nervous system function is only partially specific; one of the chief aims in development of new anticonvulsants is seizure prophylaxis without sedation. In recent years, it has become apparent that even in the absence of frank sedation, attention deficit can be a serious problem. This is especially true of the barbiturates, less so of the hydantoins, and apparently not to a significant degree with the benzodiazapine derivatives.

The Historical Perspective

From ancient times until very recently, the approach to the question of epilepsy and learning ability has been one of considerable ambiguity. The effect of epilepsy on the mind and personality is probably what accounted for the continued prominence of religion in epileptology long after its departure from other medical enterprises. On the one hand, Aretaeus of Cappodocia spoke of epileptics as "slow to learn," Celsus was aware of the relation to insanity, and the biblical concept was of an "unclean spirit." On the other hand, prominent men of history, including Julius Caesar, Caligula, and the emperor Charles V were known with some certainty to be epileptic, and during the Renaissance there was a widespread belief that most epileptics were men of intelligence (Blumer 1984, p. 7). The detailed clinical descriptions in the French and English literature of the nineteenth century certainly left little doubt about the association between epilepsy and mental defect, at least in the institutional populations where such studies were conducted in that day. This is the reason for the importance of Lennox's observation in the mid-twentieth century that when one considers epileptic children in a middle-to-upper class office practice, the picture is much more optimistic.

Recent Studies

Formal psychometry, involving quantitative concepts of intellectual function, is basically a phenomenon of the twentieth century, and thus a relative newcomer on the scene of epileptology. Early studies were much under the influence of the prejudices and superstitions of the time, as exemplified by the following statement from the study of Richmond (1921):

> . . . the characteristic features or mental stigmata are present in a more or less marked degree from birth or early childhood, and are but little affected by the presence or absence of the seizures. The epileptic is a psychopath whose psychopathy manifests itself in a hyper-development of the ego, and extreme super-sensitiveness, marked emotional poverty and a rigidity of ideation and mentation (p. 384).

Richmond's seven cases were chosen to represent a spectrum from considerable to little or no deterioration over repeated testing. She reported that attention deficit, confusion about instructions, and poor motor coordination were common features of the responses of all seven. She also claims that the mental condition, as shown by her tests, bears no relation to the frequency or severity of seizures.

In a recent study of factors responsible for intellectual deterioration in epilepsy, Thompson and colleagues from the Chalfont Centre for Epilepsy in England (Thompson, Sander, and Oxley 1987) compared two groups of 22 epileptics each, matched for age, sex, and initial IQ, one of whom showed consistent deterioration over a 15-year period (average 25 IQ points), the other of whom remained stable. The two groups did not differ with regard to seizure type, episodes of status epilepticus, medication type, or number of medications used. However there was a significantly increased incidence of episodes of clinical and biochemical drug intoxication, also of skull fractures, among those who deteriorated. Detailed information about seizure control is not furnished, and one wonders whether the high incidence of drug toxicity among the deteriorated group does not reflect greater difficulty with control. The possibility of a role of anticonvulsant effect on learning is clear, however. This argument is strengthened by the report of Trimble and Corbett (1980). They studied 312 epileptic children in a hospital school, of whom 31 showed IQ deterioration over varying periods of time. They found significantly higher levels of two anticonvulsants, phenytoin and primidone, among the deteriorating group. They also showed negative correlation coefficients between performance IQ and serum levels of phenytoin, primidone, and phenobarbital in the group as a whole.

More recently, numerous studies have sought to compare various commonly used anticonvulsants for their effect on learning, particularly on attention. Initially there was some agreement that carbamazepine is less deleterious in this respect than phenobarbital or phenytoin. Subsequent reports suggest that monotherapy is the critical variable. A high index of suspicion and prevention of overdosage are probably the most important factors in avoidance of these effects.

Other recent studies have attempted to specify more precisely both the learning abilities and the epileptic events in this relationship. Tizard and Margerison (1963) tested two epileptic subjects while they were connected to the electroencephalograph. Two continuous-performance type tests were used; a paced auditory tape test requiring a response when a particular digit name was heard among others, and a self-paced visual task requiring the subject first to press a button which would turn on any one of five lights, then to press the switch under that light to turn it off. They found first a reduction in duration of spike-wave discharges during the lights test but not during the tape test. During spike-wave discharges they found an increase in errors of omission ("misses") on the tape test, as well as a slowing in response time on the lights test. There was no evidence that even very large numbers of spike-wave discharges impaired performance between discharges. Looking at specific wave forms, Hammond and Wilder (1984) compared the performance of 19 epileptic patients (all on at least two anticonvulsants) with that of 20 control subject on a signal-noise discrimination task. They found a significant increase in the latency of the "P-300" wave form, thought to reflect some aspect of thought processing, among the epileptics. In a well-controlled experiment with epilepsy-prone rats, Holmes et al. (1990) have shown that seizures themselves (as opposed to the disease that causes them) cause detriments to learning and memory in the developing animal.

SUMMARY

By way of introduction to the concept that "behavior belongs in the brain," we have examined the special case of cognition from the very limited perspective of the effect of acquired brain disease on cognition in the developing human organism. What about the myriad disorders/errors in the way the brain is programmed to begin with? First of all, it must be recognized that as more is learned about the events of fetal life, the definition of "to begin with" becomes more complex. Fetal alcohol encephalopathy is congenital in the strict sense of being present at birth, but clearly denotes a pathologic process acquired by a previously normal fetal brain. The situation is not entirely clear even with the classic "inborn errors of metabolism." There is reasonable evidence, for example, that the brain of the child with phenylketonuria is relatively normal at birth, having been protected during gestation by the maternal circulation. On the other hand, we have genetic brain defects, neuronal migration deficits, neurotransmitter imbalances, and a host of other disorders best thought of at our present stage of understanding as "developmental."

Progress is being made in these areas as well. Much has been learned about learning deficits in Down syndrome, and recent findings suggest specific "cognitive phenotypes" for neurofibromatosis, Tourette syndrome, Fragile-X syndrome, Williams syndrome, Turner syndrome, autism and Asperger's disorder, and others. A recent monograph (Harris 1995) provides a useful catalogue from the psychiatric perspective. An adequate neurological review of this important category of disease has yet to appear.

REFERENCES

Basser, L. 1962. Hemiplegia of early onset and the faculty of speech with special reference to the effects of hemispherectom. *Brain* 85:427–60.

Bay, E. 1962. Aphasia and non-verbal disorders of language. *Brain* 85:411–46.

Bender, M., and Teuber, H. 1946. Spatial organization of visual perception following injury to the brain. *Archives of Neurology and Psychiatry* 55:721–39.

Blumer, D. ed. 1984. *Psychiatric Aspects of Epilepsy*. Washington, DC: American Psychiatric Press.

Brouwers, P., Riccardi, P., Poplack, D., and Fedio, P. 1984. Attention deficits in long-term survivors of childhood acutelymphoblastic leukemia (ALL). *Journal of Clinical Neuropsychology* 6:325–36.

Chadwick, O., Rutter, M., Shaffer, D., and Shrout, P. 1981. A prospective study of children's head injuries IV. Specific cognitive deficits. *Journal of Clinical Neuropsychology* 3:101–20.

Colby, C. 1991. The neuroanatomy and neurophysiology of attention. *Journal of Child Neurology* 6 (Supp.):90–111.

Cole, A., Andermann, F., Taylor, L., Olivier, A., Rasmussen, T., Robitaille, Y., and Spire, J. 1988. The Landau-Kleffner syndrome of acquired epileptic aphasia: Unusual clinical outcome, surgical experience, and absence of encephalitis. *Neurology* 38:31–8.

David, O., Clark, J., and Voeller, K. 1972. Lead and hyperactivity. *Lancet* 2:900–904.

English, T. 1904. The after-effects of head injuries. *Lancet* 1:485–9.

Fodor, J. 1983. *The Modularity of Mind.* Cambridge: MIT Press.

Gall, F. 1807. Craniologie ou decouvertes nouvelles, *Ouvrage Traduit de l'Allemand.* Paris.

Gardner, H. 1983. *Frames of Mind.* New York: Basic Books.

Geschwind, N. 1962. A human cerebral disconnection syndrome. *Neurology* 12:675–85.

Geschwind, N. 1964. The paradoxical position of Kurt Goldstein in the history of aphasia. *Cortex* 1:214–24.

Geschwind, N. 1965. Disconnexion syndromes in animals and man. *Brain* 88:237–94 and 585–644.

Hack, M., Breslau, N., Weissman, B., Aram, D., Kline, N., and Borawski, E. 1991. Effect of very low birth weight and subnormal head size on cognitive abilities at school age. *New England Journal of Medicine* 325:231–7.

Hammond, E., and Wilder, B. 1984. Electrophysiological index of cognitive function in epileptic patients. In *Advances in Epileptology:* XVth Epilepsy International Symposium, ed. R. J. Porter. New York: Raven Press.

Harris, J. 1995. *Developmental Neuropsychiatry.* New York: Oxford University Press.

Hecaen, H. 1972. *Introduction a la Neuropsychologie.* Paris: Larousse.

Herrnstein, R. 1971. IQ. *The Atlantic Monthly.* September.

Holmes, G., Thompson, J., Marchi, T., Gabriel, P., Hogan, M., Carl, F., and Feldman, D. 1990. Effects of seizures on learning, memory, and behavior in the genetically epilepsy-prone rat. *Annals of Neurology* 27:24–32.

Kahn, E., and Cohen, L. 1934. Organic drivenness: A brain stem syndrome and experience. *New England Journal of Medicine* 210:748–56.

Landau, W., and Kleffner, F. 1957. Syndrome of acquired aphasia with convulsive disorder in children. *Neurology* 7:523–30.

Landrigen, P., Balch, R., Barthel, W., Whitworth, R., Staehling, N., and Rosenblum, B. 1975. Neuropsychological dysfunction in children with chronic low level lead absorption. *Lancet* 1:708–12.

Lashley, K. 1929. *Brain Mechanisms and Intelligence.* Chicago: University of Chicago Press.

Leahley, S., and Sands, I. 1921. Mental disturbances in children following epidemic encephalitis. *Journal of the American Medical Association* 76:373.

Liberman, A., and Mattingly, I. 1989. A specialization for speech perception. *Science* 243:489–94.

Miller, N. 1967. Certain facts about learning relevant to the search for its physical basis. In *The Neurosciences,* eds. G. C. Quarton, T. Melnechuk, and F. O. Schmitt. New York: Rockefeller University Press.

Mohr, J. 1976. Broca's area and Broca's aphasia. In *Studies in Neurolinguistics,* eds. H. Whittaker and H. Whittaker. New York: Academic Press.

Newburger, J., Silbert, A., Buckley, L., and Fyler, D. 1973. Cognitive function and age at repair of transportation of the great arteries in children. *New England Journal of Medicine* 310:1495–99.

Nichols, P. 1980. Early antecedents of childhood hyperactivity. *Neurology* 30:439.

O'Dougherty, M., Wright, F., Loewensen, L., and Torres, F. 1985. Cerebral dysfunction after chronic hypoxia. *Neurology* 35:42–6.

Regard, M., Oelz, O., Brugger, P., and Landis, T. 1989. Persistent cognitive impairment in climbers after repeated exposure to extreme altitude. *Neurology* 39:210–13.

Reynolds, E. 1975. Chronic antiepileptic toxicity: A review. *Epilepsia* 16:310–52.

Richmond, W. 1921. Psychometric tests in essential epilepsy. *Journal of Abnormal Psychology* 16:384–91.

Rosenberger, P. 1981. The pediatrician and psychometric testing. *Pediatrics in Review* 2:301–10.

Rosenberger, P. 1991. Attention deficit. *Pediatric Neurology* 7:397–405.

Shaywitz, S., Cohen, D., and Shaywitz, B. 1980. Behavior and learning difficulties in children of normal intelligence born to alcoholic mothers. *Journal of Pediatrics* 96:978–82.

Silverman, C., Palkes, H., Talent, B., Kovnar, E., Clouse, J., and Thomas, P. 1984. Late effects of radiotherapy on patients with cerebellar medulloblastoma. *Cancer* 54:825–29.

Sprague, R., Barnes, K., and Werry, J. 1970. Methylphenidate and thioridizine: Learning, reaction time, activity, and classroom behavior in disturbed children. *American Journal of Orthpsychiatry* 40:615–28.

Strauss, A. 1944. Ways of thinking in brain-crippled deficient children. *American Journal of Psychiatry* 100:639–47.

Strecker, E., and Ebaugh, F. 1924. Neuropsychiatric sequelae of cerebral trauma in children. *Archives of Neurology and Psychiatry* 12:443–53.

Tallal, P., Miller, S., Bedi, G., Byma, G., Wang, X., Nagarajan, S., Schreiner, C., Jenkins, W., and Merzenich, M. 1996. Language comprehension in language-learning impaired children improved with acoustically modified speech. *Science* 271:81–4.

Teuber, H. 1963. Space perception and its disturbances after brain injury in man. *Neuropsychologia* 1:47–57.

Thompson, P. J., Sander, J. W. A. S., and Oxley, J. 1987. Intellectual deterioration in severe epilepsy. *Advances in Epileptology*. 16:611–14.

Tizard , B. 1958. Theories of brain organization from Flourens to Lashley. *Medical History* 3:132–44.

Tizard, B., and Margerison, J. 1963. The relationship between generalized paroxysmal EEG discharges and various test situations in two epileptic patients. *Journal of Neurology, Neurosurgery, and Psychiatry* 26:308–13.

Trimble, M., and Corbett, J. 1980. Anticonvulsant drugs and cognitive function. *Advances in Epileptology* (X Epilepsy International Symposium) 113–20.

Woods, B., and Teuber, H. 1978. Changing patterns of childhood aphasia. *Annals of Neurology* 3:273–80.

Chapter • 3

Educational Issues for Children with Neurobehavioral Dysfunction

Michael Bender

It has been within only the last decade and a half that educational issues associated with brain dysfunction have merited public attention. Children with complex problems such as seizures, autism, traumatic brain injury (TBI), and lead poisoning have been viewed primarily from a medical perspective, with little emphasis placed upon their educational needs. Reasons for this oversight include a lack of accurate data concerning the numbers of children being identified, confusing diagnostic information that did not lend itself to a prescriptive format, and the limited number of educational programs with experienced teachers to work with these populations. In addition, many parents initially viewed their children, especially those with TBI, as having lifelong medical problems and gave little thought to their need for comprehensive school programs and eventual community integration.

EDUCATIONAL NEEDS

In order to understand fully many of the current and recurring educational needs of these populations, one group, those with traumatic brain injury (TBI), will be described. They represent many of the complex issues associated with educational reintegration and the need for specialized interventions and programs.

It is important to recognize that certain types of brain dysfunction effect education and behavior in specific ways. In addition, early planning for intervention is critical. It is therefore imperative that those working with these populations understand existing clinical information in terms of how it can be incorporated into an educational program and individual education plan (IEP). Early intervention, professional and parental input, and ongoing monitoring and feedback are key aspects to successful programming for these children.

The needs of TBI children are often varied and complex. These needs have recently come to the attention of local school systems because of the growing numbers of such children and the realization that rehabilitation facilities or hospitals may no longer be appropriate placements after initial therapy and stabilization. This population has also come of age legally, having been defined under the reauthorization of Public Law 94-142 in Public Law 101-476 (United States Congress 1992) as a category of students eligible to receive special education services.

This population now represents a significant number of new "kids-on-the-block" needing special education and related services. Many educators, as well as other professionals, are unaware of the escalating number of TBI children each year. It is estimated that, each year, 150,000 to 200,000 school-age children or younger have some form of TBI. Especially worrisome is the fact that, of that number, 15,000 to 20,000 will require prolonged care or hospitalization (Ylvisaker, Kolpan, and Rosenthal 1994).

Unfortunately, the emotional trauma for parents of TBI children does not end once their child is on the medical road to recovery. The educational journey presents difficult challenges such as locating appropriate placements, programs, and teachers.

Let us assume the individuals being described in this chapter had been functioning at age level before their trauma. That is, they had been at their appropriate academic grade level or above, their behavioral or social skills were commensurate with their age, and they were in the upper elementary grades. This description is in contrast to some general thinking and data that suggest that many TBI children have had some learning and or behavioral problems before their injury. It is important to note that many children who have a TBI in the summer months are at an increased educational disadvantage because school systems during those times are usually in summer recess, thereby restricting timely educational interventions. When TBI students return to school in the fall, the teacher may know only generalities about their accident, especially concerning cognitive difficulties. While many such students can be and usually are assimilated into their expected grades, many will have difficulty. Of special concern are those children who appear to be the same physically as before the accident, but are actually different children cognitively and socially.

These children are continually haunted by residual impairments, as are many children with neurobehavioral dysfunction.

RESIDUAL IMPAIRMENTS

Residual impairments create many dilemmas for children, parents, and teachers; in addition to being a part of a child's daily repertoire, TBI-caused dilemmas may occur randomly. Examples of these impairments include disorganization, attention and concentration problems, slowness in learning and retention, and problems with abstract reasoning and problem solving. In addition, students with TBI often have impaired functions in goal setting, planning, self-monitoring, and self-evaluation. Adding to the problem, especially with young TBI children, is that educational and cognitive problems are difficult to identify because "pre-morbid developmental levels and intellectual potential usually have not been formally evaluated" (Cohen et al. 1985) and details of previous academic success, failure, or learning styles were just being developed.

ASSESSMENT AND GOALS

Before any educational programs or interventions are suggested, an assessment of a child's educational strengths and needs is warranted. These assessments are dynamic in that they typically are repeated numerous times during a specific period thereby reflecting the student's changing needs. These assessments are often interdisciplinary which allows them to capitalize on the clinical skills and experience of speech-language pathologists, psychologists, occupational and physical therapists, social workers, and others involved in the assessment process. Asking a wide range of informal questions, in addition to formal assessment, is also important. These questions can provide insight into a child's educational needs. Examples of helpful questions suggested by Gobble et al.(1987) include:

- How was the child functioning in home, school, and community just before the accident?
- What are the effects of increased environmental distractions?
- How well does the child scan an environment to make sound and safe judgments?
- What is his/her short- and long-term memory like, and can he/she use strategies to hold information together?
- What is the way the child interacts with others?
- How much external structure does the child need to organize behavior or material?

- Is the child capable of monitoring his/her performance or products?

Assessment of social and interpersonal skills is of major importance. Knowledge about these skills will help define the type of social skills program a student may need. This type of program often determines the degree of success a child will have in being reintegrated into school and community life. Questions asked in this domain (Carney and Schoenbrodt 1994) often lead to prescriptive activities and interventions. Some of these questions include:

1. Who does the child communicate with? Does he or she initiate these interactions? Are they appropriate?
2. Does the child appear to enjoy interactions or are they laborious or stressful?
3. What mannerisms does the child display, and is he or she aware of them?
4. How does the child respond to success, failure, and stress?
5. What is the child's threshold for tolerance and frustration?

Assessment of children with TBI is often a complicated process, because many display multiple information processing deficits. They often have difficulty processing information at the rate at which it is presented as well as understanding the amounts of information being provided. Cohen et al.(1985) have emphasized that educational interventions that help develop cognitive skills need to concentrate on how students process information in addition to focusing on correct responses. They list some of the processing factors as: (1) attention, (2) ability to follow concrete and abstract language concepts, (3) auditory and visual memory skills, (4) comprehension of rote and meaningful information, and (5) frustration tolerance and fatigue level. A major recommendation of these authors, as well as others working with this population, is never to take silence or resistance to answering questions without considering that these responses may be a reflection of processing problems.

ADJUSTMENTS TO LEARNING

Only recently have we realized the needs of children with TBI. Studies, past and recent, have indicated that educational problems, especially those of children who have sustained moderate to severe TBI, continue as they grow older (Fennel and Mickle 1992). The negative effect TBI may have on later developing skills is of special significance, especially in the area of academics and school performance.

The fact that many TBI children may already have had a learning disability or learning difficulties prior to their injury adds to the complexity of the problem. Szekeres and Meserve (1994) list some commonly observed factors after TBI that would be helpful for the teacher to know. These include:

- a sudden onset of impairment with retention of some high-level skills and knowledge but with a loss of low-level skills and knowledge;
- slowed processing and poor memory for personal experiences and new information, which make new learning and transitions challenging;
- difficulty in self-management, especially in the areas of initiation and inhibition, leading to a loss of friends and social opportunities;
- disorientation, confusion, and disorganization, which compound communication, memory, and new learning problems;
- inconsistent performance due to physical and mental fatigue which creates educational programming problems; goals appropriate one week may not be appropriate the next week (p. 22).

IEP PROBLEMS

Developing Individual Education Plans (IEP) for TBI children as they re-enter school can pose many difficulties. Often, their post-trauma profile in terms of functional capabilities is widely different from what it was, as well as from their present classmate's profiles. As a result, it often becomes important to provide instructional modifications in addition to curricular ones. These can include using large print during reading activities, preferential seating, allowing extra time for assignments, using teaching aids or adaptive technology devices, and allowing additional time for rest during the day. Using class mentors or trained volunteers may also be useful, if they are selected carefully. When speaking to TBI children, it is advisable to use a simple vocabulary initially and talk clearly and slowly until you are assured that the student is comprehending what you are saying.

Impaired social interactions usually have a cognitive dimension (Hartley 1995), and also require adjustments to learning. These impaired interactions can take the form of poor awareness and perception of social events, disorganization, disinhibition, inappropriate remarks, and communicating unintended nonverbal messages (Haarbauer-Krupa et al. 1985). Impaired social interactions can also create volatile situations because these children can be highly unpredictable. Teachers of children who have TBI need to be especially alert and employ consistent monitoring procedures.

Many of these children also display impulsiveness and a lack of self-control creating educational challenges that will require adjustments. Therefore, teachers need to use a wide array of techniques. One technique known as cognitive behavior modification or CBM (Meichenbaum 1977), teaches children to view their behavior through a process of self-instruction and monitoring. Reinforcement, which instantly provides clear and direct feedback addressing rules and solutions, is often paired with this system. Obviously this system may not be effective in all cases, especially for the child who is seeking attention.

Adjustments to learning are required not only during the initial back-to-school phase, but also into vocational life. Wehman et al. (1993) suggest that people who are most difficult to place on the job are younger than one might expect and present many functional deficits such as those associated with visual and fine motor limitations. Additionally, they continue to demonstrate many TBI learning problems, namely, difficulty with visual memory, sequencing, need for structure, and most important, a lack of judgment in areas involving safety. It is interesting to note that many of the communication and work-related behaviors with which these people may have problems are also the ones needed for academic success. For example, Blosser and DePompei (1994) have suggested that areas of school-related strengths or needs should be identified during the planning process. These areas include:

- active learning,
- awareness,
- communication efficiency,
- attention and concentration,
- information processing,
- internal locus of control,
- interactive learning,
- field independence,
- persistence,
- problem solving,
- organization,
- recall, and
- reflection.

There are many variables to consider before specific adjustments to learning can be implemented. For example, developmental factors such as age and pre-traumatic skills need to be considered. A child's current strengths and needs, as well as situation factors, all play major roles in determining an appropriate course of action. In addition to a cognitive and behavioral profile, the examiner also needs to determine a TBI child's readiness for learning as well as his or her motivation level. Executive functions, including ability to self-initiate, self-direct, self-monitor, and self-evaluate must all be considered. Lastly, an area often not adequately understood, especially in the school situation, are the side effects of a TBI child's medication. We may know the positive effects, but rarely are we prepared for the ones that are not so positive and can have a profound influence on a child's readiness to learn.

A final word in this area concerns parents. The expectations of professionals are sometimes quite unrealistic about how much help a parent or caregiver may provide in supporting all of the educational needs. Simply said, families are often "burned out" after endless interactions at the hospital or rehabilitation facility. Many parents feel the school should have primary educational responsibility, and they look forward to this time as a way of receiving respite from the daily and often intense routines of medical facilities.

SOCIAL CONSIDERATIONS

It is now apparent that teaching social skills to children with TBI goes beyond the routine teaching of practical interpersonal skills. This area, perhaps more than any other, needs to be carefully presented and monitored, especially if TBI children are to be integrated into school, work, and community environments. In addition, teachers in transition programs have discovered that the lack of work or job skills are often not the major reason individuals with TBI lose or fail on a job. Often it is the lack of appropriate social skills such as how they act, interact, and respond to co-workers or supervisors that determines their success or failure on the job. Some areas presented by Muklewicz and Bender (1988), and Valletutti and Bender (1982), which need to be addressed as part of curricular content for job readiness, include:

- applying for work,
- getting along with co-workers,
- responding appropriately to stressful situations,
- obeying work rules and policies,
- participating in work breaks,
- reporting information and problems, and
- participating in after-hour work activities.

Impaired social interactions are not seen in work situations only, but in everyday living as well. This deficit often has a profound effect on family members who initially cannot understand why their child may be acting in inappropriate ways. What is often overlooked is that impaired cognitive skills can have an impact on social interactions through poor perception of social events, disorganization while listening and speaking, and making inappropriate remarks. These factors, as well as others, create social liabilities that the TBI child will need to overcome.

Intervention Strategies

There are numerous strategies to use in teaching or providing service to children with neurobehavioral disorders. Examples include:

Cognitive coaching helps to develop cognitive communicative knowledge in TBI children (Szekeres and Meserve 1994). This strategy allows teachers or support personnel to act as coaches in helping their students understand their strengths and needs while mediating their social and academic experiences.

Interdisciplinary collaboration promotes jointly planned interventions such as those that might occur with a special educator and speech pathologist.

Teaching compensatory strategies can involve the phases of general strategic thinking, teaching the strategy, and generalization and maintenance of the strategy (Haarbauer-Krupa et al. 1985).

Teaching of functional academics relates academic concepts or knowledge to real-life situations whenever possible. Teaching functional academics may be especially important for TBI students. Functional academics should be viewed as components of a sociological perspective. They teach roles, skills, and activities an individual must make use of in order to function fully in society (Bender and Valletutti 1982). These roles depict the student:

- as a resident of a home,
- as a learner in traditional and non-traditional school settings,
- as a participant in the community,
- as a consumer of goods and services,
- as a worker, or
- as a participant in leisure experiences.

REINTEGRATION INTO SCHOOL PROGRAMS

An overriding educational concern for educators of children with TBI (as with most children with disabilities) is the pupil's placement back into school programs. Traditionally, medical and physical restoration of these children has been the primary focus, with psychological and educational factors only recently becoming an issue. When an educational program is found, one can only hope the teacher is well trained in TBI and has administrative support and resources to develop an appropriate and individualized program. Including these students in regular grades, even with support, is a difficult process. One tends to forget that these integrations require extensive resource support and are much more internally stressful than they might appear. This is true for parents as well as for teachers and students. Under stress, TBI children can exhibit unorthodox behaviors, noncompliance (or what appears to be noncompliance), and anxieties that result in unpredictable behavior. They often become isolated in their class. Some of the more common problems that occur upon integration listed by Cohen, et al. (1985) include:

- being disoriented or confused,
- not understanding how to begin an activity,
- not understanding how to end an activity,
- giving impulsive responses,
- recognizing the need for help and asking for it,
- having difficulty working independently, and
- perseveration.

These social and educational behaviors make success in regular classes a challenge. Stretching a student's natural environment is another factor to consider. That is, often we try to make transitions for these students so protective they border on being unrealistic. This becomes a problem when students are too old for their placement or must move to another setting that does not have appropriate safeguards.

What then should we consider when planning for placement of students with TBI? Cohen et al. (1985) offer the following to consider:

- In all likelihood some form of special education support will be needed.
- These student's learning styles can be quite different from most special education students.
- Because of these children's changing and somewhat unpredictable behavior, test scores alone should not be used to make placement decisions.
- Background and life experiences may not be known and can influence a child's information base.
- In some instances, pre-traumatic abilities may have just been developing.
- Their learning styles and characteristic behaviors may not have been established prior to the accident.

The student's readiness for rehabilitation is another important consideration. Because cognitive growth is typically greatest during the first year of rehabilitation, the educational program needs to capitalize on and be prepared for this. A child ready for educational intervention in June, cannot afford to wait until September when school typically begins. Unfortunately, until we have year-round schooling, these children will be faced with the added burden that when they are most ready to learn, the educational system may not be ready for them.

Continuing Educational Issues

Educational problems for TBI children often continue throughout most of their formal schooling (Savage and Wolcatt 1994). When one considers the overwhelming issues that currently exist for them, such as limited school resources, scarcity of trained TBI teachers, and lack of year-round schooling, it is no wonder that this population presents a challenging opportunity for educational success. Just as with all children, the stages they go through will present new and different problems.

We are rapidly learning about the educational characteristics of TBI children. Their unique strengths and concerns are prime areas for applied educational research. Their needs, which appear to be dynamic and lifelong, will require comprehensive interdisciplinary planning, innovative resources, and understanding parents and professionals.

REFERENCES

Bender, M., and Valletutti, P. 1982. *Teaching Functional Academics: A Curriculum Guide for Adolescents and Adults with Learning Problems.* Texas: PRO-ED.
Blosser, J., and DePompei, R. 1994. *Pediatric Traumatic Brain Injury.* San Diego: Singular Publishing Group.
Carney, J., and Schoenbrodt, L. 1994. Educational implications of traumatic brain injury. *Pediatric Annals* 23 (1):47–52.
Cohen, S. B., Joyce, C. M., Rhodes, K. W., and Welks, D. M. 1985. Educational and vocational rehabilitation. In *Head Injury Rehabilitation*, ed. M. Ylvisaker. San Diego: College-Hill Press.
Fennell, E., and Mickle, P. 1992. Behavioral effects of head trauma in children and adolescents. In *Advances in Child Neuropsychology*, Vol. I, eds. M. Tramontawa and S. Hooper. New York: Springer-Verlag.
Gobble, E. M. R., Dunson, C., Szekeres, S., and Cornwall, J. 1987. Avocational programming for the severely impaired head injured individual. In *Re-Entry for Head Injured Adults*, eds. M. Ylvisaker and E.M.R. Gobble. San Diego: College-Hill Press.
Haarbauer-Krupa, J., Henry, K., Szekeres, S. and Ylvisaker, M. 1985. Cognitive rehabilitation therapy: Late stages of recovery. In *Head Injury Rehabilitation*, ed. M. Ylvisaker. San Diego: College-Hill Press.
Hartley, L. 1995. *Cognitive-Communicative Abilities Following Brain Injury.* San Diego: College-Hill Press.
Meichenbauum, D. 1977. *Cognitive Behavior Modification: An Integrative Approach.* New York: Plenum Press.

Muklewicz, C., and Bender, M. 1988. *Competitive Job-Finding Guide For Persons With Handicaps*. Boston: Little, Brown and Company.

Savage, R., and Wolcott, G. eds. 1994. *Educational Dimensions of Acquired Brain Injury*. Texas: PRO-ED.

Szekeres, S. and Meserve, N. F. 1994. Collaborative intervention in schools after traumatic brain injury. *Topics in Language Disorders* 15 (1): 21–36.

United States Congress. 1992. *The Individuals with Disabilities Education Act. Public Law 101-476*. Washington: U.S. Government Printing Office.

Valletutti, P., and Bender, M. 1982. *Teaching Interpersonal and Community Living Skills*. Baltimore: University Park Press.

Wehman, P., Kregel, J., Sherron, P., Nguyen, S., Kreutzer, J., Fryer, R., and Zasler, N. 1993. Critical factors associated with the successful supported employment placement of patients with severe traumatic brain injury. *Brain Injury* 7: 31–34.

Ylvisaker, M., Kolpan, K., and Rosenthal, M. 1994. Collaboration in preparing for personal injury suits after TBI. *Topics in Language Disorders* 15 (1): 1–20.

Part • II

Autism

Chapter • 4

Autism and the Pervasive Developmental Disorders: *The Clinical Syndrome*

Nancy J. Minshew

Pervasive developmental disorders (PDD) represent a new diagnostic category introduced in 1980 for autism and clinically related disorders. At that time, the only one of these disorders that had been described was autism, but it was clear that other undescribed disorders existed in this category. Thus began a series of clinical hypotheses attempting to differentiate the other pervasive developmental disorders from autism on the basis of clinical features that were thought likely to yield valid clinical syndromes separate from autism. Some of these hypotheses have not been supported by the results of field trials of the criteria, and thus some disorders have been only temporary members of this diagnostic category. Autism remains the clinical prototype for these disorders and the best defined. The other pervasive developmental disorders are defined in terms of clinical distinctions from autism. This category will remain under development for the foreseeable future.

The classification of the pervasive developmental disorders is currently in its third version, each version being substantially different from preceding versions (table I). Major modifications should be expected to occur reflecting the outcome of field trials of DSM-IV (American Psychiatric Association 1994) assessing the validity of the proposed disorders and criteria. Awareness of all three versions of the classification for the pervasive developmental disorder is important, as more than one system is typically in use in the community at any

Table I.   Pervasive Developmental Disorders: 1980, 1987, 1994

1. *DSM-III:* 1980
   Infantile Autism
   Childhood Onset Pervasive Developmental Disorder
   Atypical Pervasive Developmental Disorder
2. *DSM-III-R:* 1987
   Autistic Disorder
   Pervasive Developmental Disorder Nos
3. *DSM-IV:* 1994
   Autistic Disorder
   Asperger's Disorder
   Pervasive Developmental Disorder Nos
   Childhood Disintegrative Disorder
   Rett's Disorder

one time. In addition, patients may have been diagnosed at different times in their lives using different versions of the classification system. Thus, a single patient may have a different diagnosis under each classification system just because of variations that have occurred in the system from one version to the next. In addition, there may be variations in the application of the same criteria by different evaluators resulting in a different diagnosis across evaluations in the same patient. Since treatment is not based on the distinctions between the disorders within this category, but on the overall quality of the deficits common to all disorders in the category, the most practical diagnostic focus is on developing a clear definition of function and behavior in each symptom category that includes several real life examples of function and behavior, rather than on a debate about specific diagnostic assignment within the pervasive developmental disorder category. The pervasive developmental disorders are defined by deficits in social skills and behavior, verbal and nonverbal language and their use for communication, toy and play skills and related behavior, and reasoning and complex behavior in situations. Each of these deficits is further defined by specific qualitative features and a particular manner of presentation and evolution in early life (reviewed in: Minshew 1996; Minshew and Payton 1988a, 1988b; Rapin 1991). Efforts continue to refine diagnostic criteria in order to incorporate new data regarding the specific nature of these deficits in complex abilities and their component skills so as to arrive at criteria with the highest degree of sensitivity and specificity feasible within the abbreviated format of DSM-IV and ICD-10 (World Health Organization 1992).

The pervasive developmental disorders selectively involve the development of higher order skills that provide the foundation for flexible, adaptive function and behavior in society. Thus, a large part of the treatment of the pervasive developmental disorders involves adapting the environment to them. In a very real sense, adaptations made in the environment have the same therapeutic status in the pervasive developmental disorders as medications have in other disorders. A second consequence of the selective involvement of higher order skills in these disorders is that preserved skills do not predict the status of higher order abilities, as they do when brain development proceeds in a normal fashion. Thus, mathematical calculations, expressive language, and reading level do not accurately predict reasoning and comprehension abilities, and in fact are misleading, causing observers to overestimate substantially competence in higher order abilities.

The current classification of the pervasive developmental disorders is provided in the *Diagnostic and Statistical Manual*, fourth edition (DSM-IV) and the *International Classification of Diseases*, 10th edition (ICD-10). The definition of autism is the same in both systems and thus there is now world-wide agreement on the criteria for autism and the view of autism as a single disorder of widely varying severity. The DSM-IV classification for the pervasive developmental disorders includes four other disorders: Asperger's disorder, pervasive developmental disorder not otherwise specified (PDDNOS), childhood disintegrative disorder, and Rett's disorder. The addition of the "disorder" modifier to autism, Asperger's and Rett's reflects a general practice in the DSM system beginning with DSM-III-R, and is not indicative of a difference in the clinical syndrome from that previously known. Likewise, the deletion of the term "infantile" from the designation for autism was a reflection of the need to make this term equally applicable to individuals regardless of their age.

All of the pervasive developmental disorders in DSM-IV are defined in terms of clinical differences from autism. Asperger's disorder is defined as the syndrome of autism minus the early developmental language abnormalities. Asperger's disorder is therefore confined to verbal individuals with IQ scores in the normal or near normal range. PDDNOS is most simply defined as the syndrome of autism minus the symptoms of a restricted range of interests and activities, but also refers to individuals who have less prominent symptoms in any area than expected for autism relative to their age and IQ. Use of the latter distinction requires extensive clinical experience with autism at all levels of age and IQ and a working knowledge of the research issues in diagnosis. Such distinctions are not amenable to the checklist format of DSM or ICD and are not feasible outside of a research center. Two disorders, childhood onset disintegrative disorder and Rett's disorder, share with autism a presentation in the form of regression which is the mode of onset in about one-fourth of autistic children. Childhood onset disintegrative disorder refers to children who present with regression between 2 and 10 years of age and generally past the usual age for autism. This category includes the clinical syndrome resulting from a variety of serious neurologic degenerative disorders, such as adrenoleukodystrophy (Volkmar 1994). Rett's disorder is classified in the PDD category because of regression and loss of social, language, and reasoning skills in the first to second year of life. Rett's disorder is otherwise very different from autism and the two can be distinguished at presentation by the deceleration in head growth and microcephaly typical of Rett's disorder, in contrast to the average or above average head circumference typical for autism in the absence of a fetal viral infection. Rett's disorder is furthermore exceedingly rare with only about 800 identified cases in the United States, making this a very low probability diagnosis in children with "autistic symptomatology." Since Rett's disorder is associated with early death, it is important that this diagnostic possibility not be raised with the family until it is documented by the many findings specific to Rett's disorder.

Notable for their absence from DSM-IV are the nonverbal learning disability syndrome (NLD) (Rourke 1989), also known as the Syndrome of the Developmental Disabilities of the Right Hemisphere (Weintraub and Mesulam 1983), and pervasive developmental disorder resulting from tuberous sclerosis. Individuals presenting with NLD resemble high functioning autistic individuals but are readily distinguished by the presence of prominent difficulty with arithmetic and visual-spatial abilities that worsen with age due to lack of developmental progress. The NLD syndrome is defined by a distinctive neuropsychologic profile of right frontal and right parietal lobe deficits, which provided the basis for the description of this syndrome. NLD individuals were also generally described as having few friends but as being able to function within the mainstream of society, suggesting that their social and reasoning deficits were not as severe as in autism. The characterization of the behavioral expression of this syndrome was likely insufficient at this point for it to fit within the existing diagnostic framework for the pervasive developmental disorders, and thus it was not included in the DSM-IV classification of the PDDs. Nonetheless, NLD remains an important clinical disorder of the PDD type and a consideration in differential diagnosis. Tuberous sclerosis is associated with a PDD clinical syndrome in up to 40% to 60% of cases, and their behavioral management is therefore inextricably linked to the PDD manifestations. In addition, the investigation of individuals with PDD resulting from tuberous sclerosis has become an important research strategy in the pursuit of the neurobiologic bases for autism. Although the current practice is to classify individuals with an identified genetic, metabolic, or infectious basis for their PDD syndrome under the existing PDD diagnoses, individuals with these etiologies constitute less than 5% of those with PDD and have specific issues related to their underlying etiology that should not be obscured by classification with the other 95% of the PDDs. Conversely, this practice obscures the importance of the distinctive familial inheritance patterns of the PDDs, which include occurrence of affective disorder, anxiety disorder, and fragments of the clinical syndrome among first degree relatives. The 95% of the individuals with pervasive developmental disorder without a defined infectious, metabolic, or genetic basis does not mean that a comparable etiology exists for these individuals that has yet to be discovered, but rather that there is a distinct neurobiology for 95% of cases that is not mediated by other disorders (Minshew 1996).

The disorders comprising the PDD category in DSM-IV make it readily apparent that PDD occurs across a wide range of severity, and that IQ scores, level of verbal ability, or inclination to interact should not be used in differential diagnosis as exclusions for autism or other pervasive developmental disorders. Approximately one-half of the individuals with a pervasive developmental disorder will interact socially, speak, make eye contact, and be viewed as intelligent in at least some areas, thus defying the outdated but still common stereotype of the autistic child as having no social interactions, no language, no eye contact, and no cognitive abilities. Some of the pervasive developmental disorders (Asperger's disorder and the nonverbal learning disability syndrome) occur only in the presence of normal or near normal intelligence. Some of these disorders (autistic disorder, PDDNOS, and childhood onset pervasive developmental disorder) occur both in individuals with normal intelligence and in mentally retarded individuals. Finally, some PDDs (Rett's disorder and tuberous sclerosis) occur only or predominately in the presence of mental retardation.

Pervasive developmental disorder should be considered in the differential diagnosis of individuals, regardless of general level of intelligence, who exhibit developmental delays, a learning disability that does not conform to the developmental specific learning disabilities diagnosis, or a behavior problem that involves socially inappropriate behavior and behavior resulting from very poor common sense. Some clinical complaints that should suggest the possibility of a pervasive developmental disorder are provided in tables II and III. Young children with PDD will generally have complaints (table II) related to delayed and deviant development of social, language, play, and complex motor skills. The tendency in dealing with young children is to focus on the language impairment, and the diagnostic significance of other impairments is often overlooked. Young, less severely impaired, autistic children are often described as "autistic-like but not autistic" or "having autistic features or tendencies but not autistic," indicating that they have the qualitative features typical of autism but the severity of these symptoms is less than the examiner is accustomed to for autism. Higher

Table II.   Clues to PDD in Young Child

- Not talking and no alternate form of communication
- Doesn't respond to name but runs to TV commercial
- Echolalic, pronoun reversals, memorizes TV scripts
- Limited to no social reaction to peers
- Little to no social know-how
- Little to no interest in toys
- Odd play with toys: lines up, collects, but no play
- Smell, taste, or texture interests or sensitivities
- Irritable, unhappy, and difficult to console
- Dislikes new things or routines; dislikes change
- Very controlling of others' actions
- Odd ways of doing things
- Few interests but obsessions: TV credits, numbers
- Unusual fears but no sense of danger

Table III.   Clues to PDD in Older, More Able Child

- Viewed as strange, odd, or weird by peers
- Inappropriate, offensive behavior
- But also very gullible
- Doesn't understand social scene
- Says too much or too little—doesn't get it right
- Odd word choices, misuse of idioms or metaphors
- Canned sayings, overused
- Monotone or odd tone of voice
- Doesn't use facial expression for communication
- Obsessions with facts, details, or collections
- Phenomenal memory for detail (excel in academics)
- Poor understanding of concepts, themes, cause-effect
- No common sense
- Complains about new routines and unexpected change
- KD-3: honeymoon after difficult early childhood
- Lots of problems, many diagnoses, nothing fits

functioning, older children with PDD will have complaints related to social and reasoning behavior (table III) requiring clinicians to determine the skill deficits underlying the undesirable behavior in order to arrive at the proper diagnosis. Because training programs and textbooks have traditionally devoted little time to the analysis of complex social, communication, and problem solving behavior in children and adolescents, it is often difficult for clinicians to relate these behavior problems to a diagnosis of pervasive developmental disorder. It is therefore important for clinicians wanting to develop competence in the recognition of the pervasive developmental disorders to analyze abnormal behavior for likely underlying deficits, rather than accepting it at face value and attributing all undesirable or negative behavior to tantrums, poor parental discipline, adolescent acting out, or sociopathy.

The pervasive developmental disorders are as common as childhood leukemia, type 1 neurofibromatosis, and meningomyelocele, conditions which all clinicians are expected to recognize and refer but for which they are not expected to provide primary care in treatment. Similarly, with the pervasive developmental disorders, the goal of the majority of clinicians will be to suspect the presence of these disorders as a cause for their patient's difficulties and to make a referral for diagnosis and treatment when appropriate, as would be the case for other developmental cognitive disorders.

Because the pervasive developmental disorders in DSM-IV are all defined in terms of the clinical syndrome of autism, the following description of the deficits and abnormal behavior is based on autism. Until a theoretical framework has been developed for classifying variations in the social, communication, and reasoning deficits that exist within this category, the clinical description of pervasive developmental disorders will remain linked to autism and the capacity for delineating the various disorders will remain limited. DSM-IV diagnostic criteria for autism are provided in table IV. These criteria specify impairments in three areas related to social function, language function and play skills, and a restricted range of interests and activities. The goal of the criteria has been to identify the overall quality of the deficit in each area and provide examples of how this deficit would be manifested at different age and severity levels. The criteria for the social deficit comes closest to achieving this goal. The criteria for the language deficit approximates this goal primarily by specifying deviant features of language development and use, but do not identify a unifying quality to the impairments. The criteria in autism for the third category of symptoms, referred to as the restricted range of activities and interests, falls far short of ideal; there is no attempt to specify the underlying qualitative impairment that might unite a group of superficially disparate behaviors. At present, it appears most likely that the various types of abnormal behavior clustered in this category are related to a combination of a severe deficit in abstract reasoning and preserved or heightened awareness of the elementary features of the environment. The goal of further research is to determine the overall quality of these three symptoms, identify deficient component skill deficits responsible for the qualitative impairment in each area, and specify the behavioral expression of each impairment as a function of early development and severity at outcome.

ONSET

In the majority of cases, autism presents in the form of developmental delays and related but often overlooked oddities in behavior. Deficits are first noticed when language milestones are missed. Most parents

Table IV. DSM-IV Diagnostic Criteria for Autistic Disorder

A. A total of at least six items from (1), (2), and (3), with at least two from (1), and one each from (2) and (3):
  (1) Qualitative impairment in social interactions, as manifested by at least two of the following:
      (a) marked impairment in the use of multiple nonverbal behaviors such as eye-to-eye gaze, facial expression, body postures, and gestures to regulate social interaction.
      (b) failure to develop peer relationships appropriate to developmental level
      (c) markedly impaired expression of pleasure in other people's happiness
      (d) lack of social or emotional reciprocity
  (2) Qualitative impairments in communication as manifested by at least one of the following:
      (a) delay in, or total lack of, the development of spoken language (not accompanied by an attempt to compensate through alternative modes of communication such as gesture or mime)
      (b) in individuals with adequate speech, marked impairment in the ability to initiate or sustain a conversation with others
      (c) stereotyped and repetitive use of language or idiosyncratic language
      (d) lack of varied spontaneous make-believe play or social imitative play appropriate to developmental level
  (3) Restricted repetitive and *stereotyped patterns of behavior, interests, and activities*, as manifested by at least one of the following:
      (a) encompassing preoccupation with one or more stereotyped and restricted patterns of interest that is abnormal either in intensity or focus
      (b) apparently compulsive adherence to specific, nonfunctional routines or rituals
      (c) stereotyped and repetitive motor mannerisms (e.g., hand or finger flapping or twisting, or complex whole body movements)
      (d) persistent preoccupation with parts of objects
B. Delays or abnormal functioning in at least one of the following areas, with onset peer to age three: (1) social interaction, (2) language as used in social communication, or (3) symbolic or imaginative play.
C. Not better accounted for by Rett's Disorder or Childhood Disintegrative Disorder.

are not aware of developmental abnormalities prior to this, but research analysis of home videotapes has demonstrated evidence of abnormalities in social interactions, nonverbal language, and play in the first year of life in such children (Osterling and Dawson 1994). In the absence of siblings in the home, the social deficit may not be apparent to parents until a child is enrolled in a play group, as there are so few children in neighborhoods today. Formal evaluations also often identify delays in complex fine and gross motor skills, producing an apparent global pattern of delays. However, the social, language, play skill, and reasoning delays have considerably more impact on daily life function than do motor impairments.

About one-fourth to one-third of autistic children exhibit a loss or deterioration in previously acquired skills, after 12 to 24 months of normal or largely normal development. Regression occurs in social, language, and play skills, but does not extend to gross motor skills. As with other autistic children, the focus is often on the loss of language. Autism appears the same thereafter, regardless of mode of presentation. It is not clear if mode of presentation effects severity of outcome.

AGE AND IQ AS MODIFIERS OF THE EXPRESSION OF AUTISM

Autism is a disorder of widely varying severity (Kanner 1943, 1971; Kanner, Rodriquez, and Ashenden 1972). Despite a common presentation in early childhood, there is a wide divergence in outcome thereafter (Kanner 1971; Kanner, Rodriquez, and Ashenden 1972). Thus, development of social, language, and reasoning skills is delayed, and the progress that ultimately occurs varies from none to substantial gains. Autistic individuals may have made so little developmental progress as to be profoundly mentally retarded; or may have made such substantial gains that they are socially interactive, have communicative language, and have IQ scores in the normal range but, nonetheless, retain all of the qualitative features of autism.

As a result of these age-related and severity-related modifiers, the expression of autism varies widely as a function of age and inherent severity of the disorder. The most severe symptoms in all autistic individuals will be manifested during the three- to five-year age range, when it is apparent that skills that should have developed have not done so and distinctive abnormalities are present in the skills of those children who have made developmental gains. Thus, the clinical syndrome of autism is characterized by a period of developmental delays or regression, a phase of developmental progress in which deviant features become apparent in the development of skills, and outcome in which the qualitative features of autism are present regardless of the level of skills attained.

In autism, the majority of the gains from early developmental progress will have taken place by 8 years of age, and the developmental acquisition of language thereafter is rare. The earlier that developmental gains begin to occur, the better the prognosis for ultimate outcome. The level of functional language achieved by age 5 years is commonly viewed as the best early prognostic index of later outcome. Thereafter, the best overall indicators of outcome and autism severity are language level and Full Scale and Verbal IQ scores. The younger or severely impaired older autistic individual will bear little clinical similarity to the school age or adult high functioning autistic individual, just as the normal infant and adolescent appear to have little in common. As will become apparent below, the quality of the deficits remains the same regardless of level of function.

SOCIAL SKILLS AND BEHAVIOR

The social deficit in autism is defined by its quality and not by the quantity of interactions. Indeed, some individuals with autism are intrusive and the quantity of interactions is excessive. However, individual's inclination to interact and degree of tolerance for contact with others is an important consideration in creating an appropriate environment. Whether autistic persons interact too little or too much, they are missing the social cues as to what is appropriate to the situation. Fundamentally, autistic persons do not have the skills to interact appropriately and they do not understand the interactions of others. Variations in the severity of autism simply reflect variations in the degree to which these skills are effected.

The essential quality of the social deficit in autism is in the reciprocity of the interactions, not whether they occur or not. Reciprocity reflects a clear grasp of the social situation, the reactions of others, and the capacity for manipulating both. A nonverbal toddler demonstrates social reciprocity in the interactions that take place in attempting to open a forbidden drawer when the parent is on the telephone. With an eye on the parent, the toddler opens the drawer, smiles, and quickly closes it when the parent glares. This continues until the situation deteriorates into anger or laughter. Regardless of outcome, the toddler in this situation has demonstrated a grasp of social cause and effect, awareness of and the capacity for predicting the reactions of the adult, and the capacity to manipulate both. A verbal child or adult demonstrates reciprocity in the capacity for flexible conversation known as chitchat. Chitchat is conversation that is not structured by questions from an interviewer, a set topic, or a pre-planned, rote script. The willingness of verbal autistic individuals to answer questions during an interview or to talk on topics of their choice should not be equated with reciprocity. Repeated observations in such individuals, or a comparison of interactions across observers and situations, will often reveal that "conversation" is following a rote script with little variation from time to time. Likewise an excursion into public, which eliminates all structure and reliance on over-trained etiquette rules for class-room-like situations, is likely to unveil a remarkable lack of appropriateness of social interactions to the situation.

The behavioral expression of the social deficit in autism varies with age and with ultimate severity of the disorder apparent at outcome of development. Approximately one-half of autistic individuals fail to develop any capacity for interacting with others or for comprehending the meaning of the social overtures of others. In severely impaired individuals, the lack of reciprocity is manifested by absence of an appropriate response to the social overtures of others. In moderately severe cases, a few rote strategies or scripts are used for all interactions; these autistic individuals have a short list of questions or statements that are repeated verbatim at every encounter, and this is the sum total of their capacity to interact. In its least severe form, the social deficit in autism is manifested by "big time" socially inappropriate and offensive behavior, as well as by a naivete and gullibility about social situations, both reflecting a partial understanding of social situations. Although these individuals will generally answer a wide range of questions, it will be apparent after several unstructured visits that their innate capacity for interactions is considerably more limited than previously suspected.

The deficit in social reciprocity is multifactorial with regard to defective component skills contributing to the overall impairment in reciprocity. Some of the component skill deficits have been identified and their characterization has made significant contributions to understanding of the social impairment in autism. Two components have been particularly informative, namely referential looking, or the use of eye contact for social communication, and theory of mind abilities, or the capacity for predicting other peoples' views, feelings, and needs. Referential looking refers to the use of eye contact to direct the attention of others to an object of interest and to check that conversational partners are sharing the focus of attention. The use of nonverbal language for social communication is impaired in autism regardless of the quantity of eye contact made. The use of facial expression and tone of voice for social communication are similarly impaired in autism. Autistic individuals also have deficits in the comprehension of messages communicated with these modalities. Theory of mind abilities refer to the cognitive capacity for predicting other people's viewpoints which begins to develop in early childhood. This perspective-taking ability refers to the capacity to infer what others see, feel, or think from their perspective. The absence of this capacity in autistic individuals has been referred to as "mindblindness" (Baron-Cohen 1995) and is a significant factor in their inability to respond appropriately to people and situations. This cognitive deficit contributes significantly to the autistic person's lack of awareness of the feelings and needs of others, and to the perception of them by others as "self-centered" and interested only in their own needs, feelings, and thoughts. Because of the cognitive deficit in theory of mind abilities, autistic individuals cannot have an awareness of another's perspective as expected by society.

LANGUAGE AND COMMUNICATION IMPAIRMENT

The language deficit in autism is defined by the global involvement of all verbal and nonverbal language skills, by abnormalities in their use for communication, and by particular abnormalities in their development. As with social skills, approximately one-half of autistic individuals fail to develop language of any type and developmental progress in the remainder ranges widely. The diagnostic criteria for autism require documentation of the delay in development of verbal and nonverbal language, documentation of the typical deviant features of language development in those who develop language, and documentation at outcome of residual abnormalities in comprehension, expression, and use of all forms of language.

Verbal language in autism is characterized by a delay in development or by loss of previously acquired language most commonly between 14 and 24 months of age. Development of language in autism, when it occurs, is characterized by particular abnormal features that include: immediate, delayed, and then the functional use of echolalia; pronoun reversal as a consequence of the functional use of echolalia in the presence of incomplete comprehension of language; use of stereotyped language scripts; early reading without comprehension; and an expressive language level that exceeds comprehension. In addition to these impairments, there are abnormalities in the use of language for social communication that include a lack of awareness of the basic principles of conversation and later of the rules that govern conversation. At outcome of developmental progress, language abilities in autism range from: (1) echolalia of a few words or phrases without comprehension and without any awareness of language as a tool to be used for communication; to (2) the use of a small number of sentences that are repeated verbatim at each encounter with little awareness of their use in communication other than to direct them at others; to (3) grammatically correct, non-echoed sentence language, a level of comprehension that is below that of expressive language, a basic appreciation of conversational rules but lack of capacity for chit-chat, and a lack of understanding of what is and is not appropriate to say under the circumstances.

Nonverbal language, which includes eye contact, facial expression, tone of voice, gestures, pantomime, and body language, has impairments that are analogous to those described for verbal language in autism. Development of nonverbal language is delayed, accounting for the failure of autistic children with delayed verbal language development to use alternate forms of communication. The development of nonverbal language abilities typically parallels that of verbal language development, and thus the autistic child with echolalia makes glancing eye contact but does not use eye contact in social situations. The autistic child who uses grammatically correct sentence language will generally have a normal quantity of eye contact in social situations but lacks the capacity to comprehend the meaning of eye contact and to

use it in qualitative ways for social communication. Referential looking is one example of this level of development. As with verbal language, the amount of eye contact is greater than comprehension of its
meaning and its use as a tool for communication. Facial expression,
tone of voice language (prosody), gestures, and pantomime (gestures
with symbolic meaning) follow this same developmental and outcome
profile in autism. Abnormalities in body language, such as awareness
of appropriate social distance and messages communicated in pos-
ture, are present but are less problematic for function other than the
need for appropriate social distance.

IMPAIRMENTS IN PLAY

Impairments in play with toys and with other children are also typical
of autism. The abnormalities in toy play and the associated odd behavior relate to a failure to comprehend the symbolic meaning of toys and
are reflected early in life by an absence of interest in toys and then a preoccupation with the elementary sensory features of toys. Thus toys are
played with in ways other than those for which they were designed.
Interest in toys, when it develops in autism, is characterized by lining up
toys, spinning the moving parts, collecting but not playing with toys, arranging them in precise ways, or hoarding particular toys or objects but
not using them according to function. At the next stage of toy play development, if it occurs, the autistic child appreciates the symbolic meaning of the toy and displays isolated appropriate functional use of the toy
and later the emergence of sequences of appropriate actions. However,
toy play never achieves the creativity or variability typical of normal
children. The capacity of some high functioning autistic children for precise imitation of play observed in videotapes and movies can be remarkable, but its identity with the videotape distinguishes it from true
creative play. Ultimately, high functioning autistic children became pre-
occupied with playing computer or video games, at which they are su-
perb, or with collecting facts or objects related to an obsession.

Play with other children involves a number of skills including
social interactions, communication, and the capacity to comprehend
and create themes of play. As with other impairments, very young autistic children typically have no interest in or skills for playing with
other children. With developmental progress, an interest in the play of
others appears and then parallel play emerges. Those autistic children
who acquire sentence language also typically acquire interactive play,
but as with other forms of play, imagination and creativity are essentially non-existent. These children do best if they can play simple games
with much younger children or computer games with severely limited
demands on interactive play skills.

RESTRICTED RANGE OF INTERESTS AND ACTIVITIES

This symptom category contains an assortment of behaviors that superficially appear to have no relationship to each other. These signs and symptoms include: self-stimulatory behavior such as rocking and flapping as well as preoccupation with lights; preoccupation with the elementary sensory aspects of objects and with object parts; resistance to change; ritualistic or prescribed ways of doing things that are rigidly adhered to; a narrow range of interests, and interests that have the quality of an obsession and a focus on details or facts. Although superficially unrelated, Kanner (1971) observed that as higher functioning autistic children in his clinic became older, the resistance to change and stereotyped repetitive ways of doing things "assumed the form of obsessive preoccupations." This observation on the natural history suggests that the resistance to change and ritualistic behavior in autism have the same underlying basis as the narrow range of interests. It appears likely that all of the behavior in this category reflects the peculiar reasoning deficit in autism, which is composed equally of a phenomenal perception and memory of trivial details and equally poor abstract reasoning. Thus, the narrow range of interests with an extensive range of facts or details about each interest may reflect the poor conceptual ability and the enhanced awareness of detail. To autistic persons, each fact is a separate detail and thus, from their perspective, they have a very large range of information. By ordinary standards, their interests are viewed as narrow because they involve only one or two conceptual categories. Similarly, the enhanced appreciation of details and the severe difficulty with abstract reasoning makes even trivial change a frightening experience in the absence of a capacity to determine the significance of change and to predict its consequences. Within this context, resisting change at all costs or having a precise ritual for regulating change become good coping strategies. In a similar vane, the focus on the elementary aspects of objects and object parts may also be seen as a reflection of an enhanced awareness of trivial details and a lack of appreciation of higher order meaning and concepts. Self-stimulatory behavior is not specific to autism, but in autism this behavior appears to a greater degree than would be predicted by general level of ability. That is, skills that are present would normally predict the capacity for participation in more adaptive behavior in other individuals; but in autism these skills do not accurately predict higher order abilities. Thus, autistic people engage in less adaptive behavior than would be expected had higher order abilities developed in concert with more elementary abilities.

Although not included in the list of behaviors in this category in DSM-IV, other behaviors typical of autism are also likely to be related to the peculiar cognitive profile in autism. These behaviors include:

exaggerated fears of specific objects or situations, lack of awareness of danger, lack of common sense and judgement, and inability to understand cause and effect relationships that others automatically understand without the need for explanations.

ASSOCIATED SIGNS AND SYMPTOMS

Several additional and assorted features are commonly associated with autism, but are not considered to be central features of the disorder. Hyperactivity is common early in the course of autism, and may persist, with or without the signs of attention deficit disorder, throughout life. It is estimated that approximately 20% of autistic individuals will respond to stimulants with a reduction in hyperactivity or improvement in attention span. Relative insensitivity to pain and heightened sensitivity to sounds, smells, tastes, and the textures of objects occur in about one-fourth of autistic individuals. The sensitivities, particularly the sound sensitivity, become an important consideration in environmental modification. Gross motor development is delayed in a minority of autistic individuals but usually not past 22 months of age. Deficits in complex or skilled aspects of motor movements have been recently appreciated to be a feature of autism. Reports of motor deficits in autism have ranged from motor apraxia and a complete lack of imitative and pantomime capacity, to awkwardly performed correct movements (limb apraxia), to a generalized deficit in skilled motor movements (Hughes 1996; Minshew, Goldstein, and Siegel 1996; Smith and Bryson 1994).

Mental retardation is also a common feature in autism, and is present in 70% to 75% of autistic individuals. The mental retardation in autism does not represent the coexistence of a separate diagnostic entity but rather the logical extension of progressively more severe deficits in social, language, and reasoning abilities. Thus, mentally retarded individuals with autism do not have two separate disorders. Rather IQ is a reflection of the severity of autism.

NEUROLOGIC EXAMINATION

The neurologic physical examination, other than presence of the above signs and symptoms, is unremarkable in autism. Dysmorphic features are absent, as are abnormalities in growth. Head circumference is typically in the average or above average range. Muscle tone is generally normal, or subtly hypotonic. Deep tendon reflexes are either generally increased, or absent in the upper extremities and at the knees but increased at the ankles. Plantar reflexes are down-going.

The presence of dysmorphic features, abnormalities in body or head size, blindness, deafness, or cerebral palsy is indicative of the presence of an infectious, genetic, or metabolic disorder that is associated with a PDD clinical syndrome. For example, microcephaly resulting from fetal cytomegalic or rubella virus infection or macrocephaly related to Soto's syndrome, have been reported to be associated with a PDD clinical syndrome. Likewise, the presence of unusually tall or unusually short stature should trigger a search for a genetic syndrome. An exhaustive list of the infectious, genetic, metabolic disorders that have been reported in association with a PDD clinical syndrome is provided in Gillberg and Coleman (1992). These various conditions should not be viewed as causes of autism, but rather as other disorders that also have a selective impact on the development of social, language, and reasoning abilities and behavior. Some of these entities produce a clinical syndrome that is more similar to autism than dissimilar, but others, as exemplified by the undersocialized conduct disorder in XYY syndrome, appear only superficially similar to autism. Although the list of disorders reported to be associated with PDD is extensive, many such associations are based on single case occurrences and collectively account for a very small segment of individuals with those disorders and with PDD. Most such disorders can be identified by the presence of atypical features on the physical examination, and extensive laboratory testing is rarely productive in the absence of such atypical features.

COMPLICATIONS

Seizure disorder and mood disorder are two well established complications of autism. The presence of either one is typically associated with an exacerbation in the severity of the autistic symptomatology.

An increased incidence of seizures has been reported in autism for several decades, but the types of seizures reported have changed over time. In the 1960s and 1970s, fetal infection with rubella, complicated meningitis, tuberous sclerosis, and probably also severe hypoxic injury were common in individuals diagnosed with autism. During that era, hypsarrhythmia on the electroencephalogram and infantile spasms were reported to be common expressions of epilepsy in autism. With the improvement in the characterization of autism and the appreciation of the role of associated disorders in producing neurologic dysfunction in autism, this form of epilepsy has been separated from autism. It is now thought that autism itself is associated with an increased incidence of partial complex and secondarily generalized seizures. Generalized convulsions have been found to effect about 20% to 25% of autistic individuals by age 21, with a predilection for mentally retarded individuals, early childhood, and puberty. However, seizures can develop as a complication of autism at any age and IQ. The detection of partial complex seizures associated with lapses in consciousness or with irritability-rage-aggression have been documented with electroencephalographic assistance, but are difficult to detect clinically because of the impact of autism on clinical behavior. Partial complex seizures should be included in the differential diagnosis of autistic individuals exhibiting a sustained deterioration in function or aggression not related to change in the environment.

Depression and mania also occur in autistic individuals. In most autistic individuals, the diagnosis of depression depends on documenting a sustained deterioration in function and behavior that cannot be attributed to any other cause. Vegetative signs may be present to suggest the presence of depression, but even verbal autistic individuals have such poor insight and problem solving ability that they often are unable to relate a history that would be typical of depression in the general population. Mania is rare but occurs, and must also be suspected on the basis of a deterioration in function and behavior, since the autistic individual may be incapable of verbalizing the more typical history associated with mania, and the manifestations of autism may distort the presentation sufficiently that mania or depression are not separately recognizable.

A rare individual with autism will develop obsessive compulsive behavior that is considerably beyond that expected for the degree of autism and does not appear to be associated with more generalized signs of depression. Such individuals may step back and forth across a threshold innumerable times before being able to pass through a doorway, or may sit down and stand up repeatedly before being able to leave a chair. Such behavior is thought likely to be responsive to a sertonergic antidepressant. However, the usual ritualistic behavior in non-depressed individuals with autism is not responsive to antidepressants beyond the minor effect that may result from anxiety control.

TREATMENT

The treatment of autism is primarily environmental, as there are no medications with demonstrated efficacy against the skill deficits. However, the value of medications targeting secondary or associated signs such as anxiety, attention deficit, seizures, depression, or mania cannot be underestimated. Anxiety is particularly disabling, and is a constant consequence of the patient's difficulty handling the social, language, and problem solving demands of life in the presence of sufficient awareness that these demands exist. The treatment of autism is otherwise largely environmental and behavioral. The majority of efforts should be focused on adapting the environment to the autistic individual and on having reasonable expectations. It is essential that autism be recognized as a disorder defined by deficits in the capacity for adapting and functioning in society. Thus, the first line of treatment in addressing any problem behavior is to adapt the environment and task demands to the autistic individual, rather than expecting the autistic person to adapt to the environment. If an autistic person becomes agitated or aggressive at having to pass through a group of peers to hang up his coat, then the coat hook should be moved or an alternate, low social route to the hook should be identified, rather than embarking on medications and extensive behavior modification aimed at enabling him to pass through the group. It is equally important that teachers and staff acquire a detailed understanding of the deficits and intact abilities in autism and of their specific manifestations in real life behavior in each affected individual, so that expectations for behavior and achievement are truly appropriate to the individual. Odd behavior and limitations in tolerance of social contact and of environmental change should be respected as hard-wired expressions of the brain abnormality in autism. Odd behavior that is not hindering the autistic individual should not be targeted for behavior modification simply because it looks odd to others. The autistic individual's limits in tolerance for social contact and environmental change should be clearly identified and steps taken to prevent over-stimulation and the consequence of undesirable behavioral outbursts.

Behavior modification is a standard tool for dealing with problem behaviors in autism, once the environment and demands of the situation have been determined to be appropriate to the individual. However, the principles of behavior modification must be applied within the context of autism. For verbal autistic individuals, the social story method has proven useful in identifying those things that other people automatically know about situations that autistic people do not know but must know in order to act appropriately (Gray 1994).

With regard to academic intervention, a reverse mainstreaming approach should be utilized, so that integration takes place in academic situations that are highly structured and supervised to prevent inappropriate behavior or scape-goating from getting out of hand before redirection is provided. Maximal support should be provided in free social situations that are characterized by minimal adult supervision, such as bus rides, lunch rooms, hallways between classes, and recess. The autistic child should be protected in these situations from becoming a scape-goat and from the provocations of peers who may purposely try to elicit behavioral outbursts. Often, adult staff are not sufficiently accessible in these large group settings to provide the needed supervision to prevent scape-goating, and so peer groups may need to be formed with the specific purpose of providing protection of the autistic individual from becoming a scapegoat. Maintenance of a constant student cohort throughout school and major transitions between schools can also be a very powerful protective influence. The oddities of behavior in the autistic child who enters a school at a young age and remains there as part of a group of children will be accepted as part of that individual, and peers are likely to move to protect him or her from outsiders who are immediately struck by his or her differences. However, a bad placement should not be continued just to avoid a change in environment. The most successful integrations in school and in the work place occur when peers are made aware of the autistic individual's oddities and limitations and provided with specific guidelines about how to respond in a helpful manner. School is a highly structured and restricted life experience. Moderately impaired autistic individuals go on to job settings that are equally structured and supervised, and thus continue in essentially the same level of support. Many high functioning autistic individuals, however, are never again as successful in life as they were during the school years. Once they exit school, the level of support and structure in their lives declines significantly. Vocational rehabilitation services are not yet generally available in a form that would provide the adaptations that these high functioning autistic individuals need in order to function successfully in jobs that they would otherwise be capable of doing. The tendency is to enroll such individuals in course work in an effort to develop a career or job path, but choice of college or major often focuses on their remarkable talents, and fails to consider their limitations, or the availability of a job they can do utilizing their classroom education.

Job training and placement should take into consideration the autistic individual's tolerance of social contact and the demands of the job for communication and problem solving. As in school, peers on the job site and the supervisor will need to be provided with a clear understanding of the autistic person's behavior in all spheres and recommendations as to how to respond to inappropriate behavior.

ACKNOWLEDGMENT

I would like to gratefully acknowledge the support for my research in autism provided by grant number NS33355 from the Child Neurology Branch of the National Institute of Neurologic Disorders and Stroke.

REFERENCES

American Psychiatric Association. 1994. *Diagnostic and Statistical Manual of Mental Disorders*-Fourth Ed. Washington, DC.

Baron-Cohen, S. 1995. *Mindblindness: An Essay on Autism and Theory of Mind.* Massachusetts: MIT Press.

Gillberg, C., and Coleman, M. 1992. *The Biology of the Autistic Syndromes.* 2nd ed. London: Mac Keith.

Gray, C. 1994. *The Social Story Book 1994.* Jenison, Michigan: Jenison Public Schools.

Hughes, C. 1996. Brief report: Planning problems in autism at the level of motor control. *Journal of Autism and Developmental Disorders* 26:99–107.

Kanner, L. 1943. Autistic disturbances of affective contact. *Nervous Child* 2:217–50.

Kanner, L. 1971. Follow-up study of eleven autistic children originally reported in 1943. *Journal of Autism and Childhood Schizophrenia* 2:119–45.

Kanner, L., Rodriguez, A., and Ashenden, B. 1972. How far can autistic children go in matters of social adaptation? *Journal of Autism and Childhood Schizophrenia* 2:9–33.

Minshew, N. J. 1996. Neurobehavioral disorders in children; Pervasive developmental disorders: Autism and similar disorders. In *Behavioral Neurology and Neuropsychology*, eds. T. Feinberg and M. Farah. New York: McGraw-Hill.

Minshew, N. J., and Payton, J. B. 1988a. New perspectives in autism: The clinical spectrum of autism. Part I. *Current Problems in Pediatrics* 18:561–610.

Minshew, N. J., and Payton, J. B. 1988b. New perspectives in autism: The differential diagnosis and neurobiology of autism. Part II. *Current Problems in Pediatrics* 18:613–94.

Minshew, N. J., Goldstein, G., and Siegel, D. J. 1996. Complex memory impairments in autism. *Journal of the International Neuropsychological Society* 2:190.

Osterling, J., and Dawson, G. 1994. Early recognition of children with autism: A study of first birthday home videotapes. *Journal of Autism and Developmental Disorders* 24:247–57.

Rapin, I. 1991. Autistic children: Diagnosis and clinical features. *Pediatrics* [Suppl] 5:751–60.

Rourke, B.P. 1989. *Nonverbal Learning Disabilities: The Syndrome and the Model.* New York: Guilford Press.

Smith, I. M., and Bryson, S. E. 1994. Imitation and action in autism: A critical review. *Psychological Bulletin* 116:259–73.

Volkmer, F. R. 1994. Childhood disintegrative disorder. *Psychosis and Pervasive Developmental Disorders* 3:119–29.

Weintraub, S., and Mesulam, M. M. 1983. Developmental learning disabilities of the right hemisphere: Emotional, interpersonal, and cognitive components. *Archives of Neurology* 40:463–68.

World Health Organization. 1992. *International Classification of Diseases-10 Classifications of Mental and Behavioral Disorders: Clinical Descriptions and Diagnostic Guidelines.* Geneva: WHO.

Chapter • 5

The Neuroanatomy of Autism:
Clinical Implications

Margaret L. Bauman

Early infantile autism is a behaviorally defined disorder, first described by Kanner in 1943, in which symptoms become evident during the first three years of life. Features of the syndrome include atypical social interaction, disordered language, speech, and cognitive skills, impaired imaginary play, poor eye contact, and an obsessive insistence on sameness. Repetitive and stereotypic behavior, perseveration, and a restricted range of interests may be present in some cases. Many affected individuals have unusual islands of rote memory, and some show exceptional talents in the presence of otherwise global functional disability. Intelligence in autistic individuals may vary from profound mental retardation to superior, and it has been estimated that between 5% and 30% have cognitive abilities that fall within the normal range (DeMyer 1979). Although not dysmorphic in physical appearance, a significant number of autistic individuals exhibit hypotonia, dyspraxia, and disordered modulation of sensory input (Rapin 1994). Some clinical features of the disorder have been observed in conditions such as phenylketonuria, tuberous sclerosis, and fragile X syndrome, but the majority of the cases are without an identifiable etiology. Although the cause of autism is believed by many to be multifactorial, twin and family studies have suggested evidence of a genetic liability, the mechanism of which remains unknown (Piven and Folstein 1994).

For many years, autism was believed to be related to parenting and environmental factors. However, over time, evidence for a neurobiologic basis for the disorder has mounted. Over the past thirty-five years, a significant number of autistic individuals have been reported to have abnormalities on neurological examination and on electroencephalographic study (EEG) and many have been found to develop seizures at some time during their lives (Schain and Yannet 1960; Deykin and MacMahon 1979). In addition, it has been observed that a disproportionate number of children affected by the rubella epidemic in 1964 appeared to be at high risk for autism (Chess, Korn, and Fernandez 1971). Neurophysiologic studies have demonstrated abnormalities of auditory nerve and brainstem evoked responses (Student and Schmer 1978; Tanguay et al. 1982) and REM sleep patterns (Tanguay et al. 1976). In 1985, Rumsey at al. reported diffuse cerebral hypermetabolism on positron emission tomography (PET) in a series of adult autistic males as compared with controls. When subjected to correlation analysis, reduced frontal-parietal intercorrelations were found in the autistic subjects which were hypothesized to be related to an imbalance in mutually inhibitory neural circuits associated with attention (Horwitz et al. 1988).

With the recognition that autism was probably a disorder of neurobiologic origin, a number of regions of the brain were suggested as possible candidate sites of abnormality. These included the basal ganglia (Vilensky, DeMasio, and Maurer 1981), the thalamic nuclei (Coleman 1979), the vestibular system (Ornitz and Ritvo 1968) and structures of the medial temporal lobe (Boucher and Warrington 1976; Delong 1978; Demasio and Maurer 1978; Maurer and Demasio 1982). However, definitive neuroanatomic evidence of abnormality remained elusive. The few autopsy studies reported by the mid-1970s showed sparse and inconsistent findings.

IN VIVO NEUROANATOMY

In 1975, a pneumoencephalographic (PEG) study involving 18 children less than 18 years of age who presented with retarded language development and autistic behavior was reported (Hauser, DeLong, and Rosman 1975). Enlargement of the left temporal horn was found in 15 cases, with some patients showing enlargement of both temporal horns or mild enlargement of the lateral ventricles, primarily on the left. The authors suggested that dysfunction of medial temporal lobe structures might play a contributing role in the symptomatology of autism.

With the introduction of computerized tomographic scanning (CT) technology in the mid-1970s, in vivo neuroanatomic studies of the brain in autism increased substantially. In 1979, Hier, LeMay, and Rosenberger reported a reversal of the normal left-right parietal-occipital asymmetry in 57% of the autistic subjects studied in comparison with mentally retarded and neurologic control groups. The authors hypothesized that the failure of normal language development in autism might be related to a morphologic inferiority of the left hemisphere in affected individuals. However, subsequent CT scan studies of hemispheric asymmetry failed to support these initial findings (Damasio et al. 1980; Tsai, Jacoby, and Stewart 1983; Rumsey et al. 1988).

Imaging studies have also suggested abnormalities of ventricular size in a small subgroup of autistic individuals (Campbell et al. 1982; Jacobson et al. 1988). However, many of these studies have been confounded by the inclusion of subjects with other neurologic disorders such as neurofibromatosis as well as the inconsistency of measurement techniques and statistical data. Further, the relationship between these findings and the pathogenesis and symptomatology in autism is unclear. The majority of studies have failed to find any significant differences between autistic subjects and controls (Jacobson et al. 1988; Rumsey et al. 1988; Garber et al. 1989; Piven et al. 1992a; Kleiman, Neff, and Rosman 1992).

With the emergence of magnetic resonance imaging (MRI) technology, morphometric analysis of specific brain structures has become the focus of neuroimaging research. The major emphasis of these studies in autism has been the cerebellum. The initial investigations of Courchesne et al. (1987, 1988), and the later remeasurement of the same cases by Murakami et al. (1989), reported a selective hypoplasia of lobules VI and VII of the vermis on midsaggital MR images in autistic subjects. Since these initial reports, there have been multiple attempts to replicate these findings (Ritvo and Garber 1988; Holttum at al. 1992; Piven et al. 1992; Kleiman, Neff, and Rosman 1992). In these studies, subjects were matched for age, sex, IQ, and socioeconomic status, and were screened for fragile X syndrome, which is known to be associated with cerebellar hypoplasia (Reiss et al. 1991). Taken together, the subjects in these studies represent a cross-section of ages and cognitive abilities within the autism spectrum. Using the same imaging methods as the original study (Courchesne et al. 1988), these investigators failed to find evidence of vermal hypoplasia in autism. Although Piven et al. (1992) noted no differences in the size of lobules VI and VII, lobules I-V were noted to be increased in size in the autistic subjects as compared with age and socioeconomic status matched controls, but not when compared with age and IQ matched controls. It has been suggested that socioeconomic status may be a significant variable and may be a more accurate reflection of intellect than IQ.

In a more recent study, Courchesne, Townsend, and Saitoh (1994) reanalyzed data from previously published MRI midsaggital vermal measurements on 78 autistic subjects. Two subgroups were identified.

Although the large majority of these subjects were reported to have hypoplasia of lobules VI and VII, a small subgroup were noted to have hyperplasia of these same lobules. The authors concluded that, because of the averaging of these measurements, cerebellar midline abnormalities had failed to be detected in several previously reported series. However, the possibility that neocerebellar size might be a variable of IQ or other methodological factors and therefore non-specific to autism is not addressed.

Nowell et al. (1990) studied 53 autistic patients and 32 controls matched for age but not for sex, socioeconomic status, or IQ. All males were screened for fragile X syndrome. The authors found that only five patients (7.6%) had evidence of vermian atrophy and noted that the degree of the atrophy, when present, did not appear to correlate with the severity of the patient's autism. These authors did not find any specific morphologic criteria to be associated with autism. They concluded that either vermian atrophy was too subtle to be detected on their 10-mm images or that it was some type of epiphenomenon unrelated to autism that might develop later in life. More recently, Schaefer et al. (1996) measured the cerebellar vermis in 125 normal individuals in comparison with 102 patients with a variety of neurological abnormalities. Hypoplasia of lobules VI and VII of the vermis was found in a variety of neurologically based conditions unassociated with autistic behavior and was not uniformly seen in subjects with autism. The authors concluded that hypoplasia of lobules VI and VII was a non-specific finding, that it was not a specific marker for autism and that cerebellar dysgenesis was unlikely to be solely responsible for clinical autistic behaviors.

Posterior fossa structures, other than the cerebellum, have received relatively little attention from the perspective of neuroimaging. Although early neurophysiological research (Ornitz and Ritvo 1968; Ornitz 1985) had suggested that abnormalities of the brainstem might play a significant role in the pathogenesis of autism, many of these studies were later determined to be confounded by the presence of other neurological and audiological conditions (Rumsey et al. 1985) and methodologic deficiencies (Ornitz 1985). Because of the limitations of CT, in vivo neuroanatomic investigations of posterior fossa structures have been confined to MRI technology and results to date have been inconsistent (Gaffney et al. 1988; Hsu et al. 1991; Piven et al. 1992b).

Cortical and subcortical structures of the cerebral hemispheres have likewise received little attention and the few available studies of these regions have not been definitive. In an MRI study, Piven et al. (1992a) noted a significant enlargement of the cerebral hemispheric midsaggital area in autistic subjects as compared with controls. Observations of the cerebral cortex in this same group of patients suggested the presence of cortical gyral malformations consistent with developmental errors of neuronal migration. Some preliminary data indicate an increase in the volume of the cerebral cortex in autistic children as compared with language-delayed and normal control children (Filipek et al. 1992). More recently, Piven et al. (1995) measured total brain volume in 22 male autistic subjects in comparison with controls. The autistic subjects were found to have enlargement of both brain tissue and lateral ventricular volume. These findings are in contrast to the observation of decreased parietal lobe volume reported in an earlier series (Courchesne, Press, and Yeung-Courchesne 1992a). Further morphometric analysis of specific cortical regions in large carefully controlled samples of autistic subjects will be necessary in order to clarify what, if any, of these abnormalities may be significant to the pathogenesis and clinical features of autism.

A small number of imaging studies have subjected some subcortical structures, including the basal ganglia, thalamus, and the corpus callosum, to quantitative analysis (Creasey et al. 1986; Gaffney et al. 1988). The findings so far have not been persuasive. While no volumetric differences were noted in the corpus callosum between autistic subjects and controls in two studies (Gaffney et al. 1987b; Filipek et al. 1992), callosal volume of the autistic subjects in one series was found to be disproportionally small relative to the volume of the cortex and white matter, both of which were enlarged (Filipek et al. 1992). Since the size and configuration of the corpus callosum provides an indication of interhemispheric connectivity, further quantitative analysis of this structure may be an important area of future imaging research.

HISTOANATOMY OF THE BRAIN

Few neuropathological studies of the brain in autism have been reported. "Slight thickening of the arterioles, slight connective tissue increase in the leptomeninges and some cell increase" were described by Aarkrog (1968) in biopsy material obtained from the right frontal lobe of an autistic patient. Later, in a review of 33 cases of childhood psychosis, Darby (1976) suggested a relationship between limbic system lesions and the affective features of autism, but cited no specific pathological abnormalities. In 1980, Williams et al. studied autopsy material from four individuals with autistic features, looking primarily for cell loss or gliosis, and found no consistent abnormalities. Quantitative analysis of glial and neuronal cell number was performed by Coleman et al. (1985) in multiple areas of the cerebral cortex of a single autistic patient and two age- and sex-matched controls. No differences were observed and the authors concluded that abnormalities during the early stages of nervous system development and neuronal migration were not a feature of autism. They hypothesized that the probable pathogenetic process in this disorder was more likely to occur later in development, possibly during the elaboration of neuronal processes and synapses. Ritvo et al. (1986), who quantitatively studied the cerebellar hemispheres and vermis obtained from four autistic subjects and controls, found decreased numbers of Purkinje cells and speculated on the possible relationship of these findings to some of the clinical features of autism.

In the mid-1980s, histoanatomic analysis of the brain of a well-documented 29-year-old autistic man, studied in comparison with an identically prepared age- and sex-matched control and using the technique of whole brain serial section (Yakovlev 1970) was reported (Bauman and Kemper 1984, 1985). Observations were made with a Zeiss comparison microscope whereby sections of both brains could be seen side by side at the same magnification and in the same field of view. Quantitative analysis of neuronal cell size and cell packing density (the number of neurons per unit volume) was performed in areas of the brain that were found to be abnormal. Since this initial report, eight additional clinically well-documented cases have been similarly studied including six children, two girls and four boys ranging in age from 5 to 12 years, and two young adult males, ages 22 and 28 years, for a total of three young adults.

None of the brains studied to date have shown any gross abnormalities. Myelination has been found to be comparable to controls in all cases. Except for the anterior cingulate gyrus, detailed microscopic examination of multiple cortical regions of the autistic brains has shown no evidence of abnormality. Specifically, no disorder of cortical lamination, neuronal size or number, or cellular migration has been observed, consistent with the findings of Coleman et al. (1985). Similarly, systematic study of the autistic basal ganglia, thalamus, basal forebrain, and hypothalamus has failed to show any differences when compared with controls.

Areas of the forebrain that have been found to be abnormal have been confined to the hippocampus, subiculum, entorhinal cortex, amygdala, mamillary body, anterior cingulate cortex, and septum. When compared with controls, neuronal cell size has been found to be reduced and cell packing density increased in these areas (figures 1 and 2) and the findings appeared to be equal bilaterally. Study of the CA1 and CA4 pyramidal neurons of the hippocampus, using the rapid Golgi technique, demonstrated reduced complexity and extent of dendritic arbors in these cells (Raymond, Bauman, and Kemper 1989, 1996). In the amygdala, reduced cell size and increased packing density were found to be most pronounced in the most medially located cortical, medial, and central nuclei. In eight of the nine cases studied, the lateral nucleus appeared to be similar to controls. Similar

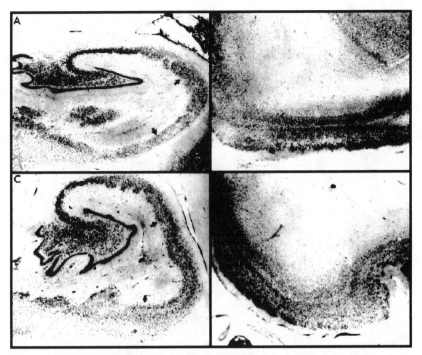

Figure 1.   Nissl-stained sections from the hippocampal complex (A) and entorhinal cortex (B) in the brain of a 29-year-old autistic male, with comparable sections from an age and sex-matched control subject (C and D). Neuronal cell packing density is increased throughout these areas in the autistic brain. This can best be appreciated by comparing area CA4 in the hilum of the fascia dentata in A and C (Bauman and Kemper 1985).

neuronal findings were also noted in the mamillary bodies and in the anterior cingulate gyrus. All forebrain areas found to be abnormal in these autistic cerebra are known to be related to each other by interconnecting circuits (figure 3), and make up a major portion of the limbic system of the brain.

Increased cell packing density and reduced neuronal cell size were also noted in the medial septal nucleus (MSN) of the septum in all cases, a pattern similar to that seen in other regions of the limbic system. However, a different pattern of abnormality was observed in the nucleus of the diagonal band of Broca (NDB). In the brains of all of the autistic patients 12 years of age and younger, the neurons of the NDB appeared to be unusually large and present in adequate numbers. In contrast, these same neurons were found to be small in size and markedly reduced in number in all of the autistic patients, ages 22 years and older, when compared with controls.

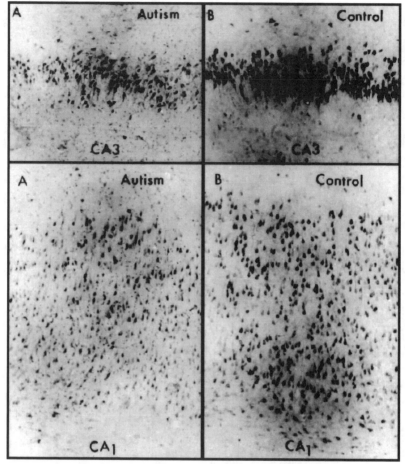

Figure 2. Photomicrograph of a Nissl-stained section of the hippocampus at higher power. Note the abnormally small, tightly packed cells in the CA3 and CA1 hippocampal subfields in the autistic brain as compared with the control (Kemper and Bauman 1992).

Outside of the forebrain, the only other abnormalities in these autistic brains have been confined to the cerebellum and related inferior olive. A significant reduction in the number of Purkinje cells has been demonstrated in all cases throughout the cerebellar hemispheres, most pronounced in the posteriolateral neocerebellar cortex and adjacent archicerebellar cortex (figure 4) (Arin, Bauman, and Kemper 1991). In contrast, no statistically significant difference in the size or number of Purkinje cells has been observed in any area of the vermis (Bauman and Kemper 1996). A variable decrease in the number of granule cells has also been noted in two patients. In addition, abnormalities have been found in the fastigial, globose, and emboliform nu-

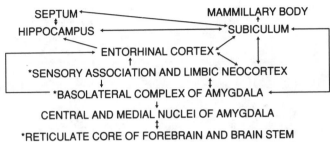

Figure 3.   Diagram of forebrain circuits mentioned in the text. The * indicates regions of the brain anatomically related to the areas of abnormality but which appear unaffected (Bauman and Kemper 1985).

clei in the roof of the cerebellum which, similar to the findings in the NDB of the septum, appear to differ with the age of the patient. As in the NDB, small pale neurons that are reduced in number are seen in these nuclei in the three young adult autistic patients (figure 5). In all of the younger cases, however, these neurons as well as those of the dentate nucleus, are enlarged in size and present in adequate numbers (figure 6) (Kemper and Bauman 1992).

No evidence of retrograde cell loss or atrophy was found in the principal inferior olivary nucleus of the brainstem in the autistic brains, areas that are known to be related to the abnormal regions of the cerebellar cortex (Holmes and Stewart 1908). In human pathology, neuronal cell loss and atrophy of the inferior olive have been invariably observed following perinatal and postnatal Purkinje cell loss (Norman 1940; Greenfield 1954). The olivary neurons in the three oldest cases were small and pale but no cell loss was observed. In the younger brains, these same neurons were significantly enlarged but were otherwise normal in appearance and number. In all cases, some of the olivary neurons tended to cluster at the periphery of the inferior nuclear convolutions, a pattern which has been observed in some syndromes of prenatal origin associated with mental retardation (Sumi 1989; DeBassio, Kemper, and Knoefel 1985).

POSSIBLE RELATIONSHIP OF LIMBIC SYSTEM FINDINGS TO THE CLINICAL FEATURES OF AUTISM

Systematic neuroanatomic analysis of the cerebra of nine clinically well-documented autistic individuals has revealed microscopic abnormalities that have been consistently confined to the limbic system and to the cerebellum and related inferior olive. Decreased neuronal cell size and increased cell packing density characterize the hippocampal complex, the amygdala and areas related to them. This pattern of small, closely packed neurons is characteristically seen during early stages of brain maturation and may, therefore, represent a selective

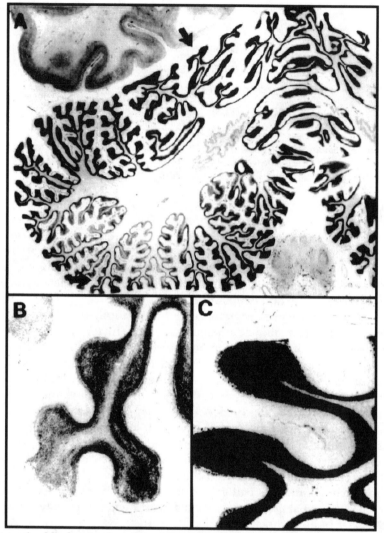

Figure 4.   Nissl-stained section of the cerebellum from an adult autistic male. Note the atrophy of the cerebellar cortex in the lateral and inferior regions of the hemispheres, and the relatively normal-appearing anterior hemisphere and vermis. In (B), the markedly reduced numbers of Purkinje cells, and to a lesser extent, granule cells, can be appreciated as compared with a section from the more normal-appearing section from the anterior cerebellum (C) (Bauman and Kemper 1985).

curtailment of normal development in these autistic brains. This notion is further supported by the appearance of reduced complexity and extent of dendritic arbors observed in the hypocampal pyramidal cells of autistic subjects.

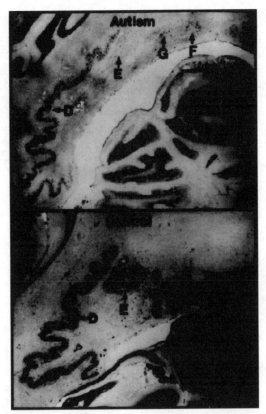

Figure 5.   Photomicrograph of the deep cerebellar nuclei from the brain of an adult autistic man. The neurons of the fastigial (F), globose (G), and emboliform (E) nuclei are small and pale and reduced in number in the autistic brain. The dentate nucleus (D) appears distorted and the neurons small but present in adequate numbers (Bauman and Kemper 1985).

Because of the extent of its connections to other parts of the brain, abnormalities of the limbic system could have far-reaching consequences. The hippocampal complex is related by sequential projections from the dentate gyrus through the ammonic subfields and into the subiculum (Rosene and Van Hoesen 1987). The entorhinal cortex projects to all areas of the hippocampus and has reciprocal projections with the subiculum (Van Hoesen and Pandya 1975a, 1975b; Rosene and Van Hoesen 1977). The perirhinal and entorhinal cortices and, to a lesser extent, the subiculum are the site of afferent projections from multiple limbic neocortical areas, auditory and visual association cortex, and the polysensory cortical area on the bank of the superior temporal sulcus (Van Hoesen and Pandya 1975a; Van Hoesen, Pandya, and Butters 1972; Van Hoesen, Pandya, and Butters 1975; Van Hoesen, Rosene, and Mesulam 1979; Amaral, Inshusti, and Cowan 1983; Rosene

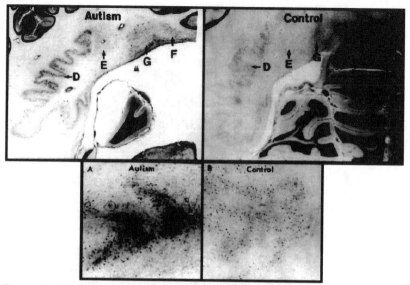

Figure 6. Nissl-stained section of the deep cerebellar nuclei from the brain of an autistic child. Note the prominent cerebellar nuclei with neuronal enlargement which characterizes this autistic brain. Similar findings are seen in the dentate nucleus in the lower panels (Kemper and Bauman 1992).

and Van Hoesen 1987). In addition, nearly all efferent projections from the hippocampal complex are from the prosubiculum and/or the subiculum, and to a lesser extent from the CA1 subfields, and include projections back to the limbic nuclei of the thalamus and the limbic neocortical areas (Rosene and Van Hoesen 1977; Rosene and Van Hoesen 1987). The mamillary body receives a dense projection from the subiculum, and both septal nuclei (NDB and MSN) are related to the hippocampal-subiculum complex by reciprocal projections (Rosene and Van Hoesen 1977; Rosene and Van Hoesen 1987). The cingulate cortex also has complex interrelationships with many of these areas (Papez 1937; Pandya, Van Hoesen, and Mesulam 1981). Thus, the central focus of these anatomically related circuits is the hippocampal-subiculum complex, with many of the abnormal areas of the forebrain in these autistic cerebra related to it by direct projections.

Like the hippocampal complex, small neuronal cell size and increased cell packing density characterize the amygdala, with the most marked increase in cell packing density found in the cortical, medial, and central nuclei. The cortical nucleus terminates in the molecular layer of the CA3 and CA2 subfields of the hippocampus as well as in the subiculum and prosubiculum (Rosene and Van Hoesen 1987). The medial and central nuclei represent the most lateral extension of the rostral part of the reticulate core of the brain, and are directly related to it by reciprocal connections from the hypothalamus to the medulla oblongata (Leontovich and Zhukova 1963; Price and Amaral 1981; Amaral, Veazel, and Cowan 1982). These nuclei also receive afferent projections from the basolateral complex of the amygdala (Price and Amaral 1981; Krettek and Price 1978), which in turn is directly related to many of the limbic, auditory, and visual association cortices. These association cortices are connected, both directly and reciprocally, to the hippocampal-subicular complex of circuits. Recent studies suggest that the amygdala also massively projects to the perirhinal and entorhinal cortices (Saunders and Rosene 1988). Thus, given this extensive network of interconnecting circuits, the abnormalities observed in the forebrain of the autistic cerebra could significantly disrupt the functional circuitry of the hippocampal complex and the amygdala as well as much of the limbic and sensory association neocortex and the reticulate core of the brain.

The findings in the NDB of the septum are difficult to interpret. In the brains of the autistic children under the age of 12 years, the neurons of this nucleus were unusually large, while those of the young adults were small and deceased in number. The timing and the clinical significance of these changes remain unknown. It is possible that the alteration in cell size may reflect an unstable circuitry involving the NDB. In the adult monkey, this nucleus provides a strong highly focused cholinergic projection to the amygdala and hippocampus (Rosene and Van Hoesen 1987). The distribution and extent of this nuclear projection during fetal life is unknown. It is possible that the small neurons observed in the hippocampal complex and amygdala in the autistic brains may fall within the fetal distribution of this septal projection.

The behavioral significance of these medial temporal lobe structures has been demonstrated experimentally in animals. Lesions in these areas have shown pronounced effects on emotion, behavior, memory, motivation, and learning, many of which resemble the clinical features of autism. Purposeless hyperactivity, hyperexploratory behavior, severe impairment of social interaction, and the inability to remember or recognize the significance of visually or manually examined objects has been observed in monkeys following bilateral surgical ablation of the medial temporal lobe (Kluver and Bucy 1939). Similar behaviors have also been reported in humans following comparable neurosurgical lesions (Terzian and Delle-Ore 1955).

Selective lesions to specific medial temporal lobe structures in adult animals have provided more definitive behavioral information. Bilateral ablations in rats, confined to the hippocampus, have resulted in hyperactive animals who exhibit stereotypic motor behavior and disordered responses to novel stimuli (Roberts, Dember, and Brodwick

1962; Kimble 1963). Similar bilateral lesions in adult monkeys, limited to the amygdala, have produced animals who showed loss of fear to normally adversive stimuli, withdrawal from previously rewarding social interaction, compulsive indiscriminate examination of objects, and a reduced ability to attach meaning to events based on past experience, resulting in the inability to adapt to new environmental situations (Mishkin and Aggleton 1981). When bilateral surgical lesions were limited still further to the central, medial, and cortical nuclei of the amygdala, the influence of familiarization on learning was significantly repressed, particularly when compared to behavior exhibited following more laterally placed amygdalar lesions (Vergnes 1981).

One of the more important observations from this animal research was reported in 1985 by Murray and Mishkin. These authors noted that, following bilateral ablations of the amygdala, monkeys experienced severely impaired cross-model associative memory which was long-term. The lesioned monkeys failed to recognize visually an object which they had previously examined by touch or taste. These observations suggest that one of the major functions of the amygdala may be the facilitation of cross-model associations. Thus, dysfunction in this circuitry could lead to difficulty in generalizing information from one experience to another, a characteristic seen in may autistic individuals.

Severe loss of recognition and associative memory has been observed following bilateral ablations of both the amygdala and the hippocampus in adult monkeys (Mishkin 1978), as well as following bilateral hippocampal lesions alone (Mahut, Zola-Morgan, and Moss 1982). In addition, profound loss of tactile memory has been noted following combined lesions of the hippocampus and the amygdala, suggesting that damage to these structures results in a severe memory deficit that is at least bimodal and that is comparable to the global retrograde amnesia seen following medial temporal lobe surgery or pathology in humans (Murray and Mishkin 1983). More recent studies suggest that the amygdala and the hippocampus appear to participate equally in object-recognition memory (Parkinson, Murray, and Mishkin 1988). However, the amygdala may be particularly important for memory related to object-reward, object-object, and object-punishment associations across modalities. In contrast, the hippocampus appears to be critical to object-place associations, lesioned monkeys being incapable of associating objects with their spatial locations.

In 1991, Squire and Zola-Morgan re-examined the relationship of the medical temporal lobe structures to memory. They found that the severe memory loss, which had been previously attributed to combined bilateral lesions of the amygdala and hippocampus, was the result of inadvertent damage to the cortical regions adjacent to the amygdala during the ablation procedure, and not to the specific inclusion of the amygdala as had been previously thought (Mishkin 1978). From this work, it has been determined that the medial temporal lobe memory system probably consists of the hippocampal formation, including the entorhinal cortex and the perirhinal and parahippocampal cortices which are anatomically related to it. The amygdala does not appear to be a component of this system, nor does it appear to contribute any kind of memory related to this system.

Current research in human and nonhuman primates has suggested the presence of at least two memory systems, procedural or habit memory, and representational or associative memory (Mishkin and Appenzeller 1987; Murray 1990; Squire and Zola-Morgan 1991). Habit memory is involved in skill learning and automatic connections between a stimulus and a response. Habit learning is not accessible to conscious recollection and is acquired by repeated presentation of the same stimulus until the task has reached criteria. Representational memory involves all sensory modalities and mediates the processing of facts, experiences and events, and the integration and generalization of information that leads to higher-order cognition and learning. The two systems are believed to be anatomically separate, with representational memory depending on the structures of the limbic system, while the substrate for habit memory is believed to reside in the striatum and neocortex of the cerebral hemispheres.

Microscopic analysis of the brain in autism has failed to demonstrate any abnormality in the striatum. Likewise, with the exception of the anterior cingulate gyrus, the neocortex also appears to be uninvolved. In contrast, the hippocampal complex, amygdala, entorhinal cortex, septum, and mamillary body have shown consistent and significant abnormalities in all brains studied to date. Thus, the substrate for representational memory appears to be selectively abnormal in the autistic brain, while that for habit memory appears to be spared. This dichotomy may help explain the remarkable ability of some autistic individuals to acquire and retain large amounts of factual information on specific topics, while at the same time having difficulty utilizing that information reliably and functionally.

The majority of experimental studies have been performed in adult animals. While providing information about the functional significance of the specific areas lesioned, they lend little insight into the effect that damage or dysfunction in these same areas, occurring early in life, may have on behavioral and cognitive development. While little information is available on the developmental effects of experimentally induced prenatal lesions, studies in neonatal animals have been revealing. Following bilateral amygdaloidectomies performed in infant monkeys, the surgically treated animals initially appeared to be behaviorally similar to controls (Thompson 1981). However, by 8 months of age, the lesioned animals exhibited poor social skills, and by 3 years of age, hyperactivity had become evident. Thus, the lesioned monkeys appeared to "grow into" their symptoms, a profile not unlike the early clinical developmental pattern reported in some autistic children. More recently, Bachevalier (1991, 1994) lesioned both the hippocampus and the amygdala bilaterally in neonatal monkeys. As in the Thompson study, behavioral abnormalities developed gradually with increasing age and included gross motor stereotypies, tantrums in novel situations, blank and expressionless facies, poor eye contact, and deficits in cognitive function. Although identical surgical lesions were made in all animals, some variability in behavioral characteristics was observed. Thus, variability in phenotypic expression may result from a common locus of pathology and may not necessarily imply differing etiologies or severity of involvement.

While the effects of surgical resection of the hippocampus, amygdala, and adjacent structures on memory function in adult humans has been described, the possible result of a congenital disturbance to this memory system is unknown. However, it is likely that the clinical picture resulting from surgical removal of specific areas of the limbic system in postnatal human and nonhuman primates may be substantially different from that resulting from prenatal abnormalities in these same areas. Early lesions and curtailments of development within these structures could be in a position to disrupt or distort the acquisition and meaning of information derived from the continually occurring novel stimuli characteristic of daily life. Such a disturbance in the processing of information could result potentially in disordered social interaction and language development as well as atypical cognitive abilities, features that characterize the clinical presentation of autism.

The development of memory and learning has been studied both in monkeys and in humans. For example, it has been observed that infant monkeys can accomplish tasks very early in life that rely on a well-developed noncognitive habit memory system. However, these same monkeys were unsuccessful when presented with tasks that required the presence of a functional representational memory system. With maturation, the monkeys began to acquire these skills in late infancy but did not achieve adult-level mastery until 2 years of age. Thus, the ability to make cognitive associations (representational memory) appears to develop gradually over time in the normal monkey, presumably because the neuronal circuitry upon which it relies matures slowly over time (Bachevalier 1991). Similar observations have been reported in humans (Overman 1990). When presented with an object discrimination task, a skill dependent on procedural memory, 12-month-old infants were able to complete the task as well as adults. However, when these same infants were presented with a delayed nonmatching-to-sample task (DNMS), which required the learning of the rules of the test in order to be successful, they were unable to solve the task. By 19 months of age, however, the children began to show some success. Although the children, ages 45 through 81 months, became more able to perform the DNMS task at increasingly higher levels with increasing age, their scores remained significantly below those seen in adults. Thus, in both human and nonhuman primates, these different cognitive processes seem to be mediated by two independent neural systems that appear to mature at different rates (Overman et al. 1992).

Based on the above data, it appears that the limbic system, which is believed to be the substrate for representational memory, is a later developing information processing system in both human and nonhuman primates, while the habit memory system seems to be fully functional very early in life. Given this maturational pattern, it could be suspected that a developmentally immature and possibly dysfunctional neuronal circuitry involving the limbic system would have little clinical impact during the first one or two years of life. However, as the brain matures and cognition gradually moves from an emphasis on skill learning to the integration and generalization of information and abstract thought, the effect of an abnormality in this circuitry would become more evident. At that point, the child might begin to exhibit what appears to be a developmental plateau or deterioration in social skills, language, and cognition, features frequently reported during the first 3 years of life in childhood autism.

CEREBELLAR FINDINGS—CLINICAL IMPLICATIONS

Outside of the forebrain, abnormalities in the autistic brains studied to date have been confined to the cerebellum and the related inferior olive. In the cerebellar cortex, the Purkinje cells of the hemispheres have been found to be bilaterally and symmetrically reduced in number, with the most marked reduction in the posterior inferior neocerebellar cortex and adjacent archicerebellar cortex, with sparing of the vermis. No evidence of significant gliosis has been observed suggesting that the lesion was acquired early in development. Studies in animals have noted a progressively decreasing glial response following cerebellar lesions at increasingly early ages (Brodal 1940). Additional evidence for the early acquisition of the cerebellar findings can be drawn from the preservation of the neurons of the principal inferior olive. It is known from studies in immature and adult animals (Brodal 1940), and from neonatal and adult human pathology (Holmes and

Stewart 1908; Norman 1940; Greenfield 1940) that retrograde loss of olivary neurons is observed regularly following cerebellar lesions that occur in the perinatal period and in postnatal life. This cell loss is presumably due to the close relationship of the olivary climbing fiber axons to the Purkinje cell dendrites (Eccles, Ito, and Szentagothai 1967). In the fetal monkey, it has been shown that prior to establishing their definitive relationship with the Purkinje cells, the olivary neurons synapse in a transitory zone located beneath the Purkinje cell layer called the lamina dissecans (Rakic 1971). In the human fetus, this zone is no longer evident after 30 to 32 weeks gestation (Rakic and Sidman 1970). Thus, given the preservation of the olivary neurons in the presence of a significant reduction in the numbers of Purkinje cells, it is likely that the events that resulted in this abnormality occurred prior to the establishment of the definitive bond between these cells, and therefore prior to 30 to 32 weeks gestation. Further support for this concept is provided by an analogous situation in which the expected retrograde cell loss of neurons in the medial dorsal nucleus of the thalamus failed to occur following prefrontal lesions in the rhesus monkey prior to but not after 106 days of gestation (Goldman and Galkin 1978).

The findings of the deep cerebellar nuclei show an inconsistent relationship to those noted in the cerebellar cortex and inferior olivary complex. The dentate, which is the least involved nulceus, normally receives direct projections from the neocerebellum, the most involved cerebellar cortical region. The fastigial nucleus, one of the most involved nuclei, typically receives direct projections from the histoanatomically normal cerebellar vermal cortex (Brodal 1940). The principal inferior olivary nucleus, which contains small neurons in the young adult patients, and abnormally enlarged neurons in the childhood cases, is reciprocally related to the dentate nucleus, which appears to be histologically normal in the young adults but shows neuronal enlargement in the younger brains. The apparently uninvolved medial and dorsal accessory olivary nuclei are reciprocally related to the globose and emboliform nuclei, which are abnormal in all cases. Therefore, because with few exceptions, the deep cerebellar nuclei provide efferent projections from the cerebellum, the combination of cerebellar cortical and nuclear lesions observed in these autistic brains are in a position to significantly disrupt these projections (Brodal 1981).

The finding of enlarged neurons in the deep cerebellar nuclei and inferior olive in the younger autistic brains and small neurons, which are decreased in number in the emboliform, fastigial, and globose nuclei in the older cases, is intriguing. A review of the work of Flechsig (1920) and Yakovlev and Lecours (1967) indicates that the olivocerebellar tracts of the inferior cerebellar peduncle show advanced myelination in the human fetus by 28 weeks gestation. This observation suggests that a functional circuit already exists between the olivary nucleus and the cerebellum at this early stage of development. Since the intimate relationship between the inferior olive and the Purkinje cells has yet to be established at this time, the prenatal olivary projection to the cerebellum is presumed to be to the cerebellar nuclei. These observations may also suggest that this pathway may be the dominant cerebellar circuit prior to 30 weeks gestation. In the infant and adult human brain, the appearance of retrograde cell loss of olivary neurons following cerebellar cortical lesions suggests that the dominant inferior olivary projection in the postnatal period is to the Purkinje cells, with the more primitive circuit remaining as a collateral projection to the cerebellar nuclei. Based on these observations, it could be hyopthesized that in the autistic brain the normal postnatal olivary to Purkinje cell circuitry cannot be adequately established because of a marked reduction in the availability of Purkinje cells. This situation might then result in the postnatal persistence of the more primitive prenatal pattern. Assuming that this hypothesis is correct, the abnormal persistence of this fetal circuit could account for the presence of "compensatory" neuronal enlargement of the cerebellar nuclei and inferior olive in the younger autistic brains. Because this fetal circuit was not "designed" to function as a dominant postnatal pathway, it is likely that it cannot be sustained over time, resulting in reduced size and eventual loss of neurons in older autistic patients.

The relationship of the cerebellar findings to the clinical features of autism is as yet unclear. Cerebellar dysfunction, beginning before birth, may be associated with few if any neurological symptoms (Norman 1940; Adams, Corelis, and Duchen 1984). Studies in animals have shown the existence of a direct pathway between the fastigial nucleus and the amygdala and septal nuclei, as well as a reciprocal relationship with the hippocampus, suggesting that the cerebellum may play some role in the regulation of higher cortical thought and emotion (Heath and Harper 1974; Heath et al. 1978). Animal and human studies have suggested that the cerebellum may be important in the regulation of affective behavior (Berman, Berman, and Prescott 1974), and in functional psychiatric disorders (Heath, Franklin, and Shraberg 1979). Studies in rabbits have implicated the dentate and interpositus nuclei in the elaboration of classical conditioned responses (McCormick and Thompson 1984).

Recent studies have suggested that the cerebellum may be important in mental imagery, anticipatory planning (Leiner, Leiner, and Dow 1987), and in some aspects of language processing (Petersen et al. 1989). In autistic subjects, the cerebellum has been implicated in the control of attention, possibly due to its relationship with the parietal association cortices through connections in the pons (Courchesne,

Akshoomoff, and Townsend 1992b). There has also been the suggestion that the cerebellum may be involved in cognitive planning which is independent of memory and which is most significant in novel situations (Grafman et al. 1992). The regulation of the speed, consistency, and appropriateness of mental and cognitive processes may be a further important function of the cerebellum (Schmahmann 1991). Thus, there is a growing body of evidence to support the role of the cerebellum in emotion, learning, behavior, and possibly language. It is likely that some of the behaviors and disorders of information processing characteristic of autism may be related, at least in part, to the histoanatomic cerebellar abnormalities seen in these cases. However, the precise functional significance of these findings, their possible relationship to the abnormalities noted in the limbic system, and their implications for the clinical features of autism remain to be clarified.

CONCLUSIONS

Consistent anatomical abnormalities which have been confined to the limbic system and cerebellar circuits have been found in the brains of nine autistic individuals. The pattern of abnormality seen in the limbic system suggests a curtailment of developmental maturation involving this circuitry. The findings in the cerebellum and related olivary nucleus further suggest that the process that results in these abnormalities has its onset before birth. Studies in animals, humans, and nonhuman primates support the role of the medial temporal lobe structures, particularly the hippocampus and the amygdala, in cognition, behavior, emotion, and learning. Further, there is growing evidence that the cerebellum may play a role in the mediation and modulation of some aspects of learning and affective behavior. Although the effects of prenatal abnormalities of the limbic system and cerebellum on development is unknown, it is likely that early dysfunction in these circuits could have a significant impact on the acquisition and processing of information during life and could account for many of the clinical features of autism.

ACKNOWLEDGMENTS

This work was supported in part by the Nancy Lurie Marks Family Foundation and the Natalie Z. Haar Foundation.

REFERENCES

Aarkrog, T. 1968. Organic factors in infantile psychoses and borderline psychoses: Retrospective study of 45 cases subjected to pneumoencephalography. *Dan Medical Bulletin* 15:283–88.

Adams, J. H., Corselis, J. A. N., and Duchen, L. W. 1984. *Greenfield's Neuro-pathology.* New York: John Wiley.

Amaral, D. G., Veazey, R. B., and Cowan, W. M. 1982. Some observations on the hypothalamoamygdaloid axonal connections. *Brain Research* 252:13–27.

Amaral, D. G., Inshusti, R., and Cowan, W. M. 1983. Evidence for direct projection from the superior temporal gyrus to the entorhinal cortex in the monkey. *Brain Research* 275:263–77.

Arin, D. M., Bauman, M. L., and Kemper, T. L. 1991. The distribution of Purkinje cell loss in the cerebellum in autism. *Neurology* 41:307 (abstract).

Bachevalier, J. 1991. An animal model for childhood autism. In C. A. Tamminga and S. C. Schultz, eds. *Advances in Neuropsychiatry and Psychopharmacology.* New York: Raven Press.

Bachevalier, J. 1994. The contribution of medial temporal lobe structures in infantile autism: A neurobehavioral study in primates. In M. L. Bauman and T. L. Kemper, eds. *The Neurobiology of Autism.* Baltimore: Johns Hopkins University Press.

Bauman, M. L., and Kemper, T. L. 1984. The brain in infantile autism: A histoanatomic report. *Neurology* 34:275 (abstract).

Bauman, M. L., and Kemper, T. L. 1985. Histoanatomic observations of the brain in early infantile autism. *Neurology* 35:866–74.

Bauman, M. L., and Kemper, T. L. 1996. Observations on the Purkinje cells in the cerebellar vermis in autism. *Journal of Neuropathology and Experimental Neurology* 55:613.

Berman, A. J., Berman, D., and Prescott, J. W. 1974. The effect of cerebellar lesions on emotional behavior in the rhesus monkey. In I. S. Cooper, M. Riklan, and R. S. Snyder, eds. *The Cerebellum, Epilepsy and Behavior.* New York: Plenum Press.

Brodal, A. 1940. Modification of the Gudden method for study of cerebral localization. *Archives of Neurological Psychiatry* 43:46–58.

Brodal, A. 1981. *Neurological Anatomy in Relation to Clinical Medicine.* New York: Oxford University Press.

Boucher, J., and Warrington, E. K. 1976. Memory deficits in early infantile autism: Some similarities to the amnestic syndrome. *British Journal of Psychology* 67:73–87.

Campbell, M. S., Rosenbloom, S., Perry, R., George, A. E., Kricheff, I.I., Anderson, L., Small, A. M., and Jenings, S. J. 1982. Computerized axial tomography in young autistic children. *American Journal of Psychiatry* 139:510–12.

Chess, S., Korn, S. J., and Fernandez, P. B. 1971. *Psychiatric Disorders of Children with Congenital Rubella.* New York: Brunner & Mazel.

Coleman, M. 1979. Studies of the autistic syndromes. In R. Katzman, ed. *Congenital and Acquired Cognitive Disorders.* New York:Raven Press.

Coleman, P. D., Romano, J., Lapham, L., and Simon, W. 1985. Cell counts in cerebral cortex in an autistic patient. *Journal of Autism and Developmental Disorders* 15:245–55.

Courchesne, E., Hesselink, J. R., Jernigan, T. L., and Yeung-Courchesne, R. 1987. Abnormal neuroanatomy in a nonretarded person with autism. *Archives of Neurology* 44:335–41.

Courchesne, E., Yeung-Courchesne, R., Press, G. A., Hesselink, J. R., and Jernigan, T. L. 1988. Hypoplasia of cerebellar vermal lobules VI and VII in autism. *New England Journal of Medicine* 318:1349–54.

Courchesne, E., Press, G. A., and Yeung-Courchesne, R. 1992a. Parietal lobe abnormalities detected by magnetic resonance in patients with infantile autism. *Society for Neuroscience Abstracts* 18:332 (abstract).

Courchesne, E., Akshoomoff, N. A., and Townsend, J. 1992b. Recent advances in autism. In H. Naruse, and E. M. Ornitz, eds. *Neurobiology of Infantile Autism*. Amsterdam: Elsevier Science Publishers.

Courchesne, E., Townsend, J., and Saitoh, O. 1994. The brain in infantile autism. *Neurology* 44: 214–28.

Creasey, H., Rumsey, J. M., Schwartz, M., Duara, R., Rapoport, J. L., and Rapoport, S. I. 1986. Brain morphometry in autistic men as measured by volumetric computed tomography. *Archives of Neurology* 43:669–72.

Darby, J. H. 1976. Neuropathological aspects of psychosis in childhood. *Journal of Autism and Child Schizophrenia* 6:339–52.

DeBassio, W. A., Kemper, T. L., and Knoefel, J. E. 1985. Coffin-Siris syndrome: Neuro-findings. *Archives of Neurology* 42:350–53.

Delong, G. R. 1978. A neuropsychological interpretation of infantile autism. In M. Rutter, and E. Schopler, eds. *Autism*. New York: Plenum Press.

Demasio, A. R., and Maurer, R. G. 1978. A neurological model for childhood autism. *Archives of Neurology* 35:777–86.

Demasio, H., Maurer, R. G., Demasio, A. R., and Chui, H. C. 1980. Computerized tomographic scan findings in patients with autistic behavior. *Archives of Neurology* 37:504–10.

DeMyer, M. K. 1979. *Parents and Children in Autism*. Washington, DC: Winston & Sons.

Deykin, E. Y., and MacMahon, B. 1979. The incidence of seizures among children with autistic symptoms. *American Journal of Psychiatry* 136:1310–12.

Eccles, J. C., Ito, M., and Szentagothai, J. 1967. *The Cerebellum as a Neuronal Machine*. New York: Springer.

Filipek, P. A., Richelme, C., Kennedy, D. N., Rademacher, J., Pitcher, D. A., Zidel, S., and Caviness, V. S. 1992. Morphometric analysis of the brain in developmental language disorders and autism. *Annals of Neurology* 32:475 (abstract).

Flechsig, P. 1920. *Anatomie des Menchlichen Gehim und Ruchenmachs auf Myelogenetischer Grundlage*. Leipzig: George Theime.

Gaffney, G. R., Kuperman, S., Tsai, L. Y., Minchin, S., and Hassanein, K. M. 1987. Midsaggital magnetic resonance imaging of autism. *British Journal of Psychiatry* 151:831–33.

Gaffney, G. R., Kuperman, S., Tsai, L.Y., and Minchin, S. 1988. Morphological evidence of brainstem involvement in infantile autism. *Biological Psychiatry* 24:578–86.

Gaffney, G. R., Kuperman, S., Tsai, L.Y., and Minchin, S. 1989. Forebrain structure in infantile autism. *Journal of American Academy of Child and Adolescent Psychiatry* 28:534–37.

Garber, H. J., Ritvo, E. R., Chui, L. C., Griswold, V. J., Kashanian, A., and Oldendorf, W. H. 1989. A magnetic resonance imaging study of autism: Normal fourth ventricle size and absence of pathology. *American Journal of Psychiatry* 146:532–35.

Garber, H. J., and Ritvo, E. R. 1992. Magnetic resonance imaging of the posterior fossa in autistic adults. *American Journal of Psychiatry* 149:245–47.

Goldman, P. S., and Galkin, T. W. 1978. Prenatal removal of frontal association cortex in the fetal rhesus monkey: Anatomic and functional consequences in postnatal life. *Brain Research* 152:452–85.

Grafman, J., Litvan, I., Massaquoi, S., Stewart, M., Sivigu, A., and Hallet, M. 1992. Cognitive planning deficit in patients with cerebellar atrophy. *Neurology* 42:1493–96.

Greenfield, J. G. 1954. *The Spino-cerebellar Degenerations*. Springfield, IL: Charles C Thomas.

Harcherik, D. F., Cohen, D. J., Ort, S., Paul, R., Shaywitz, B. A., Volkmar, F. R., Rothman, S .I. G., and Leckman, J. F. 1985. Computed tomographic brain scanning in four neuropsychiatric disorders of childhood. *American Journal of Psychiatry* 142:731–34.

Hauser, S. L., Delong, G. R., and Rosman, N. P. 1975. Pneumographic findings in the infantile autism syndrome. A correlation with temporal lobe disease. *Brain* 98:667–88.

Heath, R. G., and Harper, J. W. 1974. Ascending projections of the cerebellar fastigial nucleus to the hippocampus, amygdala and other temporal lobe sites: Evoked potential and other histiologic studies in monkeys and cats. *Experimental Neurology* 45:268–87.

Heath, R. G., Dempsey, C. W., Fontana, C. J., and Myers, W. A. 1978. Cerebellar stimulation: Effects on septal region, hippocampus and amygdala of cats and rats. *Biological Psychiatry* 113: 501–29.

Heath, R. G., Franklin, D. E., and Shraberg, D. 1979. Gross pathology of the cerebellum in patients diagnosed and treated as functional psychiatric disorders. *Journal of Nerves and Mental Disorders* 167:585–92.

Hier, D. B., LeMay, M., and Rosenberger, P. B. 1979. Autism and unfavorable left-right asymmetries of the brain. *Journal of Autism and Developmental Disorders* 9:153–59.

Holmes, G., and Stewart, T. G. 1908. On the connection of the inferior olives with the cerebellum in man. *Brain* 31:125–37.

Holttum, J. R., Minshew, N. J., Sanders, R. S., and Phillips, N. E. 1992. Magnetic resonance imaging of the posterior fossa in autism. *Biological Psychiatry* 32:1091–1101.

Horwitz, B., Rumsey, J., Grady, C., and Rapoport, S. I. 1988. The cerebral metabolic landscape in autism: Intercorrelations of regional glucose utilization. *Archives of Neurology* 45:749–55.

Hsu, M., Yeung-Courchesne, R., Courchesnes, E., and Press, G. A. 1991. Absence of magnetic resonance imaging evidence of pontine abnormality in infantile autism. *Archives of Neurology* 48:1160–63.

Jacobson, R., Lecouteur, A., Howlin, P., and Rutter, M. 1988. Selective subcortical abnormalities in autism. *Psychological Medicine* 18:39–48.

Kanner, L. 1943. Autistic disturbances of affective contact. *Nervous Child* 2:217–50.

Kemper, T. L., and Bauman, M. L. 1992. Neuropathology of infantile autism. In H. Naruse, and E. M. Ornitz, eds. *Neurobiology of Infantile Autism.* Amsterdam: Elsevier Science Publishers.

Kimble, D. P. 1963. The effects of bilateral hippocampal lesions in rats. *Journal of Physiological Psychology* 56:273–83.

Krettek, J. E., and Price, J. L. 1977. Projections from the amygdaloid and adjacent olefactory structures of the entorhinal cortex and to the subiculum in the rat and cat. *Journal of Comparative Neurology* 172:723–52.

Krettek, J. E., and Price, J. L. 1978. A description of the amygdaloid complex in the rat and cat with observations on the intra-amygdaloid axonal connections. *Journal of Comparative Neurology* 178:255–80.

Kleinman, M. D., Neff, S., and Rosman, N. P. 1992. The brain in infantile autism. *Neurology* 42:753–60.

Kluver, H., and Bucy, P. 1939. Preliminary analysis of functions of the temporal lobe in monkeys. *Archives of Neurological Psychiatry* 42:979–1000.

Leiner, H. C., Leiner, A. L., and Dow, R. S. 1987. Cerebrocerebellar learning loops in apes and humans. *Italian Journal of Neurologial Science* 8:425–36.

Leontovich, T. A., and Zhukova, G. P. 1963. The specificity of the neuronal structure and topography of the reticular formation of the brain and spinal cord in carnivora. *Journal of Comparative Neurology* 121:347–79.

Mahut, H., Zola-Morgan, S., and Moss, M. 1982. Hippocampal resections impair associative learning and recognition memory in the monkey. *Journal of Neuroscience* 2:1214–29.

Maurer, R. G., and Demasio, A. R. 1982. Childhood autism from the point of view of behavioral neurology. *Journal of Autism and Developmental Disorders* 12:195–205.

McCormick, D. A., and Thompson, R. F. 1984. Cerebellum: Essential involvement in the classically conditioned eyelid response. *Science* 223:296–99.

Mishkin, M. 1978. Memory in monkey severely impaired by combined but not separate removal of amygdala and hippocampus. *Nature* 273:297–98.

Mishkin, M., and Aggleton, J. P. 1981. Multiple functional contributors of the amygdala in the monkey from the amygdaloid complex. In Y. Ben-Ari, ed. INSERM Symposium, No. 20. Amsterdam: Elsevier/North Holland Biomedical Press.

Mishkin, M., and Appenzeller, T. 1987. The anatomy of memory. *Scientific American* 256:80–89.

Murakami, J. W., Courchesne, E., Press, G. A., Yeung-Courchesne, R., and Hesselink, J. R. 1989. Reduced cerebellar hemisphere size and its relationship to vermal hypoplasia in autism. *Archives of Neurology* 46:689–94.

Murray, E. A., and Mishkin, M. 1983. Severe tactile memory deficits in monkeys after combined removal of the amygdala and hippocampus. *Brain Research* 270:340–44.

Murray, E. A., and Mishkin, M. 1985. Amygdaloidectomy impairs crossmodal association in monkeys. *Science* 228:604–6.

Murray, E. A. 1990. Representational memory in non-human primates. In R. P. Kesner, and D. S. Olton, eds. *Neurobiology of Comparative Cognition*. Hillsdale, NJ: Lawrence Erlbaum Associates.

Norman, R. M. 1940. Cerebellar atrophy associated with etat marbre of the basal ganglia. *Journal of Neurological Psychiatry* 3:311–18.

Nowell, M. A., Hackney, D. B., Murak, A. S., and Coleman, M. 1990. Varied appearance of autism: Fifty-three patients having the full autistic syndrome. *Magnetic Resonance Imaging* 8: 811–16.

Ornitz, E. M. 1985. Neurophysiology of infantile autism. *Journal of American Academic Child Psychiatry* 24:251–62.

Ornitz, E. M., and Ritvo, E. R. 1968. Neurophysiologic mechanisms underlying perceptual inconstancy in autistic and schizophrenic children. *Archives of General Psychiary* 19:22–27.

Overman, W. H. 1990. Performance on traditional match-to-sample and nonmatch-to-sample, and object descrimination tasks by 12 and 32 month old children: A developmental progression. In A. Diamond, ed. *Developmental and Neural Basis of Higher Cognitive Function*. New York: Academic Press.

Overman, W., Bachevalier, J., Turner, M., and Peuster, A. 1992. Object recognition versus object descrimination: Comparison between human infants and infant monkeys. *Behavioral Neuroscience* 106:15–29.

Pandya, D. N., Van Hoesen, G. W., and Mesulam, M. M. 1981. Efferent connections of the cingulate gyrus in the rhesus monkey. *Brain Research* 42:319–30.

Papez, J. W. 1937. A proposed mechanism for emotion. *Archives of Neurological Psychiatry* 38:725–43.

Parkinson, J. K., Murray, E. A., and Mishkin, M. 1988. A selective mnemonic role for the hippocampus in monkeys: Memory for the location of objects. *Journal of Neuroscience* 8:4159–67.

Petersen, S. F., Fox, P. T., Posner, M. I., Mintum, M. A., and Raichle, M. E. 1989. Positron emission tomographic studies in the processing of single words. *Journal of Cognitive Neuroscience* 1:153–70.

Piven, J., Berthier, M. L., Starkstein, S. E., Nehme, E., Pearlson, G., and Folstein, S. 1992. Magnetic resonance imaging evidence for a defect in cerebral cortical development in autism. *American Journal of Psychiatry* 14:734–39.

Piven, J., Nehme, E., Simon, J., Barta, P., Pearlson, G., and Folstein, S. E. 1992. Magnetic resonance imaging in autism: Measurement of the cerebellum, pons, and fourth ventricle. *Biological Psychiatry* 31:491–504.

Piven, J., and Folstein, S. 1994. The genetics of autism. In M. L. Bauman, and T. L. Kemper, eds. *The Neurobiology of Autism*. Baltimore: Johns Hopkins University Press.

Piven, J., Arndt, S.; Bailey, J., Havercamp, C., Andreasen, N. C., and Palmer, P. 1995. An MRI study of brain size in autism. *American Journal of Psychiatry* 152:1145–49.

Price, J. L., and Amaral, D. G. 1981. An autoradiographic study of the projections of the central nucleus of the monkey amygdala. *Journal of Neuroscience* 1:1242–59.

Rakic, P., and Sidman, R. L. 1970. Histogenesis of the cortical layers in human cerebellum particularly the lamina dissecans. *Journal of Comparative Neurology* 139:473–500.

Rakic, P. 1971. Neuron-glia relationship during granule cell migration in developing cerebellar cortex: A Golgi and electron microscopic study in macacus rhesus. *Journal of Comparative Neurology* 141:282–312.

Rapin, I. 1994. Introduction and Overview. In M. L. Bauman, and T. L. Kemper, eds. *The Neurobiology of Autism*. Baltimore: Johns Hopkins University Press.

Raymond, G., Bauman, M. L., and Kemper, T. L. 1989. The hippocampus in autism: A Golgi analysis. *Annals of Neurology* 26:483–84 (abstract).

Raymond, G., Bauman, M. L., and Kemper, T. L. 1996. Hippocampus in autism: A Golgi analysis. *Acta Neuropathology* 91:117–19.

Reiss, A. L., Alyward, E., Freund, L. S., Joshi, P. K., and Bryan, R. N. 1991. Neuroanatomy of fragile X syndrome: The posterior fossa. *Annals of Neurology* 29:26–32.

Ritvo, E. R., Freeman, B. J., Scheibel, A. B., Duong, T., Robinson, H., Guthrie, D., and Ritvo, A. 1986. Lower Purkinje cell counts in the cerebella of four autistic subjects: Initial findings of the UCLA-NSAC autopsy research report. *American Journal of Psychiatry* 146:862–66.

Ritvo, E. R., and Garber, J. H. 1988. Cerebellar hypoplasia and autism. *New England Journal of Medicine* 319:1152 (abstract).

Roberts, W. W., Dember, W. N., and Brodwick, H. 1962. Alteration and exploration in rats with hippocampal lesions. *Journal of Comparative Psychiatry* 55:695–700.

Rosenbloom, S., Campbell, M., and George, A. E. 1984. High resolution CT scanning in infantile autism: A quantitative approach. *Journal of American Academic Child Psychiatry* 23:72–77.

Rosene, D. L., and Van Hoesen, G. W. 1977. Hippocampal efferents reach widespread areas of cerebral cortex and amygdala in rhesus monkey. *Science* 198:315–17.

Rosene, D. L., and Van Hoesen, G. W. 1987. The hippocampal formation of the primate brain. In E. G. Jones, and A. Peters, eds. *Cerebral Cortex, Vol. 6.* New York: Plenum Press.

Rumsey, J. M., Duara, R., Grady, C., Rapoport, J. L., Margolin, R. A., Rapoport, S. I., and Cutler, N. R. 1985. Brain metabolism in autism. *Archives of General Psychiatry* 42:448–55.

Rumsey, J. M., Creasey, H., Stepanek, J. S., Dorwart, R., Patronas, N., Hamburger, S. D., and Duara, R. 1988. Hemispheric asymmetries, fourth ventricular size and cerebellar morphology in autism. *Journal of Autism and Developmental Disorders* 18:127–37.

Saunders, R. C., and Rosene, D. L. 1988. A comparison of the efferents of the amygdala and the hippocampal formation in the rhesus monkey. I. Convergence in the entorhinal, prorhinal and perirhinal cortices. *Journal of Comparative Neurology* 271:153–84.

Schaefer, G. B., Thompson, J. N., Bodensteiner, J. B., McConnell, J. M., Kimberling, W. J., Gay, C. T., Dutton, W. D., Hutchings, D. C., and Gray, S. B. 1996. Hypoplasia of the cerebellar vermis in neurogenetic syndromes. *Annals of Neurology* 39:382–85.

Schain, R., and Yannet, H. 1960. Infantile autism. *Journal of Pediatrics* 57:560–67.

Schmahmann, J. D. 1991. An emerging concept. The cerebellar contribution to higher function. *Archives of Neurology* 48:1178–87.

Squire, L. R., and Zola-Morgan, S. 1991. The medial temporal lobe memory system. *Science* 253:1380–86.

Student, M., and Schmer, H. 1978. Evidence from auditory nerve and brain stem evoked responses for an organic lesion in children with autistic traits. *Journal of Autism and Child Schizophrenia* 8:13–20.

Sumi, S. M. 1980. Brain malformation in the trisomy 18 syndrome. *Brain* 93:821–30.

Tanguay, P. E., Ornitz, E. M., Forsythe, A. B. and Ritvo, E. R. 1976. Rapid eye movement (REM) activity in normal and autistic children during REM sleep. *Journal of Autism and Child Schizophrenia* 6:275–88.

Tanguay, P. E., Edwards, R. M., Buchwald, J., Schwofel, J., and Allen, V. 1982. Auditory brain stem evoked responses in autistic children. *Archives of General Psychiatry* 38:174–80.

Terzian, H., and Delle-Ore, G. 1955. Syndrome of Kluver and Bucy reproduced in man by bilateral removal of the temporal lobes. *Neurology* 3:373–80.

Thompson, E. I. 1981. Long-term behavioral development of rhesus monkeys after amygdaloidectomy in infancy. In Y. Ben-Ari, ed. *The Amygdaloid Complex.* INSERM Symposium, No. 20. Amsterdam: Elsevier/North Holland.

Tsai, L. Y., Jacoby, O. G., and Stewart, M. A. 1983. Morphological cerebral asymmetries in autistic children. *Biological Psychiatry* 18:317–27.

Van Hoesen, G. W., Pandya, D. N., and Butters, N. 1972. Cortical afferents to the entorhinal cortex of the rhesus monkey. *Science* 175:1471–73.

Van Hoesen, G. W., and Pandya, D. N. 1975a. Some connections of the entorhinal (area 28) and the perirhinal (area 35) cortices in the rhesus monkey.I. Temporal lobe afferents. *Brain Research* 95:1–24.

Van Hoesen, G. W., and Pandya, D. N. 1975b. Some connections of the entorhinal (area 28) and perirhinal (area 35) cortices of the rhesus monkey. III. Efferent connections. *Brain Research* 95:39–59.

Van Hoesen, G. W., Pandya, D. N., and Butters, N. 1975. Some connections of the entorhinal (area 28) and perirhinal (area 35) cortices of the rhesus monkey. II. Frontal lobe afferents. *Brain Research* 95:25–38.

Van Hoesen, G. W., Rosene, D. L., and Mesulam, M. M. 1979. Subicular input from temporal cortex in the rhesus monkey. *Science* 205:608–10.

Vergnes, M. 1981. Effect of prior familiarization with mice on elicitation of mouse killing in rats: Role of the amygdala. In Y. Ben-Ari, ed. *The Amyg-*

daloid Complex. INSERM Symposium, No. 20. Amsterdam: Elsevier/ North Holland.

Vilensky, J. A., Demasio, A. R., and Maurer, R. G. 1981. Gait disturbances in patients with autistic behavior. *Archives of Neurology* 38:646–49.

Williams, R. S., Hauser, S. L., Purpura, D. P., Delong, G. R., and Swisher, C. N. 1980. Autism and mental retardation. *Archives of Neurology* 37:749–53.

Yakovlev, P. I. 1970. Whole brain serial histological sections. In C. G. Tedeschi, ed. *Neuropathology: Methods and Diagnosis.* Boston: Little Brown.

Yakovlev, P. I., and Lecours, A. R. 1967. Myelogenetic cycles of regional maturation of the brain. In A. Minkowski, ed. *Regional Development of the Brain in Early Life.* Oxford: Blackwell Scientific Publications.

Chapter • 6

Communication in Autistic Children

Michelle Dunn and Isabelle Rapin

Disordered communication is considered one of three core deficits in autism. The purpose of this chapter is to stress the great variety of communication deficits in autistic children, a variety that the literature does not emphasize adequately. Some autistic children, especially younger ones, have no expressive language. Others speak very little, some in clear single words or short phrases, others in such distorted words as to make them difficult to understand. Many, especially by school age, speak in more or less well formed sentences or even fluently, with large vocabularies, often with odd word choices. Some are echolalic and some hyperverbal. Our assumption is that this variety arises from the highly variable severity and extent of this developmental disorder of brain function. In order to make sense of the extraordinary variability of autistic speech, we will start by briefly reviewing the structure of language and communication in order to have a framework for considering these disorders.

LEVELS OF LANGUAGE

Language is a rule governed, highly encoded communication system that supports the transmission of complex information while minimizing ambiguity. The aural-oral route dominates human communication, with the visual and somatosensory channels playing important though secondary roles. It is customary to divide language into several levels: (1) *phonology and prosody*, the rules that govern the sound units that encode the speech sounds of language, and the intonation of utterances that indicates the intention of the communicator; (2) *syntax and morphology*, the rules for arranging strings of words into well formed sentences according to the rules of grammar of the particular language spoken, and for marking words so as to indicate their role in the sentence (e.g., subject, object, plurals, possessives, tense markers, etc); (3) *semantics and the lexicon,* the rules for using words to produce meaningful messages and the structured repository of word meanings in the brain; and (4) *verbal and nonverbal pragmatics,* the rules for using language communicatively in dialogue (e.g., turn-taking, topic maintenance, providing one's partner with enough information to make one's utterances intelligible), for signaling the intention of the communication (e.g., using prosody to indicate that the utterance is a question, an assertion, a command, a joke), and for the use of body language and facial expression to clarify and augment the effectiveness of the communication (e.g., looking at one's interlocutor, smiling, gesturing).

ASPECTS OF LANGUAGE DEFICIENCY IN AUTISM

The severity of the communication deficit in autism varies a great deal among affected individuals and changes with age. Always and persistently involved, to a greater or lesser degree, are *semantics and pragmatics.* Involved in some children and at some ages are *phonology and syntax* (Tager-Flusberg 1994). In early childhood at least, all autistic children have *comprehension deficits,* even those children who are chatter boxes and use sophisticated vocabularies, or who teach themselves to decode written language at an unusually early age (hyperlexia). It is safe to assume that such children say more than they understand, a paradoxical and rather rare situation because better comprehension than expression is the usual rule in language acquisition and among most nonautistic children with specific developmental language disorders (Rapin et al. 1992; Fein et al. 1996).

Pragmatic, Prosodic, and Semantic Deficits

Pragmatic, prosodic, and semantic deficits are among the most striking and most persistent (often throughout life) deficits in autism. In DSM-IV (American Psychiatric Association 1994), the very first characteristic in the Social Interaction rubric pertains to nonverbal pragmatics: "marked impairment in the use of multiple nonverbal behaviors such as eye-to-eye gaze, facial expression, body postures and gestures to regulate social interaction." The third, which reads: "a lack of spontaneous seeking to share enjoyment, interests, or achievements with other people (e.g., lack of showing, bringing, or pointing to objects of interest)," also refers to nonverbal pragmatics. It is clear that the border between sociability and language and communication is blurred!

Among the four items in the Qualitative Impairment in Communication category in DSM IV, the first three describe classic language deficits: (a) "delay in, or total lack of, the development of spoken language (not accompanied by an attempt to compensate through alternative modes of communication such as gestures or mime)" (the latter, a pragmatic deficit, the former with multiple possible causes to be discussed later), (b) "in individuals with adequate speech, marked impairment in the ability to initiate or sustain a conversation with others" (pragmatics again), and (c) "stereotyped and repetitive use of language or idiosyncratic language" (semantics). Finally, under the third rubric, Restricted Repetitive and Stereotyped Patterns of Behaviors—the first applies to language as well as other activities: "encompassing preoccupation with one or more stereotyped and restricted patterns of interest that is abnormal either in intensity or focus"; when applied to language, it denotes pragmatic abnormality (insensitivity to the interests of one's communication partner) and semantic impoverishment (focus on only one topic).

Pragmatics.   Deficits in pragmatic functioning span the autistic spectrum. There is a lively debate in the literature on whether the pragmatic deficits in autism are due to the social deficits, to the lack of a "theory of mind" (imagining what another person may be thinking and what impact one's behavior may have on another), or to a cognitive deficit (Baron-Cohen et al. 1985). Preverbal or nonverbal autistic children do not evidence a full range of nonverbal communicative functions. There is no real attempt to compensate through gesture as is seen in nonautistic children with developmental language disorders. Autistic toddlers and preschoolers rarely point to indicate needs or to draw another's attention, a skill that develops at around one year in normal children. ("Does your child point?" is a question that should be incorporated into all developmental histories because it is so revealing—and revealing so early—of a pragmatic deficit.) Parents of autistic children will invariably respond that their children get what they want themselves, or drag them and place their hand on what it is they wanted, or else scream until they get it. Failure to shake the head to indicate "no" and later to nod to indicate "yes" are also telling. Children with some verbal skills do not use language well to request or share information (Hurtig et al. 1982; Paul 1987). Wetherby (1986) makes the point that in autistic children the developmental pattern of pragmatic functions is abnormal: normal children acquire social and nonsocial functions concurrently whereas autistic children acquire nonsocial functions very much earlier than social functions.

The conversational skills of the more verbal autistic children are very poor. They have difficulty initiating discourse, maintaining topic, taking turns, and assuming the perspective of their conversational partner. It is difficult for them to respond to different conversational partners with whom a more or less formal style would be appropriate. They often fail to make referents clear so that what they are saying may make little or no sense to someone who does not know them intimately. They have difficulty maintaining a topic unless it is a personal preoccupation of theirs and they do not signal topic shifts in conversation (Fay and Schuler 1980; Tager-Flusberg 1982). Their speech often lacks politeness markers. There is little or no relationship between competence with the structural aspects of their speech and their pragmatic competence.

Prosody. Although, technically, prosody is considered part of phonology because it has to do with speech sounds, it refers to suprasegmental aspects of language (the tonal envelope of several words) rather than to individual speech sounds. Prosody relates to the melody of speech, for example the rising intonation that enables one to indicate that one is asking a question even though one has produced a sentence with the syntax of an affirmation (e.g., "You want to go to bed?" instead of "Do you want to go to bed?"). Prosody also clarifies that when mother says "I could eat you up" she is talking of love and not cannibalism. Prosody is regularly impaired in autistic children (Rutter et al. 1967; Baltaxe and Simmons 1985): some speak in a monotonous choppy voice, so much so that they may sound like robots; others speak in a high pitched squeaky voice; still others have the rising intonation of a question even in affirmative sentences; some speak with a singsong rising/falling intonation. Many of these prosodic deficits persist, even in adults (Ornitz and Ritvo 1976).

Semantics. An early semantic deficit is lack of understanding that people and things have names (Allen et al. 1989), which results in failure to turn when called, and inability to ask for things verbally or point to body parts, people, objects, or pictures on verbal command. An impoverished vocabulary denotes deficient semantics; it may be a primary deficit in the processing or storage of words, or may be secondary to phonologic and syntactic deficits. Words are used in limited contexts. This is also true of young normally developing children, but autistic children remain at this stage for a protracted period. Word retrieval deficits (anomia) are common in young autistic children: they may denote a specific memory deficit for accessing the lexicon, or an inefficiently organized lexicon in which word meanings are not linked in conventional ways (Dunn et al. 1996). For example, instead of words being linked within a superordinate category (e.g., articles of clothing, vehicles) or relational category (e.g., dog/bone, cat/mouse), they may be stored according to some other nonconventional, idiosyncratic rule (e.g., words heard in a particular TV show or song), or stored in a rote manner, for example by contextual salience (e.g., dinosaurs), situation (e.g., what so and so said on a particular day), or order of presentation. According to Fay and Schuler (1980), inadequate concept acquisition is a fundamental deficit in autism. This might account for inadequate organization of the lexicon. Although concept formation is highly related to overall intelligence (Tager-Flusberg 1989), even the highest functioning autistic individuals may find it difficult to interrelate concepts and experiences flexibly. DeLong (1992) proposes that autism results from the failure of a central cognitive processor required "for the construction of a complex, useful and flexible structure of meaning." According to this view, this processor governs action and modifies how relations among stimuli are laid down in memory. This cognitive processor does not subserve the acquisition of specific words or concepts during language development but the ability to conjoin them. DeLong further proposes that impairment of this system limits the capacity for flexible association of existing cognitive elements (in memory or from the environment) for the production of new and unique cognitive constructs. His model of autism implies that information in long-term memory has some degree of conceptual organization but lacks the normal richness of semantic associations. DeLong's view accounts for the disruption in lexical organization, use of semantic knowledge, and processing of semantic context characteristic of autistic language.

Autistic children rely on echolalia and formulaic speech to an excessive degree (Simon 1975). This suggests a gestalt rather than analytic style of language acquisition (Prizant 1983; Schuler and Prizant 1985). As a consequence, expression precedes comprehension. These children often produce entire sentences that they have memorized and serve back verbatim, often with pronominal reversals (you = me), in marginally appropriate contexts. Such utterances are called *scripts or delayed echolalia*. Delayed echolalia, like *immediate echolalia* (repetition of what was just said) (Prizant and Duchan 1981), denotes poor comprehension and the use of incompletely processed sentences to fill a perceived communication need. This gives the children's language an odd character, already commented on by Kanner (1946): they use "big" words they cannot possibly understand and may sound like little professors; they may chain utterances by single words rather than by ideas and go off on tangents (often taken for thought disorders with the looseness of associations typical of psychosis), and they may perseverate because they produce again and again the few sentences they have at their disposal. Autistic children who produce many scripts may be little chatter boxes who speak to speak (they know that is what people do) rather than to communicate (to convey a meaningful message to another person). Such children suffer from the *semantic-pragmatic syndrome* (Rapin and Allen 1983; Bishop and Adams 1989). One is well advised to suspect that such children understand paradoxically less than they can say, inasmuch as they process and memorize the surface (phonology and syntax) of utterances rather than their meaning (semantics), and are prone to use language non-conversationally. The children's expressive vocabularies may be larger than their receptive vocabularies; in other words, they repeat, by rote, words that have an impoverished or no meaning for them. Although their use of words from different word classes (e.g., nouns, adjectives, verbs, etc.) may be comparable to that of children matched for mean length of utterances (MLU), autistic children tend to have a smaller stock of words within each category (Tager-Flusberg 1989). Older verbal autistic individuals frequently violate semantic constraints in their speech. They may use incorrect lexical items from the correct form class that correspond loosely to the meaning intended, e.g., "The only sport I like is drawing," or make idiosyncratic choices, e.g., "He thinks when he wants to please people its like an elephant" (Simmons and Baltaxe 1975; Bishop and Adams 1989). Their strategy for comprehending connected speech is to emphasize word order over information provided by the semantic content of what was said (Tager-Flusberg 1981; Paul et al.1988).

It is not always clear whether verbal perseveration (speaking about only one topic or a narrow range of topics) denotes semantic impoverishment, lack of regard for one's partner's interests (theory of mind), or reflects a generalized tendency to stereotypy or repeated motor acts—after all, speech is also a motor act. There is an equally lively debate on whether semantic deficits denote cognitive (organizational, executive) or "true" language deficits, in the sense that the structural aspects of language (phonology and syntax) may be unaffected.

Phonologic and Syntactic Deficits

Phonology. The order of emergence of classes of speech sounds in verbal autistic children parallels that in normal children, except that speech development is almost always delayed (Paul 1987). A significant minority of autistic individuals remain nonverbal into adulthood, whereas many verbal autistic individuals master the speech sound system at later stages of development than normal children, in some cases after a prolonged period during which they produce an unintelligible jargon. Because many verbal autistic persons tend to speak clearly and intelligibly (i.e., they have acquired the phonologic rules of their language) and generally speak in well-formed sentences (i.e., they have also acquired its syntactic rules), phonologic and syntactic deficits are given short shrift in many descriptions of the language of autistic persons. Yet the receptive phonologic processing of some autistic preschoolers is so severely compromised that they understand virtually nothing of what is said to them. It is of course well known that one must be able to decode speech sounds before one can encode them to speak. In a significant proportion of nonautistic dysphasic children the basic deficit is at the level of phonologic processing; these children do not understand language because they cannot make the appropriate sound discriminations to decode the acoustic signal that represents language. In its most severe form this deficit is referred to as *verbal auditory agnosia* (VAA) or word-deafness (Rapin et al. 1977). Children with VAA or the less severe phonologic-syntactic dysphasia (Rapin and Allen 1983) have a deficit in their ability to discriminate and sequence rapid speech sounds. Whether it is due to an auditory agnosia for brief non-speech auditory signals, as long proposed by Tallal (Tallal et al. 1993, 1996) or an agnosia specific to the decoding of phonemes (Studdert-Kennedy and Mody 1995) is debated. When these children do start to speak they make many phonologic errors (speech sounds missing, distorted, or substituted), which impairs their intelligibility. Their ability to acquire language through the visual channel (sign language, writing) provides evidence for a modality-specific acoustic receptive deficit for speech.

There are nonverbal or minimally verbal autistic children whose language shares all of the characteristics of nonautistic children with VAA or severe phonologic-syntactic, receptive-expressive deficits (Allen and Rapin 1992; Klein et al. 1995). Nonautistic language-impaired children differ from autistic children by their intact pragmatic skills that enable them to capitalize on gestures to communicate nonverbally, which autistic children do not do or do to a minimal degree. As is true of nonautistic dysphasic children, most young autistic children with phonologic processing deficits eventually learn to make speech sound discriminations well enough to be able to speak, though not necessarily with perfect phonology. The clinical impression that the probability of residual expressive phonologic deficits may be somewhat less in autistic than dysphasic children still lacks empirical confirmation. Persistent deficits may be manifest, if not in speech sound production, in auditory analysis (the ability to segment speech into syllables or individual speech sounds) and in the acquisition of phonetic reading (Tallal et al. 1996).

There is a significant association between lack of speech and low IQ, yet the assumption that autistic persons do not speak because they are very retarded, rather than assuming that their IQ is low because they have not acquired language, remains a speculation. Only a thorough longitudinal study of the phonologic skills and speech sound discrimination abilities of autistic children with early phonologic deficits will resolve some of these issues.

Syntax. Faulty syntax virtually never appears as an isolated deficit in childhood; it is almost always associated with defective phonology, as is also the case in adults with Broca's aphasia. At its extreme, children with syntactic deficits speak only in single, usually poorly articulated words. More often, they speak in short, uninflected, ungrammatical, telegraphic utterances. This type of utterance indicates that the word endings that mark grammatic role (e.g., tense, plural, possessive) and the small grammatic words such as articles (e.g., "the", "a"), prepositions (e.g., "on", "through"), conjunctions (e.g., "and', "but"), and pronouns (e.g., "he", "yours") are affected selectively. While it may be that word endings lack salience and are therefore not processed, selective involvement of the "small words" (closed-class words), of which there is a finite number and therefore which appear more often in language than open-class words (nouns, verbs, adjectives, adverbs), of which there is potentially an infinite number, seems somewhat paradoxical. Perhaps it is because closed-class words are abstract, rather than pointing to concrete people, things, qualities, and events, that they are more difficult to acquire. In any case, Neville's electrophysiologic recordings in dysphasic children indicate that closed-class and open-class words are processed differentially in the brain (Neville et al. 1993).

Syntax in verbal autistic children is similar to that in normal controls matched for mean length of utterance (MLU). The length and complexity of their sentences and their syntactic errors do not differ from those of language-matched normal children (Pierce and Bartolucci 1977; Tager-Flusberg 1994). Despite similarity in sequence of morphologic development, autistic children do not *use* as wide a range of morphologic markers in their spontaneous speech as normal children.

AGE AT LANGUAGE ACQUISITION; LANGUAGE REGRESSION

The majority of autistic children start to speak late (at age 2–3 years) or very late (at 4 years or even later). By listening to them, one can determine whether the probable reason for late speech is at the level of phonology/syntax (deficient production of speech sounds and sentences) or semantics/pragmatics (late onset but rapid progress into clearly spoken well-formed full sentences).

There are a minority of children on the autistic spectrum who are not delayed in language acquisition and whose comprehension is adequate or near adequate, although their pragmatic skills and, often, their prosody is off. These children are increasingly being referred to as having *Asperger syndrome* (Frith 1991). Whether Asperger syndrome is a biologically specific entity, rather than the upper tail of the autistic distribution, remains to be determined.

About a third of autistic children start to develop communicative language normally (or at least somewhat normally) at the expected age then regress, usually between the ages of 1 and 3 years, in language production and comprehension, as well as in sociability and play skills. The Diagnostic and Statistical Manual of Mental Disorders (DSM-IV) refers to children who lose their language, cognitive, and social skills after age 2 years following fully normal language acquisition, and do so before age 10 years, as suffering from *disintegrative disorder* (Kurita et al. 1992). Whether disintegrative disorder is or is not biologically distinct from the much more common autistic regression is uncertain.

The neurologic basis of autistic regression is not understood. In a minority of cases it may be associated with epilepsy (and thus overlap acquired epileptic aphasia or Landau-Kleffner syndrome [Landau and Kleffner 1957; Rapin 1995]). In our opinion, the loss of language, sociability, and play in autistic children most likely denotes more widespread brain dysfunction than in pure Landau-Kleffner syndrome, rather than autistic behaviors being the consequence of the loss of language (e.g., Stefanatos et al. 1995). Clear fluctuations in language and cognitive ability should make one consider that subclinical epilepsy may be responsible for the regression and make it *mandatory* to obtain a prolonged or overnight sleep EEG or, better, prolonged EEG monitoring to rule out this possibility, inasmuch as it has medical implications (Deonna 1991): the finding of (bilateral) spike/wave discharges or of status epilepticus in slow wave sleep (Jayakar and Seshia 1991) would suggest a trial of spike-suppressant antiepileptic medication or of ACTH/steroids, even though their efficacy is unpredictable in children with acquired epileptic aphasia. The usual course of events in autistic regression is for development to pick up after a plateau lasting from a few weeks to many months, although complete recovery is virtually never achieved and autistic characteristics of a more or less severe degree persist. There is an urgent need for serious study of the children *at the time of the regression*, rather than months or even years later, in order to address all of these unresolved issues.

Although it is often assumed that autistic children do not talk because they lack the drive to communicate, this is only part of the picture. In fact, there is considerable overlap between the language disorders of young autistic children and those of non-autistic dysphasic children (Allen and Rapin 1992). A major difference is that purely or almost purely expressive disorders are not encountered in autism, inasmuch as comprehension is always deficient, at least in early childhood. It is widely assumed that an autistic child who has not started to produce speech by age 5 years is unlikely to become verbal. Although there is considerable truth to this statement, some children will start to speak after age 5. The severity of the comprehension deficit and the response to adequate educational intervention, together with an assessment of the child's cognitive abilities, provide some prognostic guidelines.

NEUROLOGIC BASIS OF THE COMMUNICATION DISORDERS OF AUTISM

Specific information about the neurologic basis of the communication deficits of autism is scant. There is pathologic evidence of bilateral hippocampal, limbic, and neocerebellar cellular maldevelopment in autism, but none thus far in the neocortex (Bauman and Kemper 1994), even though electrophysiology is beginning to provide some functional evidence for cortical involvement (Dunn 1994; Klein et al. 1995). Therefore we have to turn to evidence from other sources, realizing that reasoning by analogy from adults to children acquiring language is dangerous (Rapin and Allen 1988). Phonologic decoding is known to take place in primary and secondary language areas of the temporal lobe bilaterally, with some predominance for consonants on the left and for vowels on the right. Therefore it makes sense that the Landau-Kleffner syndrome, almost always associated with a phonologic decoding (and encoding) deficit, occurs in the context of bilateral perisylvian epileptic discharges. In right-handed adults at least, comprehension of the meaning of language requires the integrity of Wernicke's area in the left posterior temporal lobe and there is evidence that the right hemisphere is dominant for prosodic encoding and decoding. As stated earlier, Neville's evoked response work in dysphasic and normally developing children indicates that closed-class words are processed separately from open-class words (Neville et al. 1993). In adults, lexical organization seems to require lateral prefrontal activity, and Broca's area on the left is involved in both phonologic and syntactic encoding for speech. Recent PET evidence from Raichle's laboratory shows that, in normal adults, the right cerebellar hemisphere, as well as the left frontal lobe, is involved in the generation of verbs from nouns (even when they are unexpressed vocally or otherwise), so that our knowledge about the organization of language in the brain is about to undergo a revolution (Raichle 1994). Pragmatic deficits may be a function of limbic circuits involving the amygdala and cingulate gyrus, perhaps more so on the right than the left. Finally, it is well established that hippocampal circuits are required for verbal learning. How much of this sketchy knowledge about language processing is relevant to the communication disorders of autism remains to be seen.

INTERVENTION

Before one can start specific training of language skills, it is necessary to develop joint attention and imitation on demand. Approaches such as the conditioning paradigms promulgated by Lovaas (1993) may enable children to learn to sit and focus on the task at hand and to acquire labels for objects, people, and actions. They also need to learn that one object or action can symbolize another. Once this has been accomplished, the focus should be on reciprocal communicative interactions and play and on social reinforcers. Many autistic toddlers and preschoolers do not understand that language is power, and that pointing is likely to lead to a desirable outcome. One has to teach language-less autistic preschoolers to point to objects, to pictures of objects, to communication boards, and, eventually, to written words. They need to learn that people and things have names (Allen et al. 1989). The introduction of sign language (or even reading) has helped even some older nonverbal autistic children acquire language through their less impaired visual channel, and in some cases has resulted in significant improvement in their behavior (Bonvillian et al. 1981). Therefore, the focus of language training should not be on phonology but on meaningful communication, even in children who have obvious phonologic deficits.

For verbal autistic children, training in the production of meaningful language and the conversational use of language is at the forefront. One can capitalize on children's use of scripts to teach them to produce more appropriate and flexible expressive language. One always needs to keep in mind that the severity of their comprehension deficit is easily overlooked because they often produce more complex language in scripts than they understand. One needs to assure oneself that lack of compliance with a request is not lack of comprehension, rather than oppositional behavior. It is safe to assume that failure to answer an open-ended question such as who, what, or where in the absence of a referent, and when, why, and how denotes lack of understanding of the question rather than failure to know the answer or unwillingness to answer. One needs to scale down one's utterances to facilitate understanding, and to model appropriate responses when none, or an inappropriate one, is forthcoming.

Precocious ability to recite the alphabet, count, sing the words of songs, or read is reassuring to parents because such skills rule out across-the-board mental deficiency. They do not necessarily denote comprehension. A subset of both low and high functioning autistic children has precocious ability to decode the written word (hyperlexia) with poor comprehension of written and oral language. Such children may even be obsessed with reading. Rather than seeking to extinguish this behavior it can be used as a particularly useful tool for developing language, associating the written word with objects and events to foster comprehension and expand vocabulary. Building sentences with word cards helps improve syntax. One can write classroom instructions to make sure they are understood. Daily routines in the home can be represented by pictures accompanied by single written words or brief written instructions.

The overall strategy is to use all of the child's strengths to compensate for deficits and to take the child's particular learning style into account in planning remediation. Most autistic children have a gestalt learning style and benefit through the paired presentation of auditory and visual information. For example, one should take advantage of an excellent rote memory. Instead of discouraging echolalia and the use of scripts a therapist can teach language and social scripts and then gradually model their more flexible, less deviant use in a variety of related situations and foster generalization by using the same word or utterance in different contexts. As a child acquires language it is important to focus on establishing an organized semantic base by teaching relationships in meaning among words.

Older intelligent verbal autistic children profit from straightforward feedback about their pragmatic errors, so long as it is provided in a non-judgmental non-critical way and couched as friendly matter-of-fact informative help. Areas to focus on include how to engage in meaningful dialogue, (maintaining topic, switching topic, interrupting appropriately, using appropriate tone of voice, maintaining personal space, and being formal or casual) and how to organize a coherent account of an event or summary of a story. Autistic children benefit from being taught to organize verbal material hierarchically, weighting the main topic more heavily than secondary themes or details.

SUMMARY

Analysis of what aspects of language are deficient in each autistic child will go a long way toward demystifying such children's often bizarre productions and the paradoxical aspects of their communication skills. This analysis will also provide a basis for planning remediation. Much can be done to ameliorate the communication deficits of autistic children, but early intervention, at the optimal language-learning age (toddler and preschool years), is essential. One needs to start by developing attentional and pragmatic skills in order to be able to focus on the production of words, sentences, and, eventually, meaningful connected discourse. In children who do not speak, rather than assuming that the all-too-obvious lack of drive to communicate is at the root of the problem, it is important to consider whether presentation of language through the visual channel might help processing and strengthen the use of the auditory channel. Finally, one must keep in mind that impaired comprehension plays a significant role in the negativistic behaviors that create such severe problems for the parents and educators of these children.

ACKNOWLEDGMENT

Preparation of this paper was supported in part by Program Project NS 20489 from the National Institute of Neurological Disorders and Stroke.

REFERENCES

Allen, D. A., Mendelson, L., and Rapin, I. 1989. Syndrome specific remediation in preschool developmental dysphasia. In *Child Neurology and Developmental Disabilities*, eds. J. H. French, S. Harel, P. Casaer, M. I. Gottlieb, I. Rapin, and D. C. DeVivo. Baltimore: Paul H. Brooks.

Allen, D. A., and Rapin, I. 1992. Autistic children are also dysphasic. In *Neurobiology of Infantile Autism*, eds. H. Naruse and E. Ornitz. Amsterdam: Excerpta Medica.

American Psychiatric Association. 1994. *Diagnostic and Statistical Manual of Mental Disorders* (Fourth Edition). Washington, DC: American Psychiatric Association.

Baltaxe, C., and Simmons, J. Q. 1985. Prosodic development in normal and autistic children. In *Communication Problems in Autism*, eds. E. Schopler and G. B. Mesibov. New York: Plenum Press.

Baron-Cohen, S., Leslie, A. M., and Frith, U. 1985. Does the autistic child have a "theory of mind?" *Cognition* 21: 37–46.

Bauman, M. L., and Kemper, T. L. 1994. Neuroanatomic observations in autism. In *The Neurobiology of Autism*, M. L. Bauman and T. L. Kemper eds. Baltimore: Johns Hopkins University Press.

Bishop, D. V. M., and Adams, C. 1989. Conversational characteristics of children with semantic-pragmatic disorder. I. What features lead to a judgement of inappropriacy? *British Journal of Disorders of Communication* 24: 241–63.

Bonvillian, J. D., Nelson, K. E., and Rhyne, J. M. 1981. Sign language and autism. *Journal of Autism and Developmental Disorders* 11:125–37.

DeLong, G. R. 1992. Autism, amnesia, hippocampus and learning. *Neuroscience and Behavioral Reviews* 16:63–70.

Deonna, T. W. 1991. Acquired epileptiform aphasia in children (Landau-Kleffner syndrome). *Journal of Clinical Neurophysiology* 3:288–98/

Dunn, M. 1994. Neurophysiologic observations in autism and implications for neurologic dysfunction. In *The Neurobiology of Autism*, eds. M. L. Bauman, T. L. Kemper. Baltimore: Johns Hopkins University Press. 1994:45–65.

Dunn, M., Gomes, H., and Sebastian, M. 1996 (in press). Prototypicality of responses in autistic, language disordered and normal children in a verbal fluency task. *Child Neuropsychology*.

Fay, W., and Schuler, A. L. 1960. *Emerging Language in Autistic Children*. Baltimore: University Park Press.

Fein, D., Dunn, M., Allen, D., Hall, N., Morris, R., and Wilson, B. 1996 (in press). Neuropsychological and language findings. In *Preschool Children with Inadequate Communication: Developmental Language Disorder, Autism, Low IQ*, I. Rapin ed. *Clinics in Developmental Medicine #139*. London: Mac Keith Press.

Frith, U. 1991. *Autism and Asperger Syndrome*. Cambridge, UK: Cambridge University Press.

Hurtig, R., Ensrud, S., and Tomblin, J. B. 1982. The communicative function of question production in autistic children. *Journal of Autism and Developmental Disorders* 12:57–69.

Jayakar, P. B., and Seshia, S. S. 1991. Electrical status epilepticus during slow-wave sleep. *Journal of Clinical Neurophysiology* 8:299–311.

Kanner, L. 1946. Irrelevant and metaphorical language in early infantile autism. *American Journal of Psychiatry* 103:242–46.

Klein, S. K., Kurtzberg, D., Brattson, A., et al. 1995. Electrophysiologic manifestations of impaired temporal lobe auditory processing in verbal auditory agnosia. *Brain & Language* 51:383–405.

Kurita, H., Kita, M., and Miyake, Y. 1992. A comparative study of development and symptoms among disintegrative disorder and infantile autism with and without speech loss. *Journal of Autism and Developmental Disorders* 22:175–88.

Landau, W. M., and Kleffner, F. R. 1957. Syndrome of acquired aphasia with convulsive disorder in children. *Neurology* 7:523–30.

Lovaas, O. I. 1993. The development of a treatment-research project for developmentally disabled and autistic children. *Journal of Applied Behavavioral Analysis* 26:617–30.

Neville, H. J., Coffey, S. A., Holcomb, P. J., and Tallal, P. 1993. The neurobiology of sensory and language processing in language-impaired children. *Journal of Cognitive Neuroscience* 5:235–53.

Ornitz, E. M., and Ritvo, E. R. 1976. The syndrome of autism: A critical review. *American Journal of Psychiatry* 33:609–22.

Paul, R. 1987. Communication. In *Handbook of Autism and Pervasive Developmental Disorders*, eds. D. J. Cohen and A. M. Donellan. New York: Wiley.

Paul, R., Fischer, M. L., and Cohen, D. J. 1988. Brief Report: Sentence comprehension strategies in children with autism and specific language disorders. *Journal of Autism and Developmental Disorders* 18:669–77.

Pierce, S., and Bartolucci, G. 1977. A syntactic investigation of verbal autistic, mentally retarded, and normal children. *Journal of Autism and Childhood Schizophrenia* 7:121–34.

Prizant, B. M. 1983. Language acquisition and communicative behavior in autism: Toward an understanding of the "whole" of it. *Journal of Speech and Hearing Disorders* 48:296–307.

Prizant, B. M., and Duchan, J. F. 1981. The functions of immediate echolalia in autistic children. *Journal of Speech and Hearing Research* 46:241–49.

Raichle, M. E. Positron emission tomographic studies of verbal response selection. In *Evolution and Neurology of Language*, eds. D. C. Gajdusek, G. M. McKhann, and L. C. Bolis. *Discussions in Neuroscience* 10:130–36.

Rapin, I. 1995. Autistic regression and disintegrative disorder: How important the role of epilepsy? *Seminars in Pediatric Neurology* 2:278–85.

Rapin, I., and Allen, D. A. 1988. Syndromes in developmental dysphasia and adult aphasia. In *Language, Communication, and the Brain*, ed. F. Plum. New York: Raven Press.

Rapin, I., and Allen, D. A. 1983. Developmental language disorders: Neurologic considerations. In *Neuropsychology of Language, Reading, and Spelling*, ed. U. Kirk. New York: Academic Press.

Rapin, I., Allen, D. A., and Dunn, M. A. 1992. Developmental language disorders. In *Handbook of Neuropsychology Vol. 7. Child Neuropsychology*, eds. S. J. Segalowitz and I. Rapin. Amsterdam: Elsevier Science.

Rapin, I., Mattis, S., Rowan, A. J., and Golden, G. S. 1977. Verbal auditory agnosia in children. *Developmental Medicine and Child Neurology* 19:192–207.

Rutter, M., Greenfield, D., and Lockyer, L. 1967. A five to fifteen year followup of infantile psychosis: II. Social and behavioral outcome. *British Journal of Psychiatry* 113:1183–99.

Schuler, A. L., and Prizant, B. M. 1985. Echolalia. In *Communication Problems in Autism*, eds. E. Schopler and G. Mesibov. New York: Plenum.

Simmons, J. Q., and Baltaxe, C. 1975. Language patterns of adolescent autistics. *Journal of Autism and Childhood Schizophrenia* 5:333–50.

Simon, N. 1975. Echolalic speech in childhood autism. *Archives of General Psychiatry* 32:1439–46.

Stefanatos, G. A., Grover, W., and Geller E. 1995. Case study: Corticosteroid treatment of language regression in pervasive developmental disorder. *Journal of the American Academy of Child and Adolescent Psychiatry* 34:1107–11.

Studdert-Kennedy, M., and Mody, M. 1995. Auditory temporal perception deficits in the reading-impaired: A critical review of the evidence. *Psychonomic Bulletin & Review* 2:508–14.

Tager-Flusberg, H. 1981. Sentence comprehension in autistic children. *Applied Psycholinguistics* 2:5–24.

Tager-Flusberg, H. 1982. Pragmatic development and its implications for social interaction in autistic children. In *Proceedings of the International Symposium for Research in Autism*, ed. D. Park. Washington, DC: National Society for Autistic Children.

Tager-Flusberg, H. 1989. A psycholinguistic perspective on language development in the autistic child. In *Autism: Nature, Diagnosis, and Treatment*, ed. G. Dawson. New York: Guilford Press.

Tager-Flusberg, H. 1994. Dissociation in form and function in the acquisition of language by autistic children. In *Constraints on Language Acquisition: Studies of Atypical Children*, ed. H. Tager-Flusberg. Hillsdale NJ, Lawrence Erlbaum Associates.

Tallal, P., Miller, S., and Fitch, R. H. 1993. Neurobiological basis of speech: A case of the preeminence of temporal processing. *Annals of the New York Academy of Sciences* 682:27–47.

Tallal, P., Miller, S. L., Bedi, G., Byma, G., Wang, X., Nagajaran, S. S, Schreiner, C., Jenkins, W. M., and Merzenich, M. M. 1996. Language comprehension in language-learning impaired children improved with acoustically modified speech. *Science* 271:81–84.

Wetherby, A. M. 1986. Ontogeny of communication functions in autism. *Journal of Autism and Developmental Disorders* 16:295–316.

Part • III

Fetal Influences

Chapter • 7

Fetal Teratogens:
Methodological Issues

Claudia A. Chiriboga

To be sure, exposure to illicit drugs can affect the developing nervous system. However, determining the extent to which prenatal exposure to drugs contributes to nervous system damage is complicated by myriad intervening factors (confounders) (see table I) that occur in such settings. In addition to the effects of the

Table I.   Fetal Drug Studies: Risk Factors for Adverse Outcomes

PERINATAL
Infections
Systemic infections
Human Immunodeficiency Virus (HIV)
Congenital syphilis
Maternal nutrition
Poor prenatal care
Low birth weight
Intrauterine growth retardation
Prematurity
Polysubstance exposure
Cigarettes
Alcohol
Marijuana
Opiates
Cocaine

POSTNATAL
Socioeconomical status
Home environment
Physical
Emotional
Maternal psychopathology

drug of interest, behavioral correlates of drug use, such as poor prenatal care or sexually transmitted diseases (HIV or congenital syphilis), may be operant that may be more harmful to the offspring than the drug under study. Collectively, the plethora of concomitant risk factors, including poor nutrition, social chaos, poor parenting, and multiple drug exposures, help explain why the offspring of alcohol and drug abusing women tend to fair less well neurodevelopmentally than other children of similar socioeconomical background. However, the net effect of any single drug is substantially diminished once these confounding factors are taken into account.

Unlike the experimental model where variables are fixed by the investigator, the clinical setting is laden with many factors that act in concert to influence the fetal and postnatal environment. Epidemiological methods applied in the study design or analytical phase offer some control over these extraneous or "confounding" variables, however, the erratic high-risk behaviors associated with drug use introduce additional elements that make inferences in clinical studies regarding drug-related associations more vulnerable to bias, e.g., selection bias resulting from a high level of attrition. This chapter focuses on the methodological problems that have arisen in the clinical research of fetal drug exposures and provides a broad overview of the salient clinical findings associated with its use. Fetal cocaine exposure is emphasized because of the intense research interest it has generated over the past decade.

ASCERTAINMENT

Self Report

Self report during interview and urine toxicological testing are the traditional methods of ascertaining drug and alcohol use. The information gleaned from structured interviews allows researchers to quantify and assess patterns of drug use over time, especially during the first trimester of pregnancy. However, self report of drug use is not a reliable method for ascertaining drug use as most studies show that 25% of women who deny using cocaine during pregnancy have positive urine toxicologies (Zuckerman et al. 1989). Thus, estimates of drug use, especially during pregnancy, remain problematic, mostly because of poor exposure recall, and questions regarding maternal veracity. The latter stems from the stigma and legal consequences attached to drug use during pregnancy, such as loss of child custody. For example, in New York State, children who test positive for cocaine are placed in foster care custody unless the mothers make adequate efforts to rehabilitate. Consequently, ascertainment of fetal drug exposure based solely on self report leads to substantial misclassification of exposure status that tends to obscure the strength of associations between exposure and outcome and consequently may bias study findings.

Urine Toxicology

Urine toxicology assays can confirm drug use, but, because most drugs are rapidly metabolized, this method informs solely about recent use. For example, cocaine can be detected in urine for 6 to 8 hours and cocaine metabolites can be detected up to 6 to 8 days. (Ambre et al. 1982). In exceptional cases of prolonged heavy cocaine use, however, metabolites have been detected in urine up to 22 days after use (Weiss and Gawin 1988). Even though urine toxicology is indicative of recent exposure, paradoxically this method tends to ascertain women who are heavy drug users and are, therefore, probably not representative of the general population. This is because women who use drugs regularly are more likely to test positive at the time of delivery than women who use drugs sporadically or quit early in pregnancy. With certain exceptions, e.g., cocaine-related abruptio placentae (Acker et al. 1983), most adverse effects in infants with a positive urine toxicology are not likely to be the result of a single exposure at the time of birth and instead probably reflect a pattern of high use throughout most of the pregnancy. An additional limitation of using urine toxicology to assess drug use in clinical research settings is that it does not allow quantification of use.

Hair Radioimmunoassay

New methods of drug ascertainment, namely hair radioimmunoassay and meconium analysis, have emerged that allow us to determine more remote use of drugs. So far, however, few studies have been published using these newer, more accurate methods of ascertainment. Hair radioimmunoassay determines the past use of a number of drugs, including marijuana, cocaine, opiates, and phenylcyclidine (Graham et al. 1989). Analysis of each 1.5 cms of maternal hair gives information on drug use during the previous three months. With a sufficiently long hair sample, the entire pregnancy can be screened for drug use. Hair that has been treated chemically or physically altered may provide less reliable estimates of exposure. External contamination of the hair sample by the environment is readily avoided by thorough washings of the sample prior to processing.

Meconium Analysis

Meconium develops at about 18 weeks of gestational age. Thereafter, it acts as a reservoir of drugs used by the mother. The analysis of meconium specimens collected during the first two days of life permits us to determine chronic drug exposure during the latter half of fetal life (Ostrea et al. 1989). Unlike hair analysis, meconium analysis does not inform on the timing of in utero exposure. It does, however, afford a reliable estimate of cumulative exposure to cocaine and its various metabolites, including cocaethylene, which is formed by the combined use of cocaine and alcohol. This pharmacologically active metabolite then concentrates in meconium 10 fold (Lewis, Moore, and Leiken 1994). Measures of cocaethylene in meconium, thus, promise to enhance the ascertainment of concomitant alcohol use, which is a vexing confounder of cocaine studies.

Both hair analysis and meconium analysis use cocaine metabolites as surrogates for cocaine exposure. Since chronic exposure to cocaine during fetal life results in exposure to both the parent compound and its metabolites, neither hair nor meconium analysis can be used to discern which of these substances is responsible for the deleterious effects to the fetus. Attempts to correlate blood levels of cocaine or cocaine metabolites with concurrent neurobehaviors are flawed because there is little assurance that current behaviors reflect ongoing exposures. In assessing chronic fetal exposure, animal studies that use specific cocaine metabolites are better than clinical correlation studies to elucidate whether cocaine metabolites are responsible for perceived fetal effects.

OTHER ASSOCIATIONS AND RISK FACTORS
Infections

Systemic Infections. In addition to any specific drug effects, exposed infants are at increased risk because of behaviors related to drug abuse. Women who use drugs intravenously are at risk for systemic and cutaneous infection, including hepatitis B, subacute bacterial endocarditis, brain abscesses, HIV infection, and AIDS (Shepherd, Druckenbrod, and Haywood 1990) They also tend to exchange sex for drugs (although most would deny this constitutes prostitution), thereby increasing their risks for sexually transmitted diseases.

Human Immunodeficiency Virus (HIV). The use of intravenous street drugs poses a substantial risk for HIV infection, as contaminated needles are a well-described mode of transmission. Nonparenteral cocaine use, however, is becoming an increasingly important HIV risk factor due to the exchange of sex for drugs. Women who are unemployed and use crack have nearly 3.5 fold increased risk of being HIV seropositive than employed women who use crack (Lindsay et al. 1992), suggesting that female crack addicts use sex to pay for their cocaine habit.

The transmission rate of HIV infection in offspring varies between 15% to 25% with higher rates contingent on maternal viral burden and level of immunocompromise. HIV invasion of the central nervous system often occurs in early infancy leading to a spectrum of neurodevelopmental impairments ranging from developmental delay to a HIV progressive encephalopathy. Although a connatal form of pediatric-AIDS or neuro-AIDS has thus far not been documented, high rates of neurological abnormality are reported in the United States among children born HIV antibody positive, even among those who lose passively acquired maternal antibodies (seroreverters). These high rates are in part attributable to cocaine exposure, as evidenced by a controlled study in which cocaine-positive urine, but not HIV infection, was significantly associated with hypertonia at 6 months of age (Chiriboga et al. 1993). In the same cohort, HIV antibody status at birth appeared to correlate with the level of cocaine exposure; among cocaine-positive children, those who were HIV antibody positive (HIV infected and seroreverters) showed significantly higher rates of neurological abnormalities than those who were HIV antibody negative, while among cocaine-negative children, rates were similar between the two groups (Chiriboga et al. 1995), suggesting that HIV positivity among drug-using women may be a proxy for higher levels of cocaine exposure.

Congenital Syphilis. The cocaine epidemic in the 1980s coincided with a rise in the incidence of syphilis (Webber and Hauser 1993; Anonymous 1992), which in certain urban centers reached epidemic proportions. For instance, the rate of congenital syphilis in New York City increased from 1.2 cases per 1000 births in 1982 to 5.8 cases per 1000 births in 1988 (Webber and Hauser 1993). In controlled analyses, the odds of cocaine exposure increased 4-fold among infants with congenital syphilis (Greenberg et al. 1991). Syphilis is also linked to poor prenatal care. In one study, poor prenatal care achieved the highest adjusted odds ratio associated with congenital syphilis (OR = 11.0), while cocaine use achieved the second highest adjusted odds ratio (OR = 4.9) (Webber et al. 1993). Although the impact of congenital syphilis on neurodevelopment is not well delineated in the literature, it appears that only a fraction of infants with neurosyphilis exhibit frank neurological signs (Volpe 1995).

Maternal Nutrition. The adverse impact of poor maternal nutrition on fetal well being is well documented. Picone et al. (1982) showed that poor maternal weight gain ($\leq$ 15 lbs.) was significantly associated with lower birth weights, ponderal indices, growth rates, and shorter gestations, as well as with a reduction in placental weight, even when controlling for gestational age. Total placental DNA was

14% lower among women with low weight gain during pregnancy, a phenomenon that is not observed with exposure to maternal cigarette smoking or illicit substances. Another nutritional factor that affects the offspring of drug-using women is the lack of nutritional supplements, which accounts for an additional 40 or 60 grams decrement in newborn weight (Moro et al. 1979).

Poor maternal weight gain exerts a significant and independent effect on neonatal neurobehavioral status. Using the Brazelton Newborn Behavioral Assessment Scales (BNBAS), poor maternal weight gain was associated with impaired habituation, orientation, and regulation of state. Low weight gain in the second trimester was related to impaired motor performance, visual habituation, orientation, and reflexes (Picone et al. 1982). In another study, nutritional variables predicted poor performance on the Brazelton including poor habituation, motor, orientation, reflex score, and autonomic responses (Oyemade et al. 1994).

Experimental studies show that cocaine administration during pregnancy is associated with decreased nutritional intake. When allowed equal food access, pregnant dams that are administered cocaine eat less and gain less weight than control dams (Church, Overbeck, and Andrzejczak 1990). Low nutritional intake among cocaine addicts arises from economic factors, as meager resources are spent procuring cocaine rather than food, and also from cocaine's ability to suppress appetite. The lower levels of serum folate and ferritin found in cocaine-positive pregnant women as compared with controls attest to the poor nutritional status of drug users (Knight et al. 1994).

In experimental models, maternal caloric intake may be controlled, albeit imperfectly, by pair feeding so that nutritional intake is comparable between exposed and control dams. However, in the clinical arena, the chaotic lifestyles led by cocaine addicts make it increasingly difficult to control for nutrition because erratic eating habits and poor recall make 24-hour nutritional assessments unreliable. To further complicate matters, the association between cocaine use and poor prenatal care results in an unmonitored pregnancy in which most women are unaware of their baseline weights and of their weight gain during pregnancy. Thus, the impact of nutritional factors on fetal outcome remain largely unknown in neonatal cocaine studies.

Low Birth Weight. Low birth weight is common among drug-exposed infants and can result from prematurity and/or intrauterine growth retardation (IUGR). Prematurity is a well-established risk factor for cerebral palsy, developmental delay, behavioral impairments and learning difficulties (Nelson and Broman 1977; Hunt, Tooley, and Harvin 1992; Drillien 1977). Impaired fetal growth also poses a risk to neurodevelopment. IUGR stems from numerous causes, such as exposure to cigarettes, alcohol and illicit substances, and maternal malnutrition. Regardless of its etiology, infants who are small for dates (SGA) are at risk for cognitive and neurological impairments in later life compared to infants who are appropriate for dates, especially if fetal brain growth is proportionately impaired (symmetric or proportional SGA) (Villar et al. 1984; Ounstead, Moar, and Scott 1988). Drillien reported high rates of neurological impairments among SGA infants, which resolved by age 12 months in 80% of affected children; the remaining children were diagnosed with cerebral palsy (1977). She also noted lower developmental quotients among neurologically abnormal children as compared with neurologically intact low birth weight infants. Because of their impact on neurological, behavioral, and cognitive function, prematurity and IUGR/SGA are important factors to consider in drug-related studies.

POLYSUBSTANCE ABUSE

Women who use one drug are likely to abuse multiple drugs, smoke cigarettes, and drink alcohol. Polydrug use is, therefore, a major confounder of fetal drug effects. Many of the adverse outcomes described, such as low birth weight, intrauterine growth retardation, malformations, and neurobehavioral abnormalities, are not unique to any one drug, but instead are common with prenatal exposure to other substances of abuse (Anonymous 1994). Some of the more significant outcomes associated with substances of abuse are described below.

Cigarette Smoking

Cigarette smoking correlates with drug and alcohol use and is also reported to affect fetal growth, neonatal neurobehaviors, and subsequent development. It is a major cause of low birth weight babies, with the offspring of women who smoke cigarettes weighing, on average, 150 to 250 grams less than infants of women who do not smoke (Abel 1980). Cigarette smoking exerts a level of growth retardation that is unsurpassed by the illicit substances described herein and is rivaled only by the effects of alcohol. In utero exposure to cigarette smoke is reported to impair neonatal habituation, orientation, consolability, autonomic regulation, and orientation to sound (Picone et al. 1982). Exposure is also associated with a heightened startle response and tremor.

Small but detectable effects of heavy maternal cigarette smoking have been noted on developmental quotients and subsequent behaviors. Infants exposed prenatally to more than ten cigarettes per day had a four-point lower IQ than control infants after controlling for postnatal smoke and other factors (Olds, Henderson, and Tatelbaum 1994). Behavioral effects were significantly increased among infants of heavy smokers, as reflected by overall composite scores; yet the incidence of specific behavioral disorders was not increased (Ferguson, Horwood, and Lynskey 1993).

Alcohol

Alcohol, which is frequently used in combination with cocaine, has numerous effects that tend to confound drug studies. At the upper extreme of the alcohol exposure spectrum (FAS), lies the fetal alcohol syndrome, a constellation of signs and symptoms seen with both heavy chronic and binge drinking that is characterized by impaired growth (either prenatal or postnatal), CNS abnormalities, and a typical dysmorphic fascies (Clarren and Smith 1978). Infants with FAS are commonly mentally retarded and microcephalic. At the lower end of the spectrum are fetal alcohol effects, a term that does not refer to a diagnostic entity per se, because effects cannot be distinguished at the individual level, but to effects identified in prospective studies, such as impaired fetal growth (somatic and cerebral), teratogenesis, and cognitive differences (Wright et al. 1983; Sokol, Miller, and Reed 1980; Streissguth, Barr, and Sampson 1990).

The teratogenicity of alcohol exposure in utero has been clearly established: over 30% of offspring of heavy drinkers have minor or major congenital anomalies compared to 9% in infants of abstinent women (Hanson, Streissguth, and Smith 1978) and infants with FAS commonly have multiple congenital anomalies. Neurological malformations include Klippel-Feil anomaly, agenesis of the corpus callosum, and neural tube defects. Neuropathologically, children with FAS show abnormalities in neuronal and glial migration (Clarren, Alvord, and Sumi 1977). The degree of teratogenicity displayed by alcohol is not equaled by any other substance discussed herein.

Because alcohol lacks a stable assay by which to measure exposure during pregnancy, alcohol studies rely solely on structured interview. Quantification of use is hampered by poor exposure recall, as well as by a reluctance to admit use in light of the public awareness of the hazards of alcohol use during pregnancy (Ernhart et al. 1988). Under-reporting of alcohol use leads to misclassification of alcohol exposure and consequently will bias study results.

Marijuana

Used by one in three women of childbearing age, marijuana is one of the most popular psychoactive substances used in the United States. The effects of fetal marijuana exposure on neonatal outcome are relatively minor, with only minimal effects on gestational age and inconsistent effects on fetal growth reported (Zuckerman et al. 1989; Hingson et al. 1982; Fried 1991; Day et al. 1990; Shiono et al. 1995). In a controlled study, growth effects were noted in the offspring of women who had a positive urine assay for marijuana at delivery. Yet no effects were found in those who reported use of marijuana during pregnancy but had negative urine assays, suggesting that effects occur only with heavier exposures (Zuckerman et al. 1989). Fetal marijuana exposure induces a proportional or symmetric pattern of intrauterine growth retardation (IUGR) in which fat deposition is spared and lean body mass is decreased (Frank et al. 1990). This finding is consistent with prolonged hypoxia in utero, not a nutritional deficiency.

Marijuana-induced teratogenicity is unproven. Although Hingson et al. described a 5-fold increase in the rate of fetal alcohol syndrome-like features among marijuana-exposed offspring (1982), this was not corroborated by a later study that used computerized morphometric assessments to determine such features (Astley et al. 1992). Other studies have also described no association between prenatal marijuana and minor physical anomalies (Linn et al. 1983; O'Connell and Fried 1984).

Reported adverse marijuana-related effect on neonatal neurobehavior encompass a dose-related diminution in neonatal light response and an increase in startle and tremor (Fried 1991). Children of marijuana users were also found to have slightly longer latencies for the major wave-form components of the visual evoked response, suggesting dysmaturity of the visual pathways (Tansley, Fried, and Mount 1986). The long-term effects of prenatal marijuana on cognitive and language development have not been established in analyses that controlled for prenatal and postnatal environmental factors (Fried and Watkinson 1988, 1990). Marijuana exposure through maternal breast milk in the first postpartum month was noted at age 12 months to have a negative effect on motor, but not mental, development (Little et al. 1989).

Opiates

Heroin and methadone are the chief opiates linked to fetal exposure. Pregnant heroin addicts are treated with methadone and no efforts are made during pregnancy to wean them from methadone. The rationale behind this practice is that opiate withdrawal can be more harmful to the developing fetus than continued exposure to the drug. Moreover, providing the narcotic in controlled settings eliminates many of the adverse correlates of addiction, promoting better nutrition and prenatal health care, both of which are associated with improved neonatal outcomes.

Intrauterine Growth Retardation. Harmful fetal effects, including low birth weight (LBW), intrauterine growth retardation, and prematurity, have been reported with exposure to both heroin and methadone. In one study, 50% of heroin-exposed infants suffered LBW, and 40% suffered intrauterine growth retardation (Zelson, Rubio, and Wasserman 1971). Among heroin-exposed infants, prematurity also contributed to LBW. Methadone, on the other hand, is described as having a salutary effect over heroin, with prolonged methadone exposure linked to a longer gestation (Zelson, Lee, and Casalino 1973). In controlled studies, however, associated factors such as poor prenatal care were responsible for the main effect of low birth weight (Lifschitz and Wilson 1991). Effects on fetal growth have been noted to persist in infancy. In the opiate-exposed child who is born small for gestational age, catch-up growth is described by age 6 months and approaches the mean by 2 years of life (Chasnoff, Hatcher, and Burns 1980).

Neonatal Withdrawal Syndrome. Perhaps the most detrimental effect to the offspring, especially to the central nervous system, linked to fetal opiate exposure is the neonatal withdrawal syndrome. It is characterized by signs and symptoms of central nervous hyperirritability, gastrointestinal dysfunction, respiratory distress, and autonomic disturbances. Gastrointestinal signs include diarrhea and abdominal distention. Central nervous system signs and symptoms consist of hypertonicity, tremor, hyperreflexia, irritability, sleep disturbances, feeding difficulties, and occasionally seizures (Finnegan 1984). Neonates are normal at birth, but gradually become irritable, difficult to console, and develop a high pitch cry and frantic suck. The infant becomes increasingly jittery—first only when stimulated and subsequently at rest—as well as increasingly hypertonic.

Withdrawal of varying severity has been reported in 50% to 80% of infants (Kron et al. 1976; Besunder and Blumer 1990; Finnegan 1985). Onset of withdrawal varies from shortly after birth to 2 weeks of age, but symptoms usually occur between 48 to 72 hours of age. Because of its longer half life, about 35 hours, methadone withdrawal may be delayed compared to heroin, but usually manifests itself within 48 hours. Infants suffering methadone withdrawal reportedly experience more severe symptoms for a longer time (Zelson, Lee, and Casalino 1973). Seizures occur in 5% to 20% of neonates addicted to methadone and in 2% to 4 % of heroin-exposed babies. The most common seizure type is generalized tonic-clonic. Myoclonic seizures are also quite common. There is no apparent relationship between maternal opiate dosage and the frequency or severity of seizures. Premature infants tend to display a less intense withdrawal syndrome than term infants. This may be due to immaturity of neuronal pathways responsible for withdrawal, including opiate receptors and its regulation.

Two major scales have been devised to assess the severity of withdrawal syndrome (Finnegan 1985). Finnegan's scale assesses 21 signs in three domains: central nervous system, gastrointestinal, and autonomic/sleep/respiratory. Assessments are recommended every 2 to 4 hours after birth, and treatment is suggested for withdrawal scores of 8 or higher. Paregoric or phenobarbital is then titrated according to the severity of withdrawal scores.

Mild withdrawal can be treated by swaddling the infant and diminishing external stimuli (e.g., resting in a quiet dark room). However, symptomatic infants, i.e., those with non-infectious fevers, diarrhea, poor feeding, inability to sleep, excessive irritability, or seizure, warrant pharmacological intervention. The two most popular agents used to treat withdrawal are paregoric (camphorated tincture of opium) and phenobarbital. Of the two, paregoric is more physiological because it substitutes for the substance causing withdrawal. In one study, neonates treated with paregoric exhibited a more physiological sucking pattern, higher caloric intake, and more weight gain than infants treated with phenobarbital (Kron et al. 1976). In another study, paregoric was better at preventing and treating withdrawal-related seizures and in controlling gastrointestinal disturbances (Kandall et al. 1983). In a randomly assigned clinical trial, however, no difference in efficacy between phenobarbital and paregoric was demonstrated (Carin et al. 1983). Paregoric-treated infants required a significantly longer period of treatment than phenobarbital-treated infants (17 days vs. 22 days), perhaps attributable to phenobarbital's longer half life.

Withdrawal symptoms persisting for several months after birth have been termed "subacute withdrawal." Symptoms may first appear after the neonatal period. Methadone-exposed infants who were normal as neonates were found to be irritable, hypertonic, and hyperreflexic when examined at 3 to 4 months, with the findings resolving by 6 months. (Chasnoff, Hatcher, and Burns 1980). Although one theory has proposed "subacute withdrawal" to be the result of sustained release of opiates trapped and stored in fatty tissue reservoirs (Dole and Kreek 1973), persistence of signs for such prolonged periods makes withdrawal an unlikely mechanism. Signs probably represent direct opiate effects on the developing brain. In support of this notion are neurobehavioral abnormalities besides specific "withdrawal" symptoms that were noted with the Brazelton scale among opiate-exposed infants, including poor state control, interactive behaviors, depressed ability to orient to auditory or visual stimuli (Strauss et al. 1975), and a greater resistance to cuddle. These neonatal behaviors may affect infant socialization, thereby taxing the caregiver's interaction with the infant.

Sudden infant death syndrome (SIDS) is also strongly linked with opiate exposure. Compared to infants without fetal drug exposure, infants exposed to methadone showed a 3.7 fold increase in risk, and those exposed to heroin showed a 2.3 fold increase in risk of SIDS (Kandall et al. 1993).

Neurodevelopment. Although early studies noted numerous cognitive, neurological, and behavioral impairments (Wilson, Desmond, and Verniaud 1973; Rosen and Johnson 1982; Marcus, Hans, and Jeremy 1984), controlled studies have not substantiated this claim (Bauman and Levine 1986; Hans 1989). Most of the opiate effects on subsequent cognitive function have been mediated by associated risk factors, such as poor prenatal care, maternal intelligence, and aversive behaviors or the presence of withdrawal (Marcus, Hans, and Jeremy 1984). The development of opiate-exposed children, particularly those with withdrawal symptoms, however, appears more vulnerable to the adverse effects of an impoverished environment (Bauman and Levine 1986). There is little evidence supporting long lasting sequelae on neurodevelopment resulting from intrauterine exposure to opiates.

Cocaine

In the 1980s, a drop in cocaine prices, coupled with the introduction of "crack" cocaine, fueled an unprecedented degree of cocaine abuse. During the peak of the cocaine epidemic, 30% of adults between the ages of 19 and 28 years reported using cocaine at least once (O'Malley, Johnston, and Bachman 1991). Although cocaine use declined abruptly in 1987, it is still a major public health problem, as an unfortunate high level of abuse continues unabated. Infants born to women using crack/cocaine, the so-called "crack/cocaine babies," have been stigmatized by the media because of their potential burden to society, however, little is known of the long-term consequences of fetal cocaine exposure.

Cocaine is a highly psychoactive substance with numerous effects (Johanson and Fischman 1989). It inhibits postsynaptic reuptake of catecholamines, dopamine, and tryptophan; it blocks sodium ion permeability, thus acting as a local anesthetic agent. In addition to the multiple effects exerted by the parent compound, cocaine breaks down into active metabolites (e.g., benzoylecgonine, benzoylnorecgonine), of similar or yet more powerful pharmacological activity. Many of these substances are independently neurotoxic and may be responsible for perceived cocaine effects (Kurth et al. 1993; Konkol et al. 1992). Cocaine and its metabolites readily pass the placenta, achieving variable levels in the fetus (Schenker et al. 1993). The mechanism by which cocaine affects the fetus is not fully known, but is postulated to result from either a direct effect to the fetus or an indirect effect mediated through the maternal autonomic and cardiovascular system, especially at the level of the uterus (Woods, Plessinger, and Clark 1987).

The two most common forms of cocaine used by addicts on the street are cocaine hydrochloride, a water soluble salt, and crack/cocaine, a free-base alkaloid (Brust 1993). Cocaine hydrochloride can be used by either snorting a line, applying it to various mucosal membranes (oral or genital), or injecting it intravenously. Crack/cocaine is volatile and is administered by smoking.

Cocaine Addiction. A discussion of the biological and psychological basis of cocaine addiction is warranted to gain a better understanding of the behavioral correlates associated with cocaine use. In adults, cocaine use produces a state of euphoria characterized by increased energy, and enhanced alertness. According to classical and operational conditioning theory, the degree of euphoria is a prominent positive reinforcer. The level of euphoria in turn is predicated on the speed of delivery and cerebral cocaine concentrations. Because crack/cocaine is smoked, this preparation delivers the highest levels of cocaine to the brain in the most expedient fashion (Woolverton and Johnson 1992), thus producing a more intense euphoria than other methods of delivery, i.e., snorting or injecting. This intense sensation, described by addicts as a "rush" of pleasure, gradually gives way to dysphoria, an equally intense but opposite sensation that is described as a "crash" from cocaine. Dysphoria is characterized by a strong craving for the drug, a depressed state, and hypersomnia; it acts as a powerful negative reinforcer. Fluctuations in postsynaptic levels of dopamine are postulated to account for the reinforcing properties of cocaine (Dackis and Gold 1985). Converging lines of evidence support a dopaminergic hypothesis of cocaine addiction related to a mesocortical limbic reward system. (Fischman 1984; Goeders and Smith 1986).

Despite lacking the severe physical symptoms that are associated with opiate or sedative withdrawal, abrupt cessation of cocaine use generates an unwavering craving for the drug. The overpowering grip of cocaine addiction is evident in experimental models in which animals allowed to self-administer cocaine will do so compulsively and at the expense of food intake and to the point of toxicity or death (Deneau, Yanagita, and Seevers 1969). Crack/cocaine produces high cerebral concentrations rapidly, hence it elicits a strikingly powerful addiction that tends to render crack-addicted women unable to abstain or curtail its use during pregnancy despite the hazards posed to their fetuses and at the risk of losing custody of their offspring. The human correlates of such addiction-related behaviors during pregnancy have obvious detrimental consequences to the fetus.

Prevalence. The prevalence of cocaine use during pregnancy varies across the U.S. ranging from less than 1% to 18% (Vaughn et al. 1993; Burke and Roth 1993; Bateman et al. 1993; McCalla et al. 1991;

Habel, Kaye, and Lee 1990; Zuckerman et al. 1989). Population based rates are influenced by a number of demographic factors, namely race, urban dwelling, and socioeconomic status, as well as by the method of ascertaining cocaine use (see below). Rates are lowest in smaller cities and among private patients (Vaughn et al. 1993; Burke and Roth 1993) and highest in inner cities among ward patients (Bateman et al. 1993; McCalla et al. 1991). Although drug use in general is distributed equally across racial lines, urban blacks are more likely to use cocaine than other drugs (Vaughn et al. 1993).

Estimated prevalence of cocaine use is influenced by the method of ascertaining use. With urine toxicology testing, rates of cocaine use among women giving birth in two urban hospitals ranged from 9% to 13% (Bateman et al. 1993; McCalla et al. 1991), but rates reached 18% using both self-report and urine testing (Zuckerman et al. 1989). Highest rates were found with meconium testing, which was positive for cocaine in 31% of women delivering in a high-risk urban population (Ostrea et al. 1992), and 3.4% on random testing in an urban sample more representative of the community (Rosengren 1993).

Poor prenatal care and syphilis are the risk factors associated with the highest rates of cocaine use during pregnancy. About 30% to 50% of urban women who lack prenatal care will have a positive urine toxicology for cocaine at the time of delivery; rates reach 70% to 80% with the use of meconium or hair analysis (DiGregorio et al. 1994). The profile that emerges of women most likely to use cocaine during pregnancy are those living in inner cities who are single, black, older, of low socioeconomic status, and who have syphilis, HIV, and poor prenatal care.

Neonatal Effects

The adverse effects of prenatal cocaine exposure on neonatal outcome are well documented. The spectrum of fetal cocaine effects are depicted in table 2.

Withdrawal-like Symptoms and Other Neurobehaviors. Early studies reported a transient withdrawal syndrome related to fetal cocaine exposure. Bingol (1987) described irritability, crying, and a vigorous suck in 10% of exposed infants. Others reported infants as tremulous, hypertonic, with abnormal sleep patterns, and poor feeding (Oro and Dixon 1987; Ryan, Erlichs, and Finnegan 1987; Fulroth et al. 1989). Because infants scored in the mildly elevated range when assessed with neonatal abstinence scales, findings were interpreted by some as indicative of a withdrawal syndrome. Other studies have failed to note evidence of withdrawal (Chasnoff et al. 1985, 1989; Neuspiel et al. 1990). Instead infants were depressed and exhibited

Table II. Fetal Cocaine Effects and Associations

Pregnancy
    Spontaneous abortions
    Abruptio placentae
    Stillbirths
    Premature delivery
Growth
    Low birth weight
    Intrauterine growth retardation
    Small head size
Infections
    Perinatal HIV
    Congenital syphilis
Malformations
    Urogenital
    Brain
        Midline defects (agenesis of corpus callosum, septo-optic dysplasia)
        Skull defects, encephaloceles
    Ocular
    Vascular disruption (limb reduction, intestinal atresia)
    Cardiac
Neurodevelopmental findings
    Neonates
        Impaired organizational state
        Hypertonia, tremor
        Strokes, porencephaly
        Seizures
        Brainstem conduction delays
        Sudden infant death syndrome
    Infants and children
        Hypertonia in infancy
        ?Abnormal behaviors

Adapted with permission from Chiriboga C. A., Abuse of children: Pediatric AIDS, fetal alcohol syndrome, fetal cocaine effects, and the battered child syndrome, in *Merritt's Textbook of Neurology*, 9th ed., Baltimore, Williams & Wilkins Farbiger, 1995.

poor state and impaired orientation (Chasnoff 1985). Most of these infants were examined shortly after birth and cocaine exposure was assessed by urine toxicology.

The timing of the neonatal assessment may explain these seemingly contradictory findings. Neusspiel et al. found significant differences in motor clusters between cocaine-exposed and unexposed infants when the Brazelton Neonatal Behavioral Assessment Scales (BNBAS) was administered at 11 to 30 days after birth (Neuspiel et al. 1991). Yet, no differences were noted on any of the clusters when the BNBAS was administered within 72 hours of birth, suggesting that neurobehavioral abnormalities may be late in emerging.

These divergent results can be reconciled by dividing neurobehaviors into two types based on the onset of symptoms: (1) an early depressed state occurring immediately after birth and resolving within 3 to 4 days (Dempsey et al. 1995) and (2) a late emerging excitable phase with variable onset ranging from 3 to 30 days. The early depressed state usually coincides with recent cocaine exposure and may be the neonatal equivalent of the "crash"-like withdrawal observed in adult cocaine addicts or due to a direct toxic effect of cocaine or its metabolites (Konkol et al. 1994). The late excitable phase with its variable onset and prolonged duration, is not a withdrawal syndrome, but probably reflects a direct cocaine effect on the developing brain.

Other abnormal neurobehaviors reported among cocaine-exposed infants are increased rates of stress-related behaviors (Eisen et al. 1991) and hypertonic tetraparesis (Chiriboga et al. 1993). Neurobehavioral abnormalities have also been noticed prior to birth, with organizational and regulatory behavioral states abnormalities observed prenatally in 13 of 20 cocaine-exposed fetuses by ultrasonic techniques (Hume, O'Donnell, and Stanger 1989). A major study flaw was the lack of control subjects and examiners not blinded to exposure status. In most neurobehavioral studies infants were selected primarily from high-risk populations, and small sample size prevented controlling for confounding variables. A study based on a non-selected cohort that was more representative of the community failed to identify neurobehavioral effects in cocaine-exposed infants with the Brazelton scale after controlling for confounders, but a high level of attrition may have affected its power to detect an association (Neuspiel et al. 1990).

Intrauterine Growth. High rates of low birth weight (LBW) and intrauterine growth retardation (IUGR) are reported among infants with cocaine-positive urine toxicologies at the time of birth feeding (Bateman et al. 1993; Oro and Dixon 1987); but not in those exposed exclusively in the first trimester (Chasnoff et al. 1989). IUGR adopts a symmetric pattern with measures of body composition revealing reduced body fat and leanness, which is consistent with a nutritional deficiency (Frank et al. 1990). In a prospective study involving 1,226 mothers, cocaine-positivity on urine toxicology accounted for a 93 gram decrease in birth weight, a 0.5 cm decrement in length, and 0.43 cm head size difference compared to non-users (Zuckerman et al. 1989). The latter was impaired independently of birth weight and gestational age. Fetal brain growth may be even more impaired than somatic growth (Little and Snell 1991). The relevance of this effect is evident in a study by Chasnoff, in which cognitive differences in toddlers were indirectly mediated through cocaine effects on brain growth (1992).

Strokes. In animal models, cocaine exerts a vasoconstrictive effect on fetal cerebral vasculature and decreases cerebral blood flow.

Clinical reports describe neonatal strokes associated with prenatal cocaine exposure (Chasnoff et al. 1986; Oro and Dixon 1987). To some extent such strokes may be mediated by other stroke risk factors, such as abruptio placentae or birth asphyxia, which are also linked to cocaine exposure, but reports of cocaine-exposed neonates with normal deliveries who evidence porencephaly and infarcts support an independent cocaine effect on cerebral vasculature (Dominguez et al. 1991). Initially a high rate of intracranial hemorrhage and cystic lucencies was reported among cocaine-exposed neonates (Bejar and Dixon 1989), but this finding has not been substantiated by later studies involving both term and premature infants (Frank et al. 1992; Dusick et al. 1993).

Seizures. EEG tracings in cocaine-exposed newborns show conflicting results. One study showed marked central nervous system irritability, with bursts of sharp waves and spikes that were mostly multifocal and did not correlate with clinical seizures or neurological abnormalities. EEG findings resolved completely within 3 to 12 months (Doberczak et al. 1988). Another study reported no frank electroencephalographic abnormalities, but did find evidence for electroclinical sleep discordance with cocaine-exposed infants displaying more mature, continuous slow wave sleep than a comparison group (Legido et al. 1992).

Focal seizures are common in cocaine-exposed newborns with strokes. A higher incidence of neonatal seizures related to fetal cocaine exposure in the absence of strokes has not been established. One uncontrolled retrospective study determined subtle seizures among cocaine-exposed infants based on a correlation between stereotypic movements and "ictal" discharges (Kramer et al. 1990). Most "seizures" were treated with anticonvulsants without improvement. It is highly likely that such behaviors were not epileptic, but rather cocaine-related neurobehaviors. A study that assessed intracranial hemorrhage in premature infants found a 3 fold higher rate of seizures among cocaine-exposed infants compared to control infants (Dusick et al. 1993). This finding should be taken with caution because seizures were not a study end-point and thus were not systematically evaluated. Infants with focal seizures or generalized tonic/clonic seizures warrant a complete neurologic evaluation, including adequate neuroimaging. Cocaine-exposed infants who exhibit only neurobehavioral abnormalities, however, do not require such intensive investigations. In clinical practice, seizures resulting from prenatal cocaine exposure, in the absence of strokes, are rare.

Malformations. Cocaine has been linked to numerous congential malformations, some of which are ascribed to vascular disruption

resulting from cocaine-induced vasoconstriction during different periods of organogenesis. Genitourinary anomalies include hydronephrosis, prune belly syndrome, and masculinization of external genitalia
(Bingol et al. 1987; Chasnoff, Chisum, and Kaplan 1988: Greenfield et
al. 1991). A controlled study reported a 4.4 fold increase risk of urinary anolmalies associated with cocaine exposure, but no increased
risk of genital anomalies (Chavez, Mulinare, and Cordero 1989). This
finding was confirmed by a large scale epidemiological study, which
reported an association between urogenital malformations and cocaine exposure in the first trimester (Anonymous 1989).

Although limb reduction deformities and intestinal atresia and infarction are reported among cocaine-exposed infants (Hoyme et al. 1990;
Hannig and Phillips 1991; Steinbaum and Badell 1992) a population-
based study found no significant increase in the prevalence of vascular disruption defects coinciding with the cocaine epidemic (Martin et
al. 1992). The heart may also be susceptible to cocaine-related vascular
disruption as suggested by an autopsy describing a cocaine-positive
fetus with a single cardiac ventricle that was secondary to a coronary
thrombus (Shepard, Fantel, and Kapur 1991). Most cases of single ventricle, however, are probably unrelated to cocaine exposure (Martin
and Khoury 1992). The risk ratio of cardiac anomalies was elevated 3.7
fold among cocaine-positive infants compared to controls (Lipschultz,
Frassica, and Orau 1991), but the study did not account for confounding factors.

Cocaine has been implicated in the genesis of brain and eye malformations. Early in the epidemic, Bingol et. al. reported skull defects,
exencephaly, encephaloceles, and delayed ossification (1987). Others
noted a 12% rate of cerebral malformations among cocaine-exposed
infants, composed mostly of encephaloceles and skull defects (Heier et
al. 1991). In a referral sample to a neurophthalomologist, Dominguez
et al. (1991) described high rates of strabismus, nystagmus, and hy-
poplastic discs. Most infants also had cerebral malformations, strokes,
or porencephaly. Many were exposed to illicit substances other than
cocaine; only two infants with malformations were exposed exclusively to cocaine: one case of agenesis of the corpus callosum and one
of septo-optic dysplasia. Other ocular anomalies noted among
cocaine-exposed infants are delayed visual maturation, optic nerve
hypoplasia, persistent eyelid edema (Good et al. 1992), tortuous abnormally dilated iris vessels (Isenberg, Spierrer, and Inekelis 1987),
and a persistent hyperplastic primary vitreous with retinopathy of
prematurity-like findings (Teske and Trese 1987). Finally, other investigators, in comparisons of 40 cocaine-positive infants with controls,
have found no differences in rates of congenital anomalies, optic disc
and nerve abnormalities, or scleral and retinal hemorrhage (Stafford et

al. 1994). However, the small size of their sample might have provided insufficient power to detect such an association.

In rodents, high doses of cocaine can induce urogenital, cardiac, cerebral, and limb reduction anomalies. Mahalik, Gautierri, and Maun (1980) reported a high incidence of malformations induced by cocaine in CF-1 mice which mirrored those reported in human infants, namely skeletal defects, exencephaly, ocular malformations, hydronephrosis, and delayed ossification. Nevertheless, the teratogenic potential for cocaine effects in animal studies are inconsistent and occur with doses much larger than those encountered in clinical settings.

The teratogenicity of cocaine in humans, with the exception of urogenital malformations, has yet to be established by large scale epidemiological studies. Most reports on cocaine-related malformations are case reports or series, where ascertainment bias is surely operant as cases are collected in a non-blinded, non-systematic fashion based on exposure status; the few population based studies have not controlled for the effects of fetal alcohol exposure, a well-known teratogen. The influence of confounders on cocaine-related teratogenic effects is exemplified in a study by Zuckerman in which cocaine-exposed infants had significantly higher rates (14%) of three minor or one major congenital anomalies compared to cocaine-unexposed infants (8%), that disappeared after controlling for confounders, including alcohol (1989).

One of the problems in making causal associations between cocaine and malformations in non-population-based studies is that both cocaine use and malformations of any type are common in clinical practice. The high frequency of both cases and exposure makes associations between the two likely the result of chance and nullifies the rare disease assumption, which is the basis for the approximation of the odds ratio to the risk ratio, thus, raising questions regarding the validity of the odds ratio in case-controlled cocaine studies (Kleinbaum, Kupper, and Morgenstern 1982).

SIDS and Other Effects. Studies on sudden infant death syndrome (SIDS) and fetal cocaine exposure have yielded somewhat discrepant results. Several studies have reported an association between prenatal cocaine exposure and SIDS (Kandall et al. 1993; Durand, Espinoza, and Nickerson 1990; Davidson et al. 1990), although others have failed to do so (Bauchner et al. 1988). The rarity of SIDS may have made findings unstable, especially in smaller studies. A large population-based study found a 1.6 fold elevation in the risk of SIDS linked to cocaine, which reached statistical significance, but was much lower than that noted with fetal opiate exposure (Kandall et al. 1993).

In pneumographic studies involving term infants, those with cocaine exposure exhibited increased episodes of longest apnea, bradycardia, and less periodic breathing than control infants (Silvestri et al. 1991). A cocaine effect on the norepinephrine system at the level of the locus coerulus, which is responsible for arousal from sleep-related apnea, has been invoked in the genesis of SIDS (Gingras and Weese-Mayer 1990).

Adverse cocaine effects on the auditory system have also been described, with separate reports showing prolonged interpeak latencies I through V on brain stem auditory evoked responses among cocaine-exposed infants that persisted up to 3 months (Salamy et al. 1990; Shi, Cone-Wesson, and Reddix 1988). Moreover, an increased startle response was reported among cocaine-exposed neonates (Anday et al. 1989). Collectively, these studies would suggest that cocaine may affect the central pathways of the developing brain at the level of the brain stem.

Long-term Neurodevelopment

The mechanism(s) by which fetal cocaine exposure affects the developing brain is not known. Neither is it known whether effects are related to cocaine or to one of its metabolites. Postulated mechanisms of action include hypoxia, direct toxicity, cortical dysgenesis (Gressens, Kosofsky, and Evrard 1992), and alterations of monoaminergic (norepinephrine, dopamine, and serotonin) or other neural pathways. Evidence for the latter mechanism derives from experiments showing a prolonged effect of cocaine on the developing rat brain producing lasting neurochemical changes in the dopaminergic system in the brain coupled with both late and early behavioral abnormalities (Dow-Edwards 1989). Dopaminergic involvement is also suggested in clinical settings where newborn infants exposed to cocaine showed lower cerebrospinal fluid levels of homo-vanillic acid than unexposed controls (Needleman et al. 1992).

Anecdotally, cocaine-exposed children seem to suffer from neurobehavioral abnormalities. Sleep disturbances, especially night terrors or inverted sleep patterns, unexplained unconsolable daytime crying, and an excessive startle response are commonly observed in a subset of cocaine-exposed infants and young children. In an uncontrolled study, high rates of autism and developmental abnormalities were reported among cocaine-exposed infants referred to a developmental clinic (Davis et al. 1992).

Cognitive Effects. In a study that assessed habituation, no differences were detected at age 3 months between cocaine-exposed and control infants (Mayes et al. 1995). A significantly larger proportion of cocaine-exposed infants, however, were unable to begin testing due to excessive irritability. Differences in psychomotor but not mental development were also noted; cocaine-related state abnormalities may have influenced these findings.

Few prospective studies have dealt with cocaine exposure and long-term neurodevelopment (Chasnoff et al. 1992; Azuma and Chasnoff 1993; Chiriboga et al. 1995; Hurt et al. 1995). Most have involved infants or toddlers and two reports refer to the same cohort of children. One of the latter involved comparisons between three groups of 2-year-old children: a cocaine/polydrug-exposed, a no-cocaine/polydrug-exposed, and a drug-negative control group (Chasnoff et al. 1992). No significant differences in mean development scores were noted between the two drug-exposed groups, a finding that was replicated by two other studies (Chiriboga et al. 1995; Hurt et al. 1995). Nonetheless, compared to controls, the polydrug (with and without cocaine) exposed groups had a significantly larger proportion of children scoring in the abnormal range. Fetal cocaine exposure was the best predictor of depressed head size, which in turn mediated effects on cognition. Another study, which involved the same cohort at age 3 years, identified through path analysis both a direct and indirect drug effect on cognitive function; indirect effects were mediated through head size, perseverance at a task, and home environment (Azuma and Chasnoff 1993). One study limitation that resulted from analyzing all illicit drugs as a single exposure category was that it did not distinguish individual cocaine effects from other drug effects.

The practice followed in most, if not all, cocaine studies of controlling for infant head size in order to assess the effect of cocaine on cognition independently raises questions regarding the introduction of bias. It is well recognized that controlling for variables that lie in the causal pathway of disease (intervening factors) or are caused by the same factor may lead to bias, often towards the null (Breslow and Day 1980). For example, abnormalities in gliogenesis and dendritic synaptogenesis have been described with cocaine exposure (Gressens, Kosofsky, and Evrard 1992), it is therefore biologically plausible that cocaine impairs brain growth and neurodevelopment through a common effect on fetal neuropil. Controlling for head size in such instances would therefore diminish or negate true cocaine effects on development (Breslow and Day 1980). Moreover, an argument has been made for not controlling for factors that are in part caused by the exposure, such as cocaine-effects on fetal brain growth, as this may also introduce bias (Weinburg 1993). It may well serve to examine the possible etiologic pathways involved and re-evaluate routine practices in order to avoid over-controlling cocaine effects.

Neurological Effects. Motor assessments in 4-month-old infants ($n = 124$) using the Movement Assessment of Infants found high scores among the cocaine/polydrug-exposed group involving tone and primitive reflexes (Schneider and Chasnoff 1992). Two prospective studies that focused on neurological function have yielded discrepant result (Chiriboga et al. 1995; Hurt et al. 1995). One reported high rates of hypertonia associated with fetal cocaine exposure among children at risk for HIV. Rates of hypertonia were maximal at age 6 months and resolved in most children by age 2 years, arms first and legs last (Chiriboga et al. 1995). A diagnosis of hypertonic tetraparesis (HTP) was more strongly associated with cocaine positivity than was all types of hypertonia combined: 27% of 51 cocaine-positive infants compared with 9% of 68 cocaine-negative infants (chi-square, $p = .006$; OR = 4.0, 95% CI = 1.5-10.8). Cocaine exposure remained significantly associated with hypertonia in logistic regression models that controlled for 11 variables, including gestational age, birth weight, head circumference, HIV infection, and opiate withdrawal. The adjusted odds of hypertonia associated with cocaine was 3.4 at age 6 months, 5.4 at age 12 months, and 8.7 at age 18 months. Development quotients were similar between cocaine-exposed and unexposed children, but among the cocaine-exposed group a diagnosis of hypertonic tetraparesis (HTP) at age 6 months appeared to be a marker for later developmental impairments. The other study found no difference between cocaine-exposed and unexposed infants in assessment of tone and reflexes (Hurt et al. 1995). The discrepancy noted between these two studies may be explained by differences in the characteristics of the study population as well as the sensitivity of the neurological instrument used.

Behavioral Effects. Whether fetal cocaine exposure results in behavioral abnormalities is not known. Anecdotally, cocaine-exposed children appear to show high rates of attention deficit disorder, but few studies, if any, focus on cocaine-related behaviors. Infants with polydrug exposure, including cocaine, exhibited significantly lower scores on the Fagan Test of Infant Intelligence, a structured test of visual memory (Struthers and Hansen 1992). Differences in attention and distractibility between groups were also noted. Although this test is a good predictor of later intelligence, it is less accurate at predicting subsequent behaviors. To date, the cohorts reported are much too young for behavioral estimates to be made reliably. Studies in older children are therefore needed to address this question.

POSTNATAL ENVIRONMENT

Barring well-defined exceptions, such as profound birth asphyxia, as the child ages, prenatal risk factors assume a smaller role in shaping child development, while the opposite is true of the postnatal environment. Although a comprehensive discussion of the numerous factors that influence child development is beyond the scope of this chapter, some that are especially relevant in settings of substance abuse include low socioeconomic status, maternal psychopathology, and multiplicity of foster care homes. The adverse effects of an impoverished environment on child development are well described, with low socioeconomic status (SES) repeatedly associated with lower scores on scholastic, cognitive, and language assessments (Duncan et al. 1994). Parental psychopathology has a negative impact on psychosocial and behavioral outcome of offspring (Weintraub 1991). The child rearing practices of drug abusing parents may also exert a negative influence. Parent-child interaction may range from benign chaos coupled to limited parenting skills to, as many news headlines attest, a total disregard of the basic physical and emotional needs of children. All too often child abuse (physical, emotional, and sexual) rears its ugly head.

Instruments have been developed to assist investigators in taking these difficult-to-measure environmental factors into account. One such instrument, the Home Observational for Measurement of Environment (HOME) scale, was devised to assess the physical and emotional environment of the child's home, including child-parent interaction, opportunities to learn, and emotional climate of the home (Caldwell and Bradley 1984). It was found to predict subsequent child cognitive development in population-based (Bradley et al. 1989), as well as high-risk populations, including drug-exposed children (Azuma and Chasnoff 1993).

SUMMARY

Clinical studies of drug effects on the exposed offspring are hindered by numerous factors that confound outcome. Behavioral correlates of drug use that may be more harmful to the offspring than the drug under study may be operant. Alcohol is an undisputed teratogen that tends to confound fetal drug studies. The teratogenicity of illicit substances has not been firmly established. The adverse effects of fetal drug exposures on neonatal neurobehaviors and intrauterine growth are well documented. Impaired brain growth may indirectly mediate drug effects on cognition, but may also lie in the causal pathway and not need to be controlled. Heavy prenatal exposure to marijuana, cigarettes, and cocaine may be associated with cognitive, neurological, or behavioral effects. The net effect of any single drug, however, is substantially diminished once these confounding factors are taken into account. Hence the importance of employing epidemiological methods in clinical studies targeting fetal drug effects.

REFERENCES

Abel, E. L. 1980. Smoking during pregnancy: A review of effects on growth and development on the offspring. *Human Biology* 52:593–625.

Acker, D., Sachs, B. P., Tracy, K. J., and Wise, W. E. 1983. Abruptio placentae associated with cocaine use. *American Journal of Obstetrics and Gynecology* 146:220–21.

Ambre, J. J., Ruo, T., Smith, G. L., Backes, D., and Smith, C. M. 1982. Ecgonine methyl ester, a major metabolite of cocaine. *Journal of the Annals of Toxicology* 6:26–29.

Anday E. K., Cohen M. E., Kelley N. E., and Leitner, D. S. 1989. Effects of in utero cocaine exposure on startle and its modification. *Developmental Pharmacology* 12:137–45.

Anonymous. 1989. Urogenital anomalies in the offspring of women using cocaine during early pregnancy-Atlanta 1968–1980. *Morbidity and Mortality Weekly Report* 38:536,541–42.

Anonymous. 1992. Epidemic early syphilis-Montgomery County Alabama, 1990-1991. *Morbidity and Mortality Weekly Report* 41:790–94.

Anonymous. 1994. Effects of in utero exposure to street drugs. *American Journal of Public Health* 83 Suppl:1–32.

Astley, S. J., Clarren, S. K., Little, R. E., Sampson, P. D., and Daling, J. R. 1992. Analysis of facial shape in children gestationally exposed to marijuana, alcohol, and/or cocaine. *Pediatrics* 89:67–77.

Azuma, S. and Chasnoff, I. J. 1993. Outcome of children prenatally exposed to cocaine and other drugs: A path analysis of three year data. *Pediatrics* 92:396–402.

Bateman, D. A., Ng, S. K., Hansen, C. A. and Heagarty, M. C. 1993. The effect of intrauterine cocaine exposure in newborns. *American Journal of Public Health* 83:190–93.

Bauchner, H., Zuckerman, B., McClain, M., Frank, D., Fried, L. E. and Kayne, H. 1988. Risk of sudden infant death syndrome among infants with in utero cocaine exposure. *Journal of Pediatrics* 113:831–34.

Bauman, P., and Levine, S. 1986. The development of children of drug addicts. *International Journal of the Addictions* 21:849–63.

Bejar, R., and Dixon, S. D. 1989. Echoencephalographic findings in neonates associated with maternal and methamphetamine use: Incidence and clinical correlates. *Journal of Pediatrics* 115:770–78.

Besunder, J. B., and Blumer, J. L. 1990. Neonatal Drug Withdrawal Syndromes. In *Maternal-Fetal Toxicology: A Clinicians Guide*, eds. G. Koren and M. Dekker. New York.

Bingol, N., Fuchs, M., Diaz, V., Stone, R. K., and Gromisch, D. S. 1987. Teratology of cocaine use. *Journal of Pediatrics* 110:93–96.

Bradley, R. H., Caldwell, B. M., Rock, S. L., Barnard, K. E., Gray, C., Hammond, M. A., Mitchell, S., Siegel, L., Ramey, C. T., Gottfried, A. W., and Johnson, D. L. 1989. Home environment and cognitive development in the first 3 years of life: A collaborative study involving six sites and three ethnic groups in North America. *Developmental Psychology* 25:217–35.

Breslow, N. E., and Day, N. E. 1980. *Statistical Methods in Cancer Research*. The analysis of case control studies. IARC Scientific publications No. 32 Lyon International Agency for Research in Cancer.

Brust, J. C. M. 1993. *Neurological Aspects of Substance Abuse*. Boston, MA: Butterworth-Heinemann.

Burke, M. S., and Roth, D. 1993. Anonymous screening in private obstetric population. *Obstetrics and Gynecology* 81:354–56.

Caldwell, B. M., and Bradley, R. H. 1984. *Home Observation for Measurement of the Environment*. Little Rock: University of Arkansas at Little Rock.

Carin, I., Glass, L., Parekh, A., Solomon, N., Steigman, J., and Wong, S. 1983. Neonatal methadone withdrawal. *American Journal of Diseases of Children* 137:1166–9.

Chasnoff, I. J., Burns ,W. J., Scholl, S. H., and Burns, K. A. 1985. Cocaine use in pregnancy. *New England Journal of Medicine* 313:666–69.

Chasnoff, I. J., Bussey, M. E., Savich, R., and Stack, C. M. 1986. Perinatal cerebral infarction and maternal cocaine use. *Journal of Pediatrics* 108:456–57.

Chasnoff, I. J., Chisum, G. M., and Kaplan, W. E. 1988. Maternal cocaine use and genitourinary tract malformations. *Teratology* 37:201–4.

Chasnoff, I. J., Griffith, D. R., Freier, C., and Murray J. 1992. Cocaine/polydrug use in pregnancy. *Pediatrics* 89:284–89.

Chasnoff, I. J., Griffith, D. R., MacGregor, S. N., Dirkes, K., and Burns, K. S. 1989. Temporal patterns of cocaine use in pregnancy. *Journal of American Medical Association* 261:171–74.

Chasnoff, I. J., Hatcher, R., and Burns, W. J. 1980. Early growth patterns of methadone-addicted infants. *American Journal of Diseases of Children* 134:1049–51.

Chavez, G. F., Mulinare, J., and Cordero, J. F. 1989. Maternal cocaine use during early pregnancy as a risk factor for congenital urogenital anomalies. *Journal of American Medical Association* 262:795–98.

Chiriboga, C. A., Bateman, D., Brust, J. C. M., and Hauser, W. A. 1993. Neurological findings in cocaine-exposed infants. *Pediatric Neurology* 9:115–19.

Chiriboga, C. A., Vibbert, M., Malouf, R., Suarez, M. S., Abrams, E. J., Heagarty, M. C., Brust, J. C., and Hauser, W. A. 1993. Children at risk for HIV infection: Neurological and developmental abnormalities. (abstract) *Annals of Neurology* 34:500–01.

Chiriboga, C. A., Vibbert, M., Malouf, R., Suarez, M. S., Abrams, E. J., Heagarty, M. C., Brust, J. C., and Hauser, W. A. 1995. Neurological correlates of fetal cocaine exposure: Transient hypertonia of infancy and early childhood. *Pediatrics* 96:1070–7.

Church, M. W., Overbeck, G. W., and Andrzejczak, A. L. 1990. Prenatal cocaine exposure in Long-Evans Rat: I. Dose dependent effects on gestation, mortality and postnatal maturation. *Neurotoxicology and Teratology* 12:327–34.

Clarren, S. K., Alvord, E. C., Sumi, M., Streissguth, A. P., and Smith, D. W. 1977. Brain malformations related to prenatal exposure to ethanol. *Journal of Pediatrics* 92:64–67.

Clarren, S. K., and Smith, D. W. 1978. The fetal alcohol syndrome. *New England Journal of Medicine* 298:1063–7.

Dackis, C. A., and Gold, M. S. 1985. New concepts in cocaine addiction: The dopamine depletion hypothesis. *Neuroscience and Biobehavioral Reviews* 9:469–77.

Davidson, W. S. L., Bautista, D., Chan, L., Derry, M., Lisbin, A., Durfee, M. J., Mills, K. S. C., and Keens, T. G. 1990. Sudden infant death syndrome in infants of substance-abusing mothers. *Journal of Pediatrics* 117:876–81.

Davis, E., Fenoy, I., and Laraque, D. 1992. Autism and developmental abnormalities in children with perinatal cocaine exposure. *Journal of the National Medical Assocication* 84:315–19.

Day, N., Sambamoorthi, U., Taylor, P., Richardson, G., Robles, N., Jhon, Y., Scher, M., Stoffer, D., Cornelius, M., and Jasperse, D. 1990. Prenatal marijuana use and neonatal outcome. *Neurotoxicology and Teratology* 13:329–34.

Dempsey, D. A., Jacobson, S. A., Allen, F., Matthiews, R., and Ferriero, D. M. 1995. Neonatal cocaine intoxication, withdrawal, and fetopathic effects. (abstract) *Annals of Neurology* 38:502.

Deneau, G. A., Yanagita, T., and Seevers, M. H. 1969. Self administration of psychoactive substances by monkeys. *Psychopharmacologia* 16:30–48.

DiGregorio, G. J., Ferko A. P., Barbieri, E. J., Ruch, E. K., Chawla, H., Keohane, D., Rosenstock, R., and Aldano, A. 1994. Detection of cocaine usage in pregnant women by urinary EMIT drug screen and GC-MS analyses. *Journal of the Annals of Toxicology* 18:247–50.

Doberczak, T. M., Shanzer, S., Senie, R. T., and Kandall, S. R. 1988. Neonatal electroencephalographic effect of intrauterine cocaine exposure. *Journal of Pediatrics* 113:354–58.

Dole, V. P., and Kreek, M. J. 1973. Methadone plasma level: Sustained by a reservoir of drug in tissue. *Proceedings of The National Academy of Sciences of the United States of America* 70:10.

Dominguez, R., Vila-Coro, A. A., Slopis, J. M., and Bohan, T. P. 1991. Brain and ocular abnormalities in infants with in-utero exposure to cocaine and other street drugs. *American Journal of Diseases of Children* 145:688–95.

Dow-Edwards, D. L. 1989. Long term neurochemical and neurobehavioral consequences of cocaine use during pregnancy. *Annals of the New York Academy of Sciences* 562:280–89.

Drillien, C. M. 1972. Abnormal neurological signs in the first year of life in low-birthweight infants: Possible prognostic significance. *Developmental Medicine and Child Neurology* 14:575–84.

Duncan, G. J., Brooks-Gunn, J., and Klebanov, P. K. 1994. Economic deprivation and childhood development. *Child Development* 65:296–318.

Durand, D. J., Espinoza, A. M., and Nickerson, B. G. 1990. Association between prenatal cocaine exposure and sudden infant death syndrome. *Journal of Pediatrics* 117:909–11.

Dusick, A. M., Covert, R. F., Schreiber, M. D., Yee, G. T., Brown, S. P., Moore, C. M., and Tebett, I. R. 1993. Risk of intracranial hemorrhage and other adverse outcomes after cocaine exposure in a cohort of 323 very low birth weight infants. *Journal of Pediatrics* 122:438–45.

Eisen, L. N., Field, T. M., Bandstra, E. S., Roberts, J. P., Morrow, C., and Larson, S. K. 1991. Perinatal cocaine effects on neonatal stress behavior and performance on the Brazelton Scale. *Pediatrics* 88:477–80.

Ernhart, C. B., Morrow-Tlucak, M., Sokol, R. J., and Martier, S. 1988. Underreporting of alcohol use in pregnancy. *Alcoholism Clinical Experimental Research* 12:506–11.

Ferguson, D. M., Horwood, L. J., and Lynskey, M. T. 1993. Maternal smoking before and after pregnancy: Effects on behavioral outcomes in middle childhood. *Pediatrics* 92:815–22.

Finnegan, L. P. 1984. Neonatal abstinence. In *Current Therapy in Neonatal and Perinatal Medicine*, ed. M. Nelson. St. Louis: CV Mosby (BC Decker).

Finnegan, L. P. 1985. Effects of maternal opiate abuse on the newborn. *Federation Proceedings* 44:2314–7.

Fischman, M. W. 1984. The behavioral pharmacology of cocaine in humans. *NIDA Research Monograph* 50:72–91.

Frank, D. A., Bauchner, H., Parker, S. Huber, A. M., Kyei-Aboagye, K., and Cabral, H. 1990. Neonatal body proportionality after in-utero exposure to cocaine and marijuana. *Journal of Pediatrics* 117:662–66.

Frank, D. A., and McCarten, K. 1992. Cranial ultrasounds in term newborns: Failure to replicate excess abnormalities in cocaine-exposed. *Pediatric Research* 31:247a.

Fried, P. A., and Watkinson, B. 1988. 12- and 24-month neurobehavioral follow-up of children prenatally exposed to marihuana, cigarettes and alcohol. *Neurobehavioral Toxicology and Teratology* 10:305–13.

Fried, P. A., and Watkinson, B. 1990. 36-48-month neurobehavioral follow-up of children prenatally exposed to marihuana, cigarettes and alcohol. *Journal of Developmental and Behavioral Pediatrics* 11:49–58.

Fried, P. A. 1991. Postnatal consequences of maternal marijuana use during pregnancy: Consequences for the offspring. *Seminars in Perinatology* 15:280–87.

Fulroth, R. F., Phillips, B., Durand, B., and Durand, D. J. 1989. Perinatal outcome of infants exposed to cocaine and/or heroin in utero. *American Journal of Diseases of Children* 243:905–10.

Gingras, J. L., and Weese-Mayer, D. 1990. Maternal cocaine addiction II: An animal model for the study of brainstem mechanisms operative in sudden infant death syndrome. *Medical Hypotheses* 33:231–34.

Goeders, N. E., and Smith, J. E. 1986. Reinforcing properties of cocaine in the medial prefrontal cortex: Primary action of presynaptic dopaminergic terminals. *Pharmacology Biochemistry Behavior* 25:191–99.

Good, W. V., Ferriero, D. M., Golabi, M., and Kobori, J. A. 1992. Abnormalities of the visual system in infants exposed to cocaine. *Ophthalmology* 99:341–46.

Graham, K., Koren, G., Klein, J., Schneiderman, J., and Greenwald, M. 1989. Determination of gestational cocaine exposure by hair analysis. *Journal of American Medical Association* 262:3328–30.

Greenberg, M. S. Z., Singh, T., Htoo, M., and Schultz S. 1991. The association between congenital syphilis and cocaine/crack use in New York City: A case control study. *American Journal of Public Health* 81:1316–8.

Greenfield, S. P., Rutigliano, E., Steinhardt, G., and Elders, J. S. 1991. Genitourinary tract malformations and maternal cocaine abuse. *Urology* 37: 455–59.

Gressens, P., Kosofsky, B., and Evrard, P. 1992. Cocaine-induced disturbances in corticogenesis in the developing murine brain. *Neuroscience* (Lett) 140:113–16.

Habel, L., Kaye, K., and Lee, J. 1990. Trends in the reporting of drug use and infant mortality among drug-exposed infants in New York City. *Women and Health* 16:41–58.

Hannig, V. A., and Phillips, J. A. 1991. Maternal cocaine abuse and fetal abnormality: Evidence for teratogenic effects of cocaine. *Southern Medical Journal* 84:498–99.

Hans, S. L. 1989. Developmental consequences of prenatal exposure to methadone. *Annals of the New York Academy of Sciences* 562:195–207.

Hanson, J. W., Streissguth, A. P., and Smith, D. W. 1978. The effect of moderate alcohol consumption during pregnancy on fetal growth and morphogenesis. *Journal of Pediatrics* 92:457–60.

Heier, L. A., Carpanzano, C. R., Mast, J., Brill, P. W., Winchester, P., and Deck, M. D. 1991. Maternal cocaine abuse: The spectrum of radiologic abnormalities in the neonatal CNS. *American Journal of Neuroradiology* 12:951–56.

Hingson, R., Alper, T. T., Day, N., Dooling, E., Kayne, H., and Morelock, S. 1982. Effects of maternal drinking and marijuana use on fetal growth and development. *Pediatrics* 70:539–46.

Hoyme, H. E., Lyons, J. K., and Dixon, S. D. 1990. Prenatal cocaine exposure and fetal vascular disruption. *Pediatrics* 85:743–47.

Hume, R. F., O'Donnell, K. J., and Stanger, C. L. 1989. In-utero cocaine exposure: Observations of fetal behavioral state may predict neonatal outcome. *American Journal of Obstetrics and Gynecology* 161:685–90.

Hunt, J. V., Tooley, W. H., and Harvin, D. 1992. Learning disabilities in children with birth weights < 1500 grams. *Seminars in Perinatology* 6:280–83.

Hurt, H., Brodsky, N. L., Betancourt, L., Braitman, L. E., Malmud, E., and Giannetta, J. J. 1995. Cocaine-exposed children: Follow-up through 30 months. *Journal of Developmental and Behavioral Pediatrics* 16:29–35.

Isenburg, S. J., Spierrer, A., and Inkelis, S. H. 1987. Ocular signs of cocaine intoxication in neonates. *Americal Journal of Ophthalmology* 103:211–4.

Johanson, C. E., and Fischman, M. W. 1989. The pharmacology of cocaine related to its abuse. *Pharmacological Reviews* 41:3–52.

Kandall, S. R., Doberczak, T. M., Mauer, K. R., Strashun, R. H., and Korts, D. C. 1983. The comparative effects of opiates vs central nervous system depressant treatment on neonatal drug withdrawal. *American Journal of Diseases of Children* 137:378–82.

Kandall, S. R., Gaines, J., Habel, L., Davidson, G., and Jessop, D. 1993. Relationship of maternal substance abuse to subsequent infant death syndrome in offspring. *Journal of Pediatrics* 123:120–26.

Kleinbaum, D. G., Kupper, L. L., and Morgenstern, H. 1982. *Epidemiological Research. Principles and Quantitative Methods.* New York: Van Norstrand Reinhold.

Knight, W. M., James, H., Edwards, C. H., Spurlock, B. F., Oyemade, U. J., Johnson, A. A., West, W. L., Cole, O. J., Westney, L. S., Westney, O. E., Manning, M., Laryea, H., and Jones, S. 1994. Relationship of serum illicit drug concentrations during pregnancy to maternal nutritional status. *Journal of Nutrition* 124:973S–980S.

Konkol, R. J., Erickson, B. A., Doerr, J. K., Hoffman, R. G., and Madden, J. A. 1992. Seizures induced by cocaine metabolite benzoylecgonine in rats. *Epilepsia* 33:420–27.

Konkol, R. J., Murphey, L. J., Ferriero, D. M., Demsey, D. A., and Olsen, G. D. 1994. Cocaine metabolites in the neonate: Potential for toxicity. *Journal of Child Neurology* 9:242–48.

Kramer, L. D., Locke, G. E., Ogunyemi, A., and Nelson, L. 1990. Neonatal cocaine-related seizures. *Journal of Child Neurology* 5:60–64.

Kron, R. E., Litt, M., Eng, D., Phoenix, M. D., and Finnegan, L. P. 1976. Neonatal narcotic abstinence: Effects of pharmacotherapeutic agents and maternal drug usage on nutritive sucking behavior. *Journal of Pediatrics* 88:637–41.

Kurth, C. P., Monitto, C., Albuquerque, M. L., Feuer, P., Anday, E., and Shaw L. 1993. Cocaine and its metabolites constrict cerebral arterioles in new born pigs. *Journal of Pharmacology and Experimental Therapeutics* 265:587–91.

Legido, A., Clancy, R. R., Spitzer, A. R., and Finnegan, L. P. 1992. Electroencephalographic and behavioral state studies in infants of cocaine-addicted mothers. *American Journal of Diseases of Children* 146:748–52.

Lewis, D. E., Moore, C. M., and Leiken, J. B. 1994. Cocaethylene in meconium specimens. *Journal of Toxicology Clinical Toxicology* 32:697–703.

Lifschitz, M. H., and Wilson, G. S. 1991. Patterns of growth and development in narcotic-exposed children. *NIDA Research Monographs* 114:323–39 Rockville, MD: U. S. Department of Health and Human Services.

Lindsay, M. K., Peterson, H. B., Boring, J., Gramling, J., Willis, S., and Klein, L. 1992. Crack/cocaine as a risk factor for Human Immunodeficiency Virus Infection type I among inner city parturients. *Obstetrics and Gynecology* 80:981–84.

Linn, S., Schoenbaum, S., Monson, R., Rosner, R., Stubblefield, P.C., and Ryan, K. J. 1983. The association of marijuana use with the outcome of pregnancy. *American Journal of Public Health* 73:1161–4.

Lipschultz, S. E., Frassica, J. J. and Orau, E. J. 1991. Cardiovascular abnormality in infants prenatally exposed to cocaine. *Journal of Pediatrics* 118:44–51.

Little, R. E., Anderson, K. W., Ervin, C. H., Worthington-Roberts, B., and Clarren, S. K. 1989. Maternal alcohol use during breast feeding and infant mental and motor development at one year. *New England Journal of Medicine* 32:425–30.

Little, R. E., and Snell, L. M. 1991. Brain growth among fetuses exposed to cocaine in utero: Asymmetrical growth retardation. *Obstetrics and Gynecology* 77:361–64.

Mahalik, M., Gautierri, R., and Maun, D. 1980. Teratogenic potential of cocaine hydrochloride in CF-12 mice. *Journal of Pharmaceutical Sciences* 111:703–06.

Marcus, J., Han, S. L., and Jeremy R. J. 1984. A longitudinal study of offspring born to methadone-maintained women. III. Effects of multiple risk factors on development at 4, 8 and 12 months. *American Journal of Drug Abuse* 10:195–207.

Martin, M. L., and Khoury, M. J. 1992. Cocaine and single ventricle: A population study. *Teratology* 46:267.

Martin, M. L., Koury, M. J., Corderos, J. F., and Waters, G. D. 1992. Trends in rate of multiple vascular disruption, Atlanta. Is there evidence for a cocaine epidemic? *Teratology* 45:647–53.

Mayes, L. C., Bornstein, M. H., Chawarska, M. A., and Granger, R. H. 1995. Information processing and developmental assessments in 3-month old infants exposed to cocaine. *Pediatrics* 95:539–45.

McCalla, S., Minkoff, H. L., Feldman, J., Delke, I., Salwin, M., Valencia, G., and Glass, L. 1991. The biological and social consequences of perinatal cocaine use in an inner city population: Results of an anonymous cross-sectional study. *American Journal of Obstetrics and Gynecology* 164:625–30.

Moro J. O., de Paredes, B., Wagner, M., de Navarro, L., Suescun, J., Christiansen, N., and Herrera, M. G. 1979. Nutritional supplementation and outcome of pregnancy. I Birth weight. *American Journal of Clinical Nutrition* 32:455–62

Needleman, R., Zuckerman, B. S., and Anderson, G. 1992. CSF monoamine precursors and metabolites in human neonates following in-utero cocaine exposure. *Pediatrics* 31:13A.

Nelson, K. B., and Broman, S. H. 1977. Perinatal risk factors in children with serious motor and mental handicaps. *Annals of Neurology* 2:371–77.

Neuspiel, D. R., Hamel, C., Hochberg, E., Greene, J., and Campbell, D. 1990. Maternal cocaine use and infant behavior. *Neurotoxicology and Teratology* 13:229–33.

O'Connell, C. M., and Fried, P. A. 1984. An investigation of prenatal cannabis exposure and minor physical anomalies in a low risk population. *Neurobehavioral Toxicology and Teratology* 6:345–50.

Olds, D. L., Henderson, C. R., and Tatelbaum, R. 1994. Intellectual impairment in children of women who smoke cigarettes during pregnancy. *Pediatrics* 93:221–27.

Oro, A. S., and Dixon, S. D., 1987. Perinatal cocaine and methamphetamine exposure: Maternal and neonatal correlates. *Journal of Pediatrics* 111:571–78.

Ostrea, E. M., Brady, M. J., Gause, S., Raymundo, A. L., and Stevens, M. 1992. Drug screening of newborns by meconium analysis: A large scale, prospective, epidemiological study. *Pediatrics* 89:107–13.

Ostrea, E. M. Jr., Brady, M. J., Parks, P. M., Asensio, D. C., and Naluz, A. 1989. Drug screening of meconium in infants of drug-dependent mothers: An alternative to urine testing. *Journal of Pediatrics* 115:474–77.

Ounstead M., Moar V. A., and Scott A. 1988. Head circumference and developmental ability at age seven years. *Acta Paediatrica Scandinavica* 77:374–79.

Oyemade, U. J., Cole, O. J., Johnson, A. A., Knight, E. M., Westney, O. E., Laryea, H., Hill, G., Cannon, E., Fomufod, A., Westney, L. S., Jones, S., and Edwards, C. H. 1994. Prenatal predictors of performance on the Brazelton Neonatal Assessment Scales. *Journal of Nutrition* 124:1000S–1005S.

O'Malley, P. M., Johnston, L. D., and Bachman, J. G. 1991. Quantitative and qualitative changes in cocaine use among American high school seniors, college students and young adults. NIDA Res Monographs, 110:19–43.

Picone, T. A., Allen, L. H., Olsen, P. N., and Ferris, M. E. 1982., Pregnancy outcome in North American women. II Effects of diet, cigarette smoking, stress and weight gain on placentas, and on neonatal physical and behavioral characteristics. *American Journal of Clinical Nutrition* 36:1214–23.

Rawstron, S. A., Jenkins, S., Blanchard, S., Li, P. N., and Bromberg, K. 1993. Maternal and congenital syphilis in Brooklyn, NY. Epidemiology transmission and diagnosis. *American Journal of Diseases of Children* 147:727–31.

Rosen, T. S., and Johnson, H. L. 1982. Children of methadone maintained mothers: Follow-up to 18 months of age. *Journal of Pediatrics* 101:192–96.

Rosengren, S. S. 1993. Meconium testing for cocaine metabolite. *American Journal of Obstetrics and Gynecology* 68:1449–56.

Ryan, L., Erlichs, T., and Finnegan, L. 1987. Cocaine abuse in pregnancy: Effects on the fetus and newborn. *Neurotoxicology and Teratology* 9:295–99.

Salamy, A., Eldredge, L., Anderson, J., and Bull, D. 1990. Brainstem transmission time in infants exposed to cocaine in-utero. *Journal of Pediatrics* 117: 627–29.

Schenker, S., Yang, Y., Johnson, R. F., Downing, J. W., Schenken, R. S., Henderson, G. I, and King, T. S. 1993. The transfer of cocaine and its metabolites across the term human placenta. *Clinical Pharmacology and Therapeutics* 53:329–39.

Schneider, J. W., and Chasnoff, I. J. 1992. Motor assessment of cocaine/polydrug exposed infants at age 4 months. *Neurotoxicology and Teratology* 14: 97–101.

Shepard, T. H., Fantel, A. G., and Kapur, R. P. 1991. Fetal coronary thrombosis as a cause for single ventricle. *Teratology* 43:113–17.

Shepherd, S. M., Druckenbrod, G. C., and Haywood, Y. C. 1990. Other infectious complications in intravenous drug users. The compromised host. *Emergency Medical Clinics of North America* 8:683–92.

Shi, L., Cone-Wesson, B., and Reddix, B. 1988. Effects of maternal cocaine use and the neonatal auditory system. *International Journal of Pediatric Otorhinlaryngology* 15:245–51.

Shiono, P. H., Klebanoff, M. A., Nugent R. P., Cotch, M. F., Wilkins, D. G., Rollins, D. E., Carey, J. C., and Behrman, R. E. 1995. The impact of cocaine and marijuana use on low birth weight and preterm birth: A multicenter study. *American Journal of Obstetrics and Gynecology* 172:19–27.

Silvestri, J. M., Long, J. M., Weese-Mayer, D. E., and Barkov, G. A. 1991. Effects of prenatal cocaine on respiration, heart rate and sudden infant death syndrome. *Pediatric Pulmonology* 11:328–34.

Sokol, R. J., Miller, S. I., and Reed, G. 1980. Alcohol abuse during pregnancy: An epidemiologic study. *Alcoholism: Clinical Experimental Research* 4:135–38.

Stafford, J. R., Rosen, T. S., Zaider, M., and Merriam, J. C., 1994. Prenatal cocaine exposure and the developing human eye. *Ophthalmology* 101:301–08.

Strauss, M. E., Lessen-Firestone, J. K., Starr, R. H., and Ostrea, E. M. J. 1975. Behavior of narcotic-addicted newborns. *Child Development* 46:887–93.

Streissguth, A. P., Barr, H. M., and Sampson, P. D. 1990. Moderate prenatal alcohol exposure: Effects on child IQ and learning at age 7 1/2 years. *Alcoholism: Clinical and Experimental Research* 14:662–69.

Steinbaum, K. A., and Badell, A. 1992. Physiatric management of two neonates with limb deficiencies and prenatal cocaine exposure. *Archives of Physical Medicine and Rehabilitation* 73:385–88.

Struthers, J. M., and Hansen, R. L. 1992. Visual recognition memory in drugs exposed in infants. *Journal of Developmental Behavioral Pediatrics* 13:108–11.

Tansley, B. W., Fried, P. A., and Mount H. T. J. 1986. Visual processing in children prenatally exposed to marijuana and nicotine: A preliminary report. *Canadian Journal of Public Health* 77:72–78.

Teske, M., and Trese, M. 1987. Retinopathy of prematurity like fundus and persistent hyperplastic primary vitreous associated with maternal cocaine use. *American Journal of Ophthalmology* 103:719–20.

Vaughn, A. J., Carzoli, R. P., Sanchez-Ramos, L., Murphy, S., Khan, N., and Chiu, T. 1993. Community wide estimation of illicit drug use in delivering women: Prevalence, demographic and associated risk factors. *Obstetrics and Gynecology* 82:92–96.

Villar, J., Smerigilio, V., Martorell, R., Brown, C. H., and Klein, R. E. 1984. Heterogenous growth and mental development of intrauterine growth-related infants during the first 3 years of life. *Pediatrics* 89:67–77.

Volpe, J. 1995. *Neurology of the Newborn*. 3rd Edition. Philadelphia, PA: W.B. Saunders Company.

Webber, M. P., and Hauser, W. A. 1993. Secular trends in New York City hospital disharge diagnosis of congenital syphilis and cocaine dependence, 1982–88. *Public Health Report* 108:270–84.

Webber, M. P., Lambert, G., Bateman, D. A., and Hauser, W. A. 1993. Maternal risk factors for congenital syphilis. A case-control study, *American Journal of Epidemiology* 137:415–22.

Weinberg, C. R. 1993. Towards a clearer definition of confounding. *American Journal of Epidemiology* 137:1–8.

Weintraub, S. A. 1991. Children and adolescents at risk for substance abuse and psychopathology. *The International Journal of the Addictions* 25:481–94.

Weiss, R. D., and Gawin, F. H. 1988. Protracted elimination of cocaine metabolites in long-term high-dose cocaine abuser. *American Journal of Medicine* 85:879–80.

Wilson, G. S., Desmond, M. M., and Verniaud, W. M. 1973. Early development of infants of heroin-addicted mothers. *American Journal of Diseases of Children* 126:457–62.

Woods, J. R., Plessinger, M. S., and Clark, K. E., 1987. Effects of cocaine on uterine blood flow. *Journal of American Medical Association* 257:957–61.

Woolverton, W. L., and Johnson, K. M. 1992. Neurobiology of cocaine abuse. *Trends in Pharmacological Sciences* 13:193–200.

Wright, J. T., Barrison, I. G., Lewis, I. G., Waterson, E. J., Toplis, P. J., Gordon, M. G., MacRae, K. D., Morris, N. F., and Murray-Lyon, I. M. 1983. Alcohol consumption, pregnancy and low birth weight. *Lancet* 1:663–65.

Zelson, C, Rubio, E, and Wasserman, E. 1971. Neonatal narcotic addiction: 10 year observation. *Pediatrics* 48:178–89.

Zelson, C., Lee, S. J., and Casalino, M. 1973. Comparative effects of maternal intake of heroin and methadone. *New England Journal of Medicine* 289:1216–20.

Zuckerman, B., Frank, D. A., Hingson, R., Amaro, H., Levenson, S. M., Kayne, H., Parker, S., Vinci, R., Aboagye, K., Fried, L. E., Cabral, H., Timperi, R., and Bauchner, H. 1989. Effects of maternal marijuana and cocaine on fetal growth. *New England Journal of Medicine* 320:762–68.

Chapter • 8

Prenatal Exposure to Cocaine and Other Drugs:
Is There a Profile?

Ira J. Chasnoff

The thalidomide tragedy of the 1960s gave rise to serious concerns that any substances a pregnant woman ingested could have a potential for impact on her developing fetus. In the early 1970s, the modern description of the fetal alcohol syndrome (Jones et al. 1973) turned clinicians' attention to recreational drugs a woman might use during gestation, and this was soon followed by the description of the neonatal abstinence syndrome in newborns undergoing withdrawal from their mothers' use of opiates, especially heroin, during pregnancy (Finnegan et al. 1975). The emergence of cocaine in the early 1980s as a drug of choice among large portions of the United States population marked a new era in children's health and development, for here was a drug that was viewed as safe and nonaddictive and did not need to be injected, all of which made it very attractive to women of child-bearing age.

As the use of cocaine has continued at high levels, the growing numbers of children affected by prenatal exposure are presenting a challenge to health, mental health, and education professionals. Multiple risk factors of addiction, poverty, inadequate parenting, and dysfunctional home situations result in children who are increasingly vulnerable to social, personal, and academic failure before they even begin formal schooling. Consequently, they often are not provided with the support and positive opportunities that will enable them to develop the attitudes, skills, and behaviors essential for arriving at school "ready to learn" and to be successful.

EPIDEMIOLOGY

The ascertainment of the epidemiology of prenatal substance exposure is made difficult because the majority of women are never diagnosed. A recent study conducted under the auspices of the National Institute on Drug Abuse (1994), "The Pregnancy and Health Survey," found that 5.5% of randomly sampled women interviewed shortly after delivery admitted to illicit drug use during the pregnancy. An additional 18% had used alcohol. These one-time interviews probably significantly underestimated the number of women who actually used the substances in question.

More important than national statistics, however, are the data developed on the community level. In 1990, the first population-based evaluation of the prevalence of drug use in pregnancy was published (Chasnoff, Landress, and Barnett 1990). In this study, every woman entering prenatal care in Pinellas County, Florida, whether at a public health clinic or at a private obstetrician's office, had urine collected for toxicology at her first prenatal visit and evaluated at a central laboratory. Results from the urine toxicology were linked to demographic data on the woman. The overall prevalence rate of a positive urine toxicology for cocaine, marijuana, or heroin was approximately 14%. There was no statistical difference in rates of positive urine toxicology between women receiving care in public health care sites and women in private obstetric offices. Neither was there a difference between racial groups, with 14% of black women and 15% of white women having a positive urine for an illicit drug. Marijuana and cocaine were by far the two most common drugs found in the women's urines. There was a difference by race in patterns of drugs used, with marijuana being the most common drug found in the urines of the white women and cocaine the most common drug found among black women, but overall rates, as noted, showed no difference. From every community-based study completed in the past few years, it has become clear that there is no racial, social, or economic group that is immune to risk for substance abuse in pregnancy.

PHYSIOLOGY OF COCAINE AND THE FETUS

The fetus may be at particular risk for central nervous system alterations when exposed to cocaine. Cocaine blocks the reuptake of the biogenic amines seratonin, dopamine, and norepinephrine (Friedman, Gershon, and Rotrosen 1975; Pitts and Marwah 1987), in this way increasing the availability of these transmitters at the receptor sites and producing the cocaine "high" by increasing neuronal excitability. Over a period of chronic exposure, a dampening effect may be produced by down-regulation of the post-synaptic dopaminergic receptors in the brain (Spear, Kirstein, and Frambes 1989). In studies of pregnant rat dams and fetuses, it was found that cocaine levels in the fetal brain are 109% to 151% higher than those in the maternal blood (Wiggins et al. 1989). The impact of exposure to such levels of cocaine during critical periods of early development could place the fetal central nervous system at risk for abnormal differentiation of key neurotransmitter systems, abnormal glial cell function, altered migrational events, and abnormal neuronal growth (Coyle and Henry 1973; Lauder and Bloom 1974; Lanier, Dunn, and VanHartesveldt 1976; Johnston and Silverstein 1986). Recent studies in adult rats who were exposed to cocaine at a period of gestation comparable to the third trimester in human pregnancies demonstrated altered brain metabolism in the motor, limbic, and sensory systems, suggesting the possibility of long-term effects on CNS function in children exposed in utero to cocaine (Dow-Edwards 1989).

From an overall perspective, it appears that cocaine could have two modes of action in placing the developing fetus at risk. The first is the indirect effect of cocaine mediated through its pharmacologic actions producing maternal and fetal vasoconstriction and tachycardia, with resultant fetal hypoxia and malnutrition, as well as stimulation of the pregnant uterus to contract. On the other hand, direct effects of cocaine induced by its interference with dopamine and norepinephrine reuptake at the post-synaptic junction, engendering increased neurotransmission and central nervous system irritability, may result in direct toxicity to the developing central nervous system of the fetus.

PSYCHOSOCIAL RISK FACTORS AND THE MATERNAL CHILD RELATIONSHIP

The lifestyle of substance abusers is replete with factors that tend to complicate pregnancy and impede parenting. Regardless of socioeconomic status, the social environment of many addicted women is one of chaos and flux. These difficulties are magnified in the woman living in poverty, for she frequently lacks the social and economic supports that could help ameliorate some of the biologic impact of the cocaine. Addicted women frequently have poor family and social support networks, have few positive relationships with other women, and are often dependent on an unreliable, abusive male, increasing their vulnerability to physical and sexual abuse. Required items for survival, such as food, shelter, clothing, transportation, and medical care, are frequently out of reach for these women and their children. Nutritional needs of the pregnant woman are often ignored for the sake of the drug, leading to high rates of anemia and malnutrition in pregnancies complicated by drug use. In addition, prenatal care is frequently not a priority for drug-using women, so that indadequate or no prenatal care is often the rule rather than the exception (Connaughton et al. 1977). The fear of loss of their children to social service agencies and the foster care system can discourage any desire to participate in social service programs. Involvement with the legal system is not unusual.

Family background complicates the social environment in which many drug-using women live. Addicted women, regardless of social class, often come from families where they did not experience their mother as a supportive, nurturing figure. This negative legacy often results in a lack of exposure to appropriate mothering and concerns on the part of the pregnant woman as to her own parenting capabilities. From these concerns come ambivalent feelings in the woman toward the pregnancy, labor, delivery, and her own self-worth. It has been found that addicted women often dread rather than anticipate events such as fetal movement and ultrasound during the pregnancy. These events unmistakably validate the reality of the pregnancy, demanding a major change in how the pregnant woman relates to the world.

Several studies have shown a remarkably high incidence of depression in substance-abusing women, with some older populations having an incidence as high as 90%. Even without the influence of substance abuse, depression can greatly impede one's ability to be an effective parent. Weismann, Payhel, and Kleinman 1972 found that in non-substance-abusing depressed women, there was less involvement with their children, impaired communication, increased friction, lack of affection, and an increase in their guilt and resentment toward the child.

NEONATAL COMPLICATIONS OF PRENATAL SUBSTANCE EXPOSURE

Prematurity

Multiple factors are associated with the delivery of a premature infant, many of which are present in the substance-using woman: lack of prenatal care, poor nutrition, and tobacco smoking, to name a few. Heavy marijuana use may also be associated with preterm delivery (Fried et al. 1984). In addition, current substance abusers are likely to have a history of preterm delivery in a previous pregnancy, a risk factor for preterm labor in the current pregnancy. However, even when prior preterm delivery history is controlled for, a significantly shorter gestational age is found among cocaine-using women (Gillogley et al. 1990). The uterine irritability and smooth muscle contractions induced by cocaine use appear to have a significant role in increasing the risk for preterm labor and delivery among cocaine-using women.

Abnormal Growth Patterns

Low birth weight has been documented in infants born to mothers who use alcohol (Oulellette et al. 1977), heroin (Naeye et al. 1973), tobacco (Butler et al. 1972), marijuana (Hatch and Bracken 1986), and/or cocaine (Chouteau et al. 1988; Neerhof et al. 1989; Ryan et al. 1987) during pregnancy. As a group, mean birth weight is significantly reduced in most studies of exposed infants, and the incidence of low birth weight infants and small-for-gestation-age infants is increased (Bingol et al. 1987; MacGregor et al. 1987; Oro and Dixon 1987; Cherukuri et al. 1988; Little et al. 1989; Frank et al. 1990; Burkett 1990). The common denominator among all of these drugs is the poor nutrition and poor prenatal care that often occur among the drug using population. The difficulty arises, of course, in accounting for the multiple factors that may produce small infants.

Impaired head growth, a reflection of poor intrauterine brain growth, has been documented in several studies of cocaine use in pregnancy (Bingol et al. 1987; Chasnoff et al. 1989; Oro and Dixon 1987; Cherukuri et al. 1988; Frank et al. 1990). This appears to be independent of tobacco use. Heavy alcohol use and heroin use have also been documented as drugs that can produce microcephaly (Jones et al. 1973; Finnegan et al. 1975). Small head circumference at birth is a significant marker for risk for poor developmental outcome (Ernhart et al. 1987; Gross et al. 1983) and should alert the clinician to the need to closely track the child's developmental course.

Congenital Anomalies

Alcohol, from its earliest recognition as a toxic substance for the developing fetus, has been linked to congenital anomalies of the heart, genitourinary tract, and the face (Oulellette et al. 1977). Early reports of maternal cocaine use suggested the possibility of genitourinary tract malformations (Chasnoff et al. 1985; Chavez et al. 1989) and were corroborated by data from previously published studies in rats (Fantel and MacPhail 1982). These reports were followed by reports of cardiac, intestinal, and central nervous system anomalies (Bingol et al. 1987; Chasnoff et al. 1988) as well as limb-reduction anomalies (Chasnoff et al. 1988; Hoyme et al. 1990). The mechanism through which these anomalies arise appears to be an interruption of intrauterine blood supply with subsequent disruption or destruction of structures that previously had formed normally from an embryologic standpoint. This interruption of blood flow is related most likely to the pharmacologic effects of cocaine: hemorrhage accompanying a rapid rise in systemic and cerebral blood pressure, hemorrhage accompanying hypoperfusion, and hypoxia secondary to uterine, placental, embryonic, or fetal vasoconstriction (Hoyme et al. 1990). The important point to be made is that these types of accidents can occur at any time during pregnancy, not just the first trimester as has been the classical thinking regarding congenital malformations.

Apnea and Sudden Infant Death Syndrome

It has long been well documented that children exposed in utero to heroin or tobacco are at increased risk for death from sudden infant death syndrome (SIDS) (Rajegowda, Kandall, and Falciglia 1978). Given the little information we have regarding the etiology or mechanism of death from SIDS, it is no wonder that this issue among cocaine-exposed infants has become so clouded. Apnea and abnormalities of respiratory patterns during sleep have been documented in these infants (Chasnoff et al. 1989b), and several studies have documented an increased risk of SIDS among cocaine-exposed infants (Chasnoff et al. 1989b; Durand, Espinoza, and Nickerson 1990), but the level of risk has not been determined. A systematic study of prenatally cocaine-exposed infants did not document an increased rate of SIDS (Bauchner et al. 1988); rather, it was felt by these authors to be the associated polydrug use and environmental factors that led to any increase in the SIDS rate among this population.

Possible mechanisms for increased SIDS in this population could include increased incidence of respiratory pattern abnormalities, abnormal cardiac conduction, chronic intrauterine hypoxia or an abnormality of the autonomic nervous system induced by the intrauterine exposure to cocaine. Several animal studies have begun to explore physiologic changes in offspring exposed to cocaine in utero (Coyle and Henry 1973; Hutchings and Dow-Edwards 1991), but a clear relationship between these changes, apnea, and SIDS has not been established. Environmental or accidental exposure to cocaine could also result in illness or death of a child and be mistakenly diagnosed as SIDS (Rivkin and Gilmore 1989). Whatever the etiology or mechanism, biologic or environmental, pediatricians should recognize that substance-exposed infants are at increased risk for SIDS.

NEURODEVELOPMENT OF THE PRENATALLY EXPOSED CHILD

Neonatal Neurobehavior

Although the physical difficulties an infant might suffer due to his mother's substance abuse occur in only about 25% to 30% of the exposed infants, the neurobehavioral deficiencies that occur as a result of that exposure are far more common. Studies of newborn behavior as measured by the Neonatal Behavioral Assessment Scale (NBAS) (Brazelton 1984) have documented deficiencies in state organization, motor function, and orientation abilities in infants exposed to heroin, cocaine, phencyclidine (PCP), and other illicit drugs. (Finnegan et al. 1975; Chasnoff et al. 1983; Chasnoff et al. 1985; Chasnoff et al. 1989; Lester et al. 1991; Singer et al. 1991). Opiate-exposed infants are the only group found to go through a true abstinence syndrome due to the prenatal exposure (Finnegan et al. 1975).

A few studies of infants prenatally exposed to illicit drugs have not found any difference in behaviors among drug-exposed groups when compared to drug-free controls. Coles and colleagues (1992), in a comparison between cocaine-exposed, alcohol-exposed and drug-free infants, found a significant impact of cocaine on birthweight and head circumference of the newborn, but few significant differences in neurobehavioral functioning as measured by NBAS cluster scores. A study by Richardson and Day (1991) found that cocaine had no impact on infant growth, morphology, or behavior. On the other hand, studies by Eisen et al. (1991) and Lester et al. (1991) have found significant deficits in neurobehavioral functioning in newborns exposed in utero to cocaine.

Differences among studies in neurobehavioral findings could be a function of several factors, especially the amount of cocaine and other drugs to which the fetus was exposed. For example, mothers in one series of studies (Chasnoff et al. 1985; Chasnoff et al. 1989a) of neonatal neurobehavior were noted to be heavy users of cocaine and other drugs while the subjects in the Richardson and Day study (1991) were mainly light to moderate cocaine users who stopped or decreased their cocaine use during pregnancy.

In summarizing current research data, overall, cocaine-exposed infants can be classified as fragile infants who have very low thresholds for overstimulation and require a great deal of assistance from the caregiver to maintain control of their hyperexcitable nervous systems. This fragility is seen clearly in the infants' responses to many of the items on the NBAS, although there is a great deal of variability from infant to infant with regard to both the severity of the response deficiencies and the rate of recovery of the infant over the first few months of life. The key areas of neurobehavior affected by intrauterine cocaine exposure appear to be motor behavior (reflexes, motor control, coordination of motor activities), state control (the infant's ability to move appropriately through the various states of arousal in response to the demands of the environment), and orientation (the infant's ability to interact actively with the outside world by attending to and responding to visual and auditory stimuli) (Chasnoff et al. 1985; Chasnoff et al. 1989a; Griffith 1988; Lester et al. 1991; Singer, Garber, and Kliegman 1991).

On motor behaviors, the cocaine-exposed infants demonstrate a variety of difficulties. Overall, these infants can be noted to be quite hypertonic, with rigid posturing and hyperextension of the trunk. They may have difficulty bringing their hands to the midline and reflexes are hyperactive. On the other hand, quite a few of these infants are very hypotonic and lethargic at birth, with poor response to handling. In either case, the abnormal motor behavior interferes with coordination of the suck and swallow, and feeding difficulties are not uncommon in these infants.

State control in the cocaine-exposed infants is poorly organized, with the infants spending most of their time in states that shut them off from external stimulation. Their state changes tend to be abrupt and inappropriate for the level of stimulation encountered.

Variations in the patterns of state control documented on the NBAS are similar to the findings of Lester et al. (1991) in analyzing cry patterns in cocaine-exposed infants. The exposed infants in that study demonstrated two neurobehavioral patterns, excitable and depressed. The authors ascribed the two patterns to direct neurotoxic effects (excitable) of cocaine versus the indirect effects of intrauterine growth retardation (depressed).

By one month of age, the state control abilities, as measured on the NBAS, of cocaine-exposed infants may show significant improvement but are still not at the level of a normal 2-day-old newborn (Griffith 1988). The main difficulty at one month is that the infants still have very low thresholds for overstimulation and require a great deal of careful handling in order to reach and maintain the alert responsive states. Biologic, foster, and adoptive parents thus often need a great deal of help and guidance when they are caring for a cocaine-exposed infant.

The orientation abilities of cocaine-exposed infants, documented in their ability to track visual stimuli with their eyes and to show alerting responses to auditory stimuli, are often quite limited. For some, this is due to the fact that they have great difficulty reaching an alert responsive state. For those who are able to reach the responsive states, most are capable of only giving fleeting attention to a stimulus before they begin to show signs of distress including color changes, rapid respiration, frantic gaze aversion, and disorganized motor activity. Swaddling the infant and giving a pacifier to help quiet him or her helps to improve the orientation capabilities. As the infant reaches one month of age, there is significant improvement in orientation capabilities but the infant still requires a great deal of parenting intervention to organize his or her behavior in order to respond appropriately.

Infancy

Very little information regarding the long-term implications for intrauterine cocaine exposure exists. The transience and chaos of the lifestyle of many of the families enmeshed in substance abuse make it extremely difficult to evaluate the impact of cocaine or other drugs on the cognitive and behavioral development of the exposed child.

Streissguth et al. (1989) examined the effects of prenatal exposure to alcohol and/or tobacco on IQ scores of 4-year-old children. They found a significant negative relationship between alcohol consumption during pregnancy by white, middle class women and the IQ scores of their offspring at 4 years of age. This relationship held after controlling for various prenatal and postnatal confounding variables. No such relationship with IQ scores existed for tobacco. Although not a focus of the Streissguth et al. study, marijuana, heroin, methadone, and other illicit drugs were used by some of the women in the sample. None of the illicit drugs were related to 4-year IQ scores.

Maternal cigarette smoking during pregnancy, a factor in and of itself, has been found to have significant impact on the health and intellectual development of children (Olds et al. 1994) long term. Fried and Watkinson (1990) examined the effects of prenatal exposure to tobacco, marijuana, and/or alcohol on developmental outcome at 36 and 48 months of age. In their predominantly white, middle class sample, Fried and Watkinson found cigarette smoking to be related to less adequate language development and cognitive functioning at both 36 and 48 months of age. Alcohol exposure was related to decreased cognitive abilities at 36 months but not at 48 months of age. Marijuana exposure was not related to cognitive abilities at 36 months, but by 48 months was associated with lower scores in the verbal and memory domains (Fried 1995).

Three-month-old infants exposed prenatally to cocaine were found in one study to be more likely to fail to habituate in a novelty responsiveness procedure and, for those who did, were more likely to react with irritability early in the procedure (Mayes et al. 1995) as compared to non-exposed infants. Data from the University of California at Los Angeles (Howard et al. 1989) found that a group of 18-month-old children who had been exposed in utero to cocaine had significantly lower developme..al scores than a group of non-drug-exposed infants from similar family and socioeconomic backgrounds. However these children still fell within the low-average range on standardized developmental scores. The drug-exposed children also showed deficits in the context of free play. They were reported to have less representational play than the control group, and the majority of drug-exposed children demonstrated a high rate of scattering, batting, and picking up and putting down of toys rather than sustained combining of toys, fantasy play, or curious exploration.

In the only published prospective evaluation of long-term outcome of cocaine-exposed infants (Chasnoff et al. 1992), a group of infants exposed to cocaine plus a variety of other nonopiate drugs was compared to a group of infants exposed to marijuana and/or alcohol and to a third group of infants exposed to no drugs during pregnancy.

The cocaine-exposed infants demonstrated catch-up growth for weight and length during the first year of life, and from that point through 2 years of age had a mean weight and length that was similar to the non-drug-exposed infants. However, mean head circumference for the group of cocaine-exposed infants remained significantly smaller through 2 years of age.

On the Bayley Scales of Infant Development (Bayley 1969), mean developmental scores of the cocaine-exposed infants were not significantly different from the scores of the control group. However, an increased proportion of the cocaine-exposed infants scored greater than two standard deviations below the standardized mean score of the Bayley Scales, indicating significant developmental delays.

When taking all patterns of polydrug use into consideration, cocaine exposure was found to be the single best predictor of head circumference. There was, in turn, a significant correlation between small head size and developmental scores for the infants between 12 and 24 months of age. The group of infants at greatest risk for poor developmental outcome at 2 years of age were those infants who had a small head circumference at birth and did not show a catch-up pattern for head size during the first 2 years of life. This was consistent with findings from studies of low birth weight infants that poor head growth is a more powerful predictor of developmental outcome than head circumference at birth (Gross, Oehler, and Eckerman 1983). Thus head growth after birth may be an important clinical marker in predicticng 2 year development in children exposed in utero to cocaine.

In the same groups of children described above, by 3 years of age there again have been no differences (Eckerman, Lynne, and Gross 1985) found in the overall performance of the cocaine-exposed children and the drug-free children (Azuma and Chasnoff 1993) as evaluated on the Stanford-Binet Intelligence Scale, 4th Edition (Thorndike, Hagen, and Sattler 1986). However, just as it is important not to overgeneralize poor outcomes for cocaine-exposed children, it is equally important not to overgeneralize positive outcomes. The mean head circumference for the cocaine-exposed infants was significantly smaller at 3 years of age, and when one looked beyond global test scores into the individual behavior and development of each child, about one-third of the drug-exposed children displayed delays in normal language development and/or problems in attention and self-regulation.

Of those children showing language delays there was considerable variance as to the severity and specific nature of the language problems. Most of the children, no matter what the difficulty, responded well, however, to speech therapy.

The majority of attentional/behavioral problems seen in the 3-year-old cocaine-exposed children were quite similar to the self-regulatory problems seen in the newborn assessments. Those children displaying behavioral problems had low thresholds for overstimulation and low tolerance levels for frustration. These children were able to obtain normal scores in one-to-one testing situations, but had difficulty regulating their behavior in more complex situations. When overwhelmed by environmental stimuli, some children with self-regulation problems withdrew either physically or emotionally from the stressful situation. Others lost control of their behavior and displayed increasing rates of activity and impulsiveness. Still other children displayed a combination of both behaviors. These bipolar children appeared to recognize their oncoming loss of control and tried to avoid it by withdrawing from the situation causing them stress.

School-Aged Children

In a large prospective study of children prenatally exposed to cocaine and other drugs, at 6 years of age, Full Scale, Performance, and Verbal IQs on the WISC-III for both the 65 cocaine/polydrug-exposed and the nonexposed children are in the low average range, an indication of the negative impact of the children's low SES environment (Chasnoff and Iaukea 1995). These findings are similar to those results found at younger ages. However, it is important to note that four of the cocaine/polydrug-exposed children were untestable on the WISC-III at 6 years of age because of severe behavior problems, namely hyperactivity and difficulty attending to the testing procedures. Educationally, these results suggest that the majority of these children would be expected to perform at approximately average levels, although there may be differences in individual schools or classrooms.

On the Child Behavior Checklist (Achenbach 1982), filled out by the mother or primary caregiver, the drug-exposed children in this study exhibited significantly higher levels of thought problems (e.g., clinically elevated levels of anxiety/depression, somatic complaints, and attention problems). Additionally, the drug-exposed children were reported to exhibit significantly higher levels of serious psychological symptoms, mainly daydreaming, getting lost in thought, and inconsistent social responsiveness.

To obtain a better perspective of the clinical manifestations of the drug-exposed children's behavior, the data were compared to the normalized scores developed by Achenbach. Any child with a score above the 90th percentile is exhibiting significant behavior problems, according to the work of Achenbach and accepted clinical criteria. To be even more stringent, the authors set the levels of clinically significant behavior at a higher level—the 95th percentile. Among the drug-exposed children, 18% had significant levels of attention difficulties and 28% demonstrated significant levels of delinquent behavior as compared to the control group that had no scale scores greater than the 95th percentile.

Teacher reports based on their CBCL evaluation of the drug-exposed children were consistent with the parents' evaluations. However, the teachers reported significantly higher levels of depression, thought problems, and aggressive behavior than did the parents. These difficulties may be more easily recognizable in the classroom situation. The random thoughts and daydreaming (internalizing behaviors) reported by the teachers contributed to the child's distractibility and interfered with the ability to concentrate on tasks presented in the classroom.

It should be noted that the behavior problems reported by parents and teachers were their *perceptions*, and may not always reflect the actual clinical picture. However, the authors used the Gordon Diagnostic System (Gordon 1986), which provides an opportunity to evaluate a child's attention skills and associated behaviors objectively in a controlled environment with no external detractors. The Delay Task of the Gordon requires the child to wait a set period of time before hitting a button. Waiting the appropriate length of time results in positive reinforcement; premature action gives no feedback. Fifty-five percent of the drug-exposed children demonstrated highly impulsive behavior with an inability to modulate their activity. One child hit the button 200 times within a ten minute period, and five children were so hyperactive they could not be tested.

On the Vigilance Task (correct responses), 47% of the cocaine/polydrug-exposed children did not have the ability to pay attention long enough to respond appropriately to the tasks, and on the Vigilance Task (commissions), 38% of the drug-exposed children were borderline, nine were abnormal, and three children again were untestable. Seventy-four percent of the children demonstrated significant levels of impulsivity, consistent with the delay task findings.

THE CONTEXT OF PRENATAL COCAINE EXPOSURE

Although an overall picture of the substance-exposed infant is beginning to emerge, it is important to remember that very few infants are prenatally exposed to only one substance. Infants whose mothers used cocaine during pregnancy in all likelihood also were exposed to alcohol, tobacco, marijuana, and a variety of other licit and illicit drugs. Therfore, it becomes essentially impossible to ascribe a specific set of signs and symptoms to prenatal cocaine exposure.

In addition, one of the most important variables in studies of prenatal drug exposure is the family environment, including mental health status of the parents and especially the mother. However, it is the one variable that perhaps is most difficult to analyze. Substance abuse has been associated with dysfunctional parenting, but few studies have specifically examined interactions between addicted mothers and their infants (Bays 1990; Black and Mayer 1980) and how these interactions are related to the process of addiction. A recent study found that major parenting problems, including the occurence of child maltreatment, are more common among mothers who used cocaine (Wasserman and Leventhal 1993), but there is no information as to how substance abuse and parenting are linked: severity of addiction, maternal intoxication or withdrawal, maternal depression, social support systems. Longitudinal research with other populations has shown that family functioning is a critical independent variable in the prediction of childhood behavioral outcome (Stanger et al. 1992) These studies have shown that family variables such as socioeconomic status, history of psychological problems, and number of adults in the household are significantly related to behavioral characteristics in early and middle childhood.

In spite of a lack of conclusive empirical evidence, prenatal cocaine exposure has been frequently attributed to a variety of developmental problems, the most common of which are behavioral (i.e., attention deficit with or without hyperactivity). As an example, the following statement was recently published in a manual designed to meet the needs of drug-exposed children.

> Research indicates that drug-exposed children differ from other children in intellectual functioning, quality of play, and security of attachment to their parents or parental figures. Their performance in school can be impaired by learning problems, attention deficit disorders, and language delays. Cocaine-exposed children often have tantrums, poor impulse control, and an inability to regulate behavior. (Wilkes 1993)

Two studies were cited for this information (Kronstadt 1985; Davis 1993). Upon review, neither of the studies could substantiate these global claims of dysfunction. Therefore, at this time there is no one set of data that can clearly define long-term outcome of prenatally substance-exposed children. However, it is clear that early intervention strategies should address the entire family complex and should be designed to meet the needs of the child rather than the implications of a specific diagnosis.

Research into the cognitive, behavioral, and learning development of cocaine-exposed children is continuing, but it can be readily seen how the behaviors described above could affect achievment in school. Certainly, however, cocaine-exposed children do not present the picture displayed in the popluar media as uneducable and a "biologic underclass" who will challenge the school systems beyond capacity. The overall outcomes of children exposed to cocaine in utero can be positive if other major risk factors in their lives are addressed and interventions to correct those factors are undertaken. Unfortunately, the child prenatally exposed to cocaine has a host of environmental risk factors that can impede developmental progress, and one can assume that the emotional, behavioral, and learning problems will occur more frequently and be more severe in those children who are lost early in the system and do not receive the interventions they need.

REFERENCES

Achenbach, T. M. 1982. *Developmental Psychopathology* (2nd ed.). New York: Wiley.

Azuma, S. D., and Chasnoff, I. J. 1993. Outcome of children prenatally exposed to cocaine and other drugs: A path analysis of three-year data. *Pediatrics* 92:396–402.

Bauchner, H., Zuckerman, B., McClain, M., Frank, D., Fried, L. E., and Kayne, H. 1988. Risk of sudden infant death syndrome among infants with in-utero exposure to cocaine. *Journal of Pediatrics* 13:831–34.

Bayley, N. 1969. *Manual for the Bayley Scales of Infant Development*. New York: Psychological Corporation.

Bays, J. 1990. Substance abuse and child abuse: Impact of addiction on the child. *Pediatric Clinics of North America* 37:881–85.

Bingol, N., Fuchs, M., Diaz, V., Stone, R. K., and Gromich, D. S. 1987. Teratogenicity of cocaine in humans. *Journal of Pediatrics* 110:93–96.

Black, R., and Mayer, J. 1980. Parents with special problems: Alcoholism and opiate addiction. *Child Abuse and Neglect* 4:45–48.

Brazelton, T. B. 1984. *Neonatal Behavioral Assessment Scale*. Philadelphia: Spastics International.

Burkett, G., Yasin, S., and Palow, D. 1990. Perinatal implication of cocaine exposure. *Journal of Reproductive Medicine* 35:35–42.

Burns, K., Melamed, J., Burns, W. J., Chasnoff, I., and Hatcher, R. 1985. Chemical dependence and clinical depression in pregnancy. *Journal of Clinical Psychology* 41:851–54.

Butler, N. R., Godstein, H., and Ross, E. M. 1972. Cigarette smoking in pregnancy: Its influence on birth weight and perinatal mortality. *British Medical Journal* 2:127–30.

Chasnoff, I. J., Burns, W. J., Schnoll, S. H., and Burns, K. A. 1983. Phencyclidine: Effects on the fetus and neonate. *Developmental Pharmacology and Therapeutics* 6:404–08.

Chasnoff, I. J., Burns, W. J., Schnoll, S. H., and Burns, K. A. 1985. Cocaine use in pregnancy. *New England Journal of Medicine* 313:666–69.

Chasnoff, I. J., Chisum, G. M., and Kaplan, W. E. 1988. Maternal cocaine use and genitourinary tract malformations. *Teratology* 37:201–04.

Chasnoff, I. J., Griffith, D. R., Freier, C., and Murray, J. 1992. Cocaine/polydrug use in pregnancy: Two-year follow-up. *Pediatrics* 89:284–89.

Chasnoff, I. J., Griffith, D. R., MacGregor, S., Dirkes, K., and Burns, K. A. 1989a. Temporal patterns of cocaine use in pregnancy. *Journal of the American Medical Association* 261: 1741–44.

Chasnoff, I. J., Hunt, C. E., Kletter, R., and Kaplan, D. 1989b. Prenatal cocaine exposure is associated with respiratory pattern abnormalities. *American Journal of Diseases in Childhood* 143:583–87.

Chasnoff, I. J., and Iaukea, K. 1995. *Educational Implications of Prenatal Drug Exposure*. Washington, D.C.: U.S. Department of Education.

Chasnoff, I. J., Landress, H. J., and Barrett, M. E. 1990. The prevalence of illicit-drug or alcohol use during pregnancy and discrepancies in mandatory reporting in Pinellas County, Florida. *New England Journal of Medicine* 322:1202–06.

Chavez, G. F., Mulinare, J., and Cordero, J. 1989. Maternal cocaine use during early pregnancy as a risk factor for congenital urogenital anomalies. *Journal of the American Medical Association* 262:795–98.

Cherukuri, R., Minkoff, H., Feldman, J., Parekh, A., and Glass, L. 1988. A cohort study of alkaloid cocaine ("crack") in pregnancy. *Obstetrics and Gynecology* 72:147–51.

Chouteau, M., Namerow, P. B., and Leppert, P. 1988. The effect of cocaine abuse on birth weight and gestational age. *Obstetrics and Gynecology* 72:351–54.

Connaughton, J., Reeser, D., Schut, J., and Finnegan, L. P. 1977. Perinatal addiction: Outcome and management. *American Journal of Obstetrics and Gynecology* 129:679–86.

Coyle, J. T., and Henry, D. 1973. Catecholamines in fetal and newborn rat brain. *Journal of Neurochemistry* 21:6–67.

Davis, E. 1993. Cocaine babies grow up. *NEA Today* 11:13.

Dow-Edwards, D. L. 1989. Long-term neurochemical and neurobehavioral consequences of cocaine use during pregnancy. In *Prenatal Abuse of Licit and Illicit Drugs*, ed. D. E. Hutchings, *Annals of the New York Academy of Science* 562:280–89.

Durand, D. J., Espinoza, A. M., and Nickerson, B. G. 1990. Association between prenatal cocaine exposure and sudden infant death syndrome. *Journal of Pediatrics* 117:909–11.

Eckerman, C. O., Lynne, A. S., and Gross, S. J. 1985. Different developmental courses for very low birthweight infants differing in early head growth. *Developmental Psychology* 21:813–27.

Eisen, L. N., Field, T. M., Bandstra, E. S., Roberts, J. P., Morrow, C., Larson, S. K., and Steele, B. M. 1991. Perinatal cocaine effects on neonatal stress behavior and performance on the Brazelton Scale. *Pediatrics* 88:477–80.

Ernhart, C. B., Marler, M. R., and Morrow-Tlucak, M. 1987. Head size and cognitive development in the early preschool years. *Psychology Report* 61:103–06.

Fantel, A. G., and Macphail, B. J. 1982. The teratogenicity of cocaine. *Teratology* 26:17–19.

Finnegan, L. P., Connaughton, J. F., Kron, R. E., and Emich, J. P. 1975. Neonatal abstinence syndrome: Assessment and management. In *Perinatal Addiction*, ed. R. D. Harbison. New York: Spectrum Publications.

Frank, D. A., Bauchner, H., Parker, S., Huber, A. M., Keyi-Aboagye, Cabal, H., and Zuckerman, B. 1990. Neonatal body proportionality and body composition after in-utero exposure to cocaine and marijuana. *Journal of Pediatrics* 117:622–26.

Fried, P. A. 1995. Prenatal exposure to marihuana and tobacco during infancy, early and middle childhood: Effects and an attempt at synthesis. *Archives of Toxicology* 17:233–60.

Fried, P. A., Watkinson, B., and Willan, A. 1984. Marijuana use during pregnancy and decreased length of gestation. *American Journal of Obstetrics and Gynecology* 150:23–27.

Fried, P. A., and Watkinson, B. 1990. 36- and 48-month neurobehavioral follow-up of children prenatally exposed to marijuana, cigarettes, and alcohol. *Developmental and Behavioral Pediatrics* 11(2):49–58.

Friedman, E., Gershon, S., and Rotrosen, J. 1975. Effects of acute cocaine treatment on the turnover of 5-Hydroxytryptamine in the rat brain. *British Journal of Pharmacology* 54:61–64.

Gillogley, K. M., Evans, A. T., Hansen, R., et al. 1990. The perinatal impact of maternal substance abuse detected by universal intrapartum screening. *American Journal of Obstetrics and Gynecology* 163:1535–41.

Gordon, M. 1986. *The Gordon Diagnostic System (GDS)*. Dewitt, NY: Gordon Systems.

Griffith, D. R. 1988. The effects of perinatal cocaine exposure on infant neurobehavior and early maternal-infant interactions. In *Drug Use in Pregnancy: Mother and Child*, ed. I. J. Chasnoff. Boston: MTP Press.

Gross, S. J., Oehler, J. M., and Eckerman, C. O. 1983. Head growth and development outcome in very low birth weight infants. *Pediatrics* 71:70–75.

Hatch, E. E., and Bracken, M. B. 1986. Effect of marijuana use in pregnancy on fetal growth. *American Journal of Epidemiology* 124:986–88.

Howard, J., Beckwith, L., Rodning, C., and Kropenski,V. 1989. The development of young children of substance-abusing parents: Insights from seven years of intervention and research. *Zero to Three* 9:8–12.

Hoyme, H. E., Jones, K. L., Dixon, S. D., Jewett, T., Hanson, J. W., Robinson, L. K., Msall, M. E., and Allanson, J. E. 1990. Prenatal cocaine exposure and fetal vascular disruption. *Pediatrics* 85:743–48.

Hutchings, D. E., and Dow-Edwards, D. 1988. Animal models of opiate, cocaine and cannabis use. In *Chemical Dependency and Pregnancy: Clinics in Perinatalogy*, ed. I. J. Chasnoff. Philadelphia: W.B. Saunders Co.

Johnston, M. V., and Silverstein, F. S. 1986. New insights into mechanisms of neuronal damage in the developing brain. *Pediatric Neuroscience* 12:87–89.

Jones, K. L., Smith, D. W., Ulleland, C. N., and Streissguth, A. P. 1973. Pattern of malformation in offspring of chronic alcoholic mothers. *Lancet* 1:1267–71.

Kronstadt, D. 1989. *Pregnancy and Cocaine Addiction: An Overview of Impact and Treatment*. San Francisco: Far West Laboratory for Educational Research and Development.

Lanier, L. P., Dunn, A. J , and vanHartesveldt, C. 1976. Development of neurotransmitters and their function in brain. *Review of Neuroscience* 2:195–256.

Lauder, J. M. , and Bloom, F. E. 1974. Ontogeny of monoamine neurons in the locus coeruleus, raphe nuclei and substantia nigra of the rat. I. Cell differentiation. *Journal of Comparative Neurology* 155:469–82.

Lester, B. M., Corwin, M. J., Sepkoski, C., Seifer, R., Peucker, M., McLaughlin, S., and Golub, H. L. 1991. Neurobehavioral syndromes in cocaine-exposed newborn infants. *Child Development* 62:694–705.

Little, B. B., Snell, L. M., Klein, V. R., and Gilstrap, L. C. 1989. Cocaine abuse during pregnancy: Maternal and fetal implications. *Obstetrics and Gynecology* 73:157–60.

MacGregor, S. N, Keith, L. G., Chasnoff, I. J., Rosner, M. A., Chisum, G. M., Shawn, P., and Minogue, J. P. 1987. Cocaine use during pregnancy: Adverse perinatal outcome. *American Journal of Obstetrics and Gynecology* 157:686–90.

Mayes, L. C., Bornstein, M. H., Chawarska, K., and Granger, R. H. 1995. Information processing and developmental assessments in 3-month-old infants exposed prenatally to cocaine. *Pediatrics* 95:539–45.

Naeye, R. L., Blanc, W., Leblanc, W., and Khatamee, M. A. 1973. Fetal complications of maternal heroin addiction: Abnormal growth, infections and episodes of stress. *Journal of Pediatrics* 83:1055–61.

National Institute on Drug Abuse. 1994. *National Pregnancy and Health Survey*. Rockville, MD: U.S. Department of Health and Human Services.

Neerhof, M. G., MacGregor, S. N., Retzky, S. S., and Sullivan, T. P. 1989. Cocaine abuse during pregnancy: Peripartum prevalence and perinatal outcome. *American Journal of Obstetrics and Gynecology* 161:688–90.

Oehlberg, S. M., Regan, D. O., Rudrauff, M. E., and Finnegan, L. P. 1981. A preliminiary evaluation of parenting, depression and violence profiles in methadone-maintained women. *National Institute on Drug Abuse Research Monograph Series* 34:380–86.

Olds, D. L., Henderson, C. R., and Tatelbaum, R. 1994. Intellectual impairment in children of women who smoke cigarettes during pregnancy. *Pediatrics* 93:221–27.

Oro, A. S., and Dixon, S. D. 1987. Perinatal cocaine and methamphetamine exposure: Maternal and neonatal correlates. *Journal of Pediatrics* 111:571–78.

Ouellette, E. M., Rosett, H. L., Rosman, N. P., and Weiner, L. 1977. Adverse effects on offspring of maternal alcohol abuse during pregnancy. *New England Journal of Medicine* 297:528–31.

Pitts, D. K., and Marwah, J. 1987. Cocaine modulation of central monoaminergic neurotransmission. *Pharmacology, Biochemistry and Behavior* 26:453–61.

Rajegowda, B. K., Kandall, S. R., and Falciglia, H. 1978. Sudden unexpected death in infants of narcotic-dependent mothers. *Early Human Development* 2(3):219–25.

Regan, D. O., Leifer, B., and Finnegan, L. P. 1985. Depressive self-concept and violent experience in drug-abusing women and their influence upon parenting effectiveness. *National Institute on Drug Abuse Research Monograph Series* 54:332–35.

Richardson, G. A. , and Day, N. L. 1991. Maternal and neonatal effects of moderate cocaine use during pregnancy. *Neurotoxicology and Teratology* 13(4):455–60.

Rivkin, M., and Gilmore, H. E. 1989. Generalized seizures due to environmentally acquired cocaine. *Pediatrics* 84:1100–01.

Ryan, L., Ehrlich, S., and Finnegan, L. 1987. Cocaine abuse in pregnancy: Effects on the fetus and newborn. *Neurotoxicology and Teratology* 9:295–99.

Singer, L. T., Garber, R., and Kliegman, R. 1991. Neurobehavioral sequelae of fetal cocaine exposure. *Journal of Pediatrics* 119:667–72.

Spear, L. P., Kirstein, C. L., and Frambes, N. A. 1989. Cocaine effects on the developing central nervous system: Behavioral psychopharmacological and neurochemical studies. In *Prenatal Abuse of Licit and Illicit Drugs*, ed. D. E. Hutchings. *Annals of the New York Academy of Sciences* 562: 290–307.

Stanger, C., McConaughy, S., and Achenbach, T. 1992. Three year course of behavioral/emotional problems in a national sample of 4- to 16-year olds: II. Predictors of syndromes. *Journal of the American Academy of Child and Adolescent Psychiatry* 31:941–50.

Streissguth, A., Sampson, P., and Barr, H. 1989. Neurobehavioral dose-response effects of prenatal alcohol exposure in humans from infancy to adulthood. *Annals of the New York Academy of Sciences* 562:145–58.

Thorndike, R. L., Hagen, E. P., and Sattler, J. M. 1986. *Stanford-Binet Intelligence Scale: 4th Edition.* Chicago: Riverside Publishing Co.

Wasserman, D. R. and Leventhal, J. M. 1993. Maltreatment of children born to cocaine-dependent mothers. *American Journal of Diseases of Childhood* 147:1324–28.

Weissman, M., Paykel, E., and Kleiman, G. 1972. The depressed woman as a mother. *Social Psychiatry* 7:98–108.

Wiggins, R. C., Rolsten, C., Ruiz, B. V., and Davis, C. M. 1989. Pharmacokinetics of cocaine: Basic studies of route, dosage, pregnancy and lactation. *Neurotoxicology* 10:367–82.

Wilkes, D. 1993. Children exposed to drugs: Meeting their needs. In *Hot Topics: Usable Research.* ed. J. Follman. Greensboro, NC: Southeastern Regional Vision for Education.

Chapter • 9

Pediatric Neuro-AIDS

Renee C. Wachtel

In the United States, the continuing epidemic of HIV infection has led to increasing numbers of children acquiring HIV infection "vertically" from their mothers during the prenatal or perinatal period. In contrast to most other causes of developmental disability in the United States which are declining, the increasing seroprevalence of HIV in women of childbearing age is causing increasing numbers of children to be exposed to HIV infection and its significant impact upon the nervous system. While early in the epidemic, perinatal transmission rates were thought to approach 50%, more careful documentation and numerous U.S. and European studies have shown the transmission rate of HIV infection from mother to child to vary between 14% (European studies [European Collaborative Studies 1992]) to 28% (U.S. studies [Pizzo and Wilfert 1994]). While the reason for this variation is unknown, this clearly indicates that the majority of children exposed to HIV infection, in fact, do not become themselves infected (frequently called seroreverters, see below). While the remainder of this chapter will focus upon the neurologic and developmental effects upon children infected with HIV, there is one study from Africa (Mellati, Lepage, and Hitimana 1993) that suggests that prenatal exposure to HIV infection even in children who are themselves uninfected may have mild neurodevelopmental consequences to the developing nervous system.

Shortly after HIV infection was described in children in 1981, the neurologic and developmental consequences of this infection was clearly documented (Belman et al. 1985). These neurodevelopmental consequences, frequently called pediatric neuro-AIDS, may vary in severity and progression and may in fact be the first sign seen by the physician of HIV infection in a child. For this reason, it is important that clinicians, particularly those who work in areas where there is a high seroprevalence of HIV infection, be alert to the possibility of HIV infection in children with developmental delay, failure to thrive, or other neurologic findings that could be consistent with previously undetected HIV infection. This is particularly true because, due to the long incubation period of HIV infection, many women are unaware of their own HIV infection and may remain asymptomatic while their child is already demonstrating signs and symptoms of HIV infection.

EPIDEMIOLOGY

The increasing seroprevalence of HIV in women of childbearing years in the United States and other countries has paralleled the increasing incidence of children whose HIV infection was acquired through vertical transmission from their mother. Early in the epidemic, children were also infected as a result of transfusion of HIV contaminated blood products, particularly when requiring repeated transfusions in such disorders as hemophilia. Currently less than 5% of HIV-infected children in the United States have been infected by transfusion (Oxtoby 1994). Since the blood supply has been screened fairly effectively for HIV since 1986, it is expected that this percentage will continue to decline. In contrast, more than 90% of children with AIDS have acquired the infection from their mother. The two most common maternal risk factors for HIV infection are injection drug use and heterosexual contact with an HIV-infected male. An additional increasing subgroup of children with HIV infection are adolescents who have engaged in heterosexual or homosexual contact with an infected individual or have engaged in intravenous drug use. HIV infection in many urban areas has become the second most common cause of mortality in children (Oleske 1994).

The screening of women for HIV infection is difficult for many reasons. Foremost, the demographics of those at greatest risk indicate that they are living in poor urban settings with limited access to health care and other resources. Moreover, one study looking at the effectiveness of screening by risk factors (Landsman et al. 1987) demonstrated that more than half of HIV-infected women would be missed if screening was solely based upon the reported presence of risk factors. Routine HIV screening at the time of delivery is less than ideal if prevention of perinatal transmission is the goal. Moreover, issues of confidentiality, social stigma, consent, denial, and cutbacks in public health outreach programs make identification of pregnant women at risk extremely problematic. Best current estimates suggest that up to 5% of women of child-bearing age in high prevalence urban areas (e.g., New York City, Miami) have HIV infection, which underscores the magnitude of the problem.

RISK FACTORS FOR TRANSMISSION

The timing of transmission of HIV infection from mother to child is still unclear. It has been demonstrated to have occurred in fetuses as early as ten weeks gestation. In contrast, it is believed that the majority of perinatal transmission occurs during the perinatal period. Early attempts to prevent perinatal transmission by performing elective Caesarean section have not proved efficacious. Similarly, studies employing vaginal disinfection to reduce peripartum exposure have not resulted in a reduction in perinatal transmission of HIV. A recent study (Landsman et al. 1996) has suggested that length of time of membrane rupture during labor may be highly correlated with perinatal HIV transmission, perhaps suggesting a role for selective Caesarian section.

Multiple factors appear to influence the transmission of HIV infection from mother to child. One important determinant may be viral load, which is measured by the presence of P24 antigenemia, low maternal CD4 cell counts, advanced maternal clinical HIV disease, and presumed initial HIV infection (Peckham 1995). There has also been some suggestion that viral characteristics may influence the perinatal transmission of HIV. Unfortunately, high levels of maternal neutralizing antibody have not consistently demonstrated reduced transmission of HIV infection, suggesting that immunization strategies may prove difficult as a means of interrupting perinatal transmission.

PREVENTION OF PERINATAL TRANSMISSION

Two recent methods of interrupting perinatal transmission have been demonstrated to be effective. In several European studies, breast feeding was shown to be independently associated with an approximate doubling of the risk of perinatal transmission (World Health Organization 1987). Bottle feeding is therefore recommended for HIV-infected women in developed countries, although this would not be appropriate in settings where economic status and/or poor sanitation would increase the risk of other infectious diseases or malnutrition.

In one of the most significant developments in prevention of perinatal transmission, the Pediatric AIDS Clinical Trials group (Connor et al. 1994) reported a significant reduction (to approximately 1/3) of maternal-infant transmission of HIV-1 with Zidovudine (ZDV) treatment. This trial provided HIV-infected pregnant women with oral ZVD during the last trimester of pregnancy, intravenous ZVD during labor and delivery, and oral ZVD to the newborn for the first six weeks of life. While quite promising, the impact of this study remains to be determined, due to the difficulty in identifying asymptomatic HIV-infected pregnant women early enough in the pregnancy to enable them to complete the course of ZVD therapy. In addition, potential teratogenic effects of ZVD treatment, particularly in the large number of uninfected children resulting from this method of treatment, remains to be determined. Nevertheless, this important advance in prevention of HIV transmission holds great promise in helping us to better understand factors that can interrupt the transmission of HIV infection.

DETERMINATION OF HIV INFECTION

Due to passive transfer of maternal antibodies to HIV through the placenta to the fetus during pregnancy, the usual tests for anti-HIV immunoglobulin G (IGG) antibodies are ineffective in distinguishing the infants who have acquired HIV infection by vertical transmission and those who are uninfected. In fact, if IGG antibodies are followed over time, the majority of children born to HIV-infected women will show declining numbers of antibodies during the first year of life, consistent with their uninfected status and therefore are termed "seroreverters." For this reason, common ELISA or other tests that measure IGG antibodies are ineffective in diagnosing HIV infection in children under 2 years of age. Currently, an early diagnosis of HIV infection in infants born to HIV-infected mothers is most effectively made by detection of the virus in culture or the HIV genome by polymerase chain reaction (PCR) after one month of age. To confirm the diagnosis, positive results on two separate blood samples are required, preferably using a combination of different tests. The diagnosis is supported by the persistence of HIV antibody after 18 months. Unfortunately the sensitivity of viral culture and PCR is only about 40% at birth, making immediate neonatal diagnosis difficult. This period of uncertainty about the child's HIV infection status is very difficult for families and health care providers alike. To further complicate matters, there is a recent report (Peckham and Gibb 1995) of a few children initially positive by PCR or viral culture where clearance of HIV infection was documented and for whom further virologic studies and antibody studies were negative. For all of these reasons, it is imperative that children born to HIV-infected women be followed in a comprehensive tertiary care center where issues of appropriate diagnosis and treatment are handled by experts familiar with the techniques, methodologies, and appropriate interpretation of test results.

NEUROPATHOGENESIS OF HIV INFECTION

Much recent work has been done in understanding the neuropathogenesis of HIV infection. Features of HIV infection of the brain that have been described include multinuclear giant cell encephalitis, evidence of a vacuolar myelinopathy, gliosis associated with proliferation of macrophages and microglia and some degree of neuronal loss. The mechanism of invasion of HIV infection into the central nervous system is still speculative. Hypotheses include the presence of circulating free virus, entry through circulating CD+4 lymphocytes or macrophages, or via endothelial cell infection. Infection of the nervous system, however, occurs early in the course of the disease, since some individuals have demonstrated the presence of DNA from HIV in the brain as early as the first month of infection. In fact, recent studies have demonstrated that HIV-1 can be recovered from cerebralspinal fluid and brain tissues in 74 out of 96 adults with neurologic symptoms (77%) and in 53% of neurologically asymptomatic HIV-infected individuals (Levy 1996). These studies have not been reported in children as yet.

Also controversial, and the subject of extensive research, is the mechanism for brain injury in HIV infection. In contrast to earlier studies, it is now clear that HIV infection, as distinguished from secondary opportunistic infection, plays a direct role in the injury to central nervous system neurons which probably precedes the symptomatic expression of neurologic and developmental symptoms. Postulated HIV effects on the brain include direct toxic effects of components of HIV including envelope GP120, GP41, or envelope proteins including TAT or NEF. Alternative hypotheses include cytotoxicity or injurious effects of the immune response. Finally, various factors have been isolated in cerebrospinal fluid or brain tissue that are thought to be produced by neuronal cells (including astrocyte microglia or macrophages) that have been demonstrated to have neurotoxic effects. These include a variety of cytokines (including tumor necrosis factor-alpha, platelet aggregating factor, interleukins 1 and 6), quinolinic acid, nitrous oxide, and arachadonic acid and other chemokines. Whether all of these different factors collaborate to produce toxic effects upon nerve cells or whether they are involved in a sequential activation following a single common pathway is at present unclear. What is clear is that one mechanism of neuronal cell injury includes aptosis, a mechanism whereby nerve cells in the central nervous system demonstrate injury without an inflammatory response. Under light microscopy, nerve cells including astrocytes, neurons, and microglia demonstrate chromatin condensation, and nuclear fragmentation, and yet preserve membrane integrity. This is in distinction to nerve necrosis, which is generally accompanied by an inflammatory response and the loss of membrane integrity. In in vitro studies, tumor necrosis factor-alpha can produce aptosis of neuronal cells. This process is facilitated by Bax (Sharer et al. 1996) which promotes program cell death and is inhibited by both BCL-2 and BCL-X. Still to be further investigated are the role of glutamate receptors, which appear to suffer neuronal injury induced by excessive production of decreased clearance of excitatory neurotransmitters, and the role of oxidative stress and oxidative products (Epstein 1996).

BIOLOGY OF NEUROLOGIC INVOLVEMENT IN HIV INFECTION

Various components of the HIV virus have been studied to determine whether some are neurotropic or particularly associated with central nervous system infection or symptoms. Recent work by Power et al. (1996) indicates that the V_1, V_2 polymorphisms of HIV appear to be related to the development of HIV dementia in adults. Also HIV dementia may be associated with HIV replication rates in macrophages which may be partially determined by specific amino acid sequences within the V_1, V_2 region. In a monkey model of simian immunodeficiency virus infection, monkeys with motor impairment have demonstrated increased somatostatin mRNA in brain frontal cortex layers and increases in glial fibrillary acidic protein (GFAP). The increase in GFAP appears to be indicative of neural tissue injury and reactive astrogliosis (Eiden 1996). In contrast, monkeys with only cognitive impairment seem to demonstrate only an increase in somatostatin M-RNA, which may be indicative of neuronal disregulation. This is similar to recent work by Cunha et al. (1996), who demonstrated in the brains of eight children who died with HIV encephalopathy, increased preprosomatostatin mRNA in interneurons in area IV of the frontal cortex and subcortical areas. It is thought that these interneurons connect to the thalamus and may be related to the evolution of HIV encephalopathy. These neuronal changes may in fact begin prior to the onset of encephalopathy. Using in situ end labeling, An et al. (1996) demonstrated that HIV-infected asymptomatic adults may demonstrate apoptotic cells in the brain matter, indicating brain injury is already taking place in the early stages of HIV infection in some patients. Further understanding of the neuropathogenesis and biology of HIV infection will undoubtedly contribute to a better understanding of the clinical neurodevelopmental manifestations of HIV infection in children and hopefully lead to more targeted therapeutic intervention.

COMMON INITIAL MANIFESTATIONS OF HIV INFECTION

Non-neurologic Manifestations

In many situations, a child's risk of HIV infection is documented due to known maternal infection or maternal screening at the time of delivery, particularly in high prevalence areas. Rarely, children themselves have risk factors that indicate the importance of HIV screening. Examples include sexual abuse or exposure to HIV contaminated blood products in a child, or intravenous drug use or unprotected homosexual/heterosexual exposure in a teenager. In many children, however, clinical presentations of HIV infection occur without the pre-existing presumption of possible HIV infection. Common clinical presentations that should cause the clinician to consider HIV infection in the differential diagnosis include failure to thrive, persistent diarrhea (especially when accompanied by skin rash), and persistent anemia. Most clinicians are now sensitized to consider HIV infection when opportunistic infections, such as *Pneumocystis carenii* or persistent yeast infections are present in a child. It is increasingly common, however, that neurodevelopmental manifestations may be either the initial presentation of HIV infection, or evolve in a child being followed medically after HIV infection has been diagnosed.

Neurologic Manifestations

While children with HIV infection at any age may be completely asymptomatic, even when careful neurologic and developmental testing is performed, the following clinical neurodevelopmental manifestations are commonly seen and may occur in up to 40% of children with HIV infection.

In a young infant, diffuse neurologic abnormalities may be seen, frequently accompanied with diffuse immunosuppression, failure to thrive and/or opportunistic infection. This may be related to early invasion of the central nervous system by HIV, perhaps during the fetal period when immuno competence is still fairly immature. Initially, the infant may have diffuse hypotonia and increased deep tendon reflexes, but generally unaccompanied by persistent or exaggerated primitive reflexes. Infants are frequently hypoactive and may be difficult to engage socially. Motor delay with poor head control is frequently present. This may progress to a generalized rigidity, with increased extensor tone. CAT scans or MRI generally show diffuse cortical atrophy.

In a prospective longitudinal study that was performed to document the neurologic and developmental manifestations of children with HIV infection from birth (Wachtel et al. 1993), we found that while a proportion of HIV-infected infants had abnormal or suspect neurologic examinations during the first 12 months of life, a substantial percentage of seroreverters and control infants with similar risk factors (predominantly prenatal drug exposure) had similar neurologic findings. These abnormalities were predominantly increased motor tone and deep tendon reflexes and appeared not to be functionally significant (that is, psychomotor development was not impaired). These findings appeared to resolve during the first year of life in most children. This points out the importance of appropriate control groups both to determine causal relationships and to allow for the control of psychosocial and environmental factors in their potential influence on neurodevelopment.

In preschool-age children (2 to 5 years) a common neurologic manifestation is the presentation of a child with a spastic diplegia-type picture, with spasticity and hypertonia of the lower extremities, particularly distally, and marked hyperreflexia generally with sustained or unsustained clonus at the ankles. This is also frequently accompanied by pathologic reflexes, such as Babinski or Chaddock's response. MRI or CT findings may be quite nonspecific and the upper extremities may remain fairly functional with no obvious neurologic impairment. Uncommon presentations include the acute onset of cerebellar ataxia with dysmetria and nystagmus. In older children an initial neurologic presentation may be development of fine motor clumsiness initially unaccompanied by changes in tone or reflexes. Mild cognitive impairment with mental slowing may present as a learning disability or school underachievement at this time.

With any of these patients, regression with loss of previously attained developmental skills may occur, or the child may fail to show expected rates of neurodevelopmental progression.

NEURODEVELOPMENTAL MANIFESTATIONS OF HIV INFECTION

Early reports of neurodevelopmental impairments in children with HIV infection (Belman et al. 1985) indicated that a substantial percentage of children with AIDS had severe neurodevelopmental disabilities. Children were described who had abnormal neurodevelopment from early infancy with a slower progression of skills over a long period of time. In contrast, other groups of children had periods of normal development with later regression or a plateau period followed by a slow loss of skills (Belman et al. 1988). It was noted as early as 1985 that developmental delay could be the initial manifestation of HIV infection. A more recent prospective study (Wachtel et al. 1993) followed a cohort of children from birth including HIV-infected children, controls who were seroreverters and others who were born to uninfected women with similar risk factors for HIV infection using standardized measures. This study demonstrated that as a group HIV-infected children demonstrate neurodevelopmental abnormalities with lower Mental Development Index on the Bayley Scales of Infant Development as early as 6 months of age as compared to the other groups, although their scores remained initially in the normal range. This study also demonstrated that many HIV-infected children show developmental skills in the normal range at least until the age of 2 or 3 years. Some children infected perinatally by HIV and followed through age 8 years demonstrate problems with visual motor performance, attentional disorders, specific learning disabilities, speech-language impairment, or abnormalities in voice quality. For a smaller group of children generalized cognitive impairment (mental retardation) is demonstrated. It should be noted that in addition to their HIV infection, this group of children is at high risk for neurodevelopmental impairment due to other confounding factors, such as prenatal drug exposure, psychosocial deprivation, recurrent illnesses and hospitalizations, and psychological effects of living with HIV infection in the family.

NEURODEVELOPMENTAL ASSESSMENT

A careful comprehensive neurodevelopmental evaluation at regular intervals by an experienced clinician is an essential part of the treatment program because the early manifestations of pediatric neuro-AIDS may be fairly subtle. This must include an evaluation of current function in each developmental area, a traditional neurologic examination including deep tendon reflexes, motor, measurement of motor tone and functional capacity, and a neuromaturational evaluation assessing the development of postural responses, the progression of primitive reflexes, and other developmental reflexes over time.

PSYCHOSOCIAL MANIFESTATIONS

Because HIV infection is generally a disorder that affects numerous family members, is progressive, and carries a social stigma, the psychosocial aspects of care of children and families living with HIV infection are exceedingly complex. Issues of confidentiality must be thoroughly understood and explored to allow for necessary information sharing while protecting the privacy rights of the child and the family. In addition, necessary social supports need to be identified and put in place to enable the child to achieve maximal function. Issues of parental illness and possible death are best handled by experienced clinicians working in an interdisciplinary supportive setting. Parent support groups, reading material, and counseling services should be offered to families to assist them with coping with HIV infection in their child.

TREATMENT ISSUES

Medical Treatment

Medical treatment of pediatric neuro-AIDS consists of several components. The first includes specific antiretroviral treatment to reduce or reverse the neurodevelopmental impairment. (presumably by reducing viral load or viral toxic products as noted above). Zidovudine (ZVD) was the first antiretroviral agent approved for use in the pediatric AIDS group. It is now used in conjunction with other antiretroviral agents such as Dideoxyinosine (DDI, Videx) as primary therapy to reduce central nervous system effects of HIV infection. Careful studies have demonstrated (Browers et al. 1990) that neurologic progression can be halted in some children and even reversed with the additional benefit of improvement in cognitive function (even in some children who are functioning at the lower range of normal) when appropriate antiretroviral treatment is initiated.

In addition, other antimicrobials may be used for prophylaxis to prevent recurrent infection, including sinusitis and recurrent otitis media which can have developmental implications. Also, nutritional therapy and careful treatment of persistent diarrhea is essential to allow the child to feel well enough to participate in developmentally based interventions. Other medical interventions may include the use of muscle relaxants to reduce spasticity and prevent development of contractures. Similarly, orthopedic appliances such as ankle-foot orthoses (AFOs) and other therapeutic equipment may enable the child to regain function or to prevent the development of conditions that may interfere with function.

In infants who present with rapidly progressive clinical disease and immunosuppression, antiretroviral therapy may not prevent a rapidly progressive course with early death generally from opportunistic infection. In some children, however, antiretroviral therapy halts the progression of neurologic and other symptoms, but progression of neurodevelopment is either not generally seen or is exceedingly slow. In contrast, infants who show initial neurologic manifestations during the second year of life may have a much slower progression, and their neurologic symptoms may in fact be reversed by appropriate antiretroviral therapy. For these children careful documentation of their neurodevelopmental abilities and abnormal neurologic signs and symptoms are important to determine whether effective antiretroviral therapy has been achieved. While a careful search for opportunistic infections in the central nervous system may be warranted in some groups of infants presenting with significant neurologic impairment, generally the etiology is progressive HIV mediated encephalopathy.

Developmental Therapy

Comprehensive interdisciplinary evaluation and treatment should be followed in neuro-AIDS as in any neurodevelopmental disability. Physical therapy can help a child with motor impairment caused by neuro-AIDS improve functional motor skills, develop a home management plan, and consult with other treating disciplines, such as special education. Occupational therapy may be helpful in developing positioning equipment for maximizing function and consultation to other treating disciplines in regard to positioning, such as speech therapy. In addition, direct services may be needed to improve adaptive, oral motor, or fine motor skills which are frequently impaired in children as neuro-AIDS progresses. Speech and language services may be needed to improve demonstrated communicative impairments and infected children may require direct speech and language therapy. Evaluation of a child's hearing status is particularly important, especially if recurrent middle ear infections have been present. For children who have more severe communicative impairment, augmentative communication devices may prove valuable in enabling the child to have an alternative means of communicating. Developmental pediatricians play an important role in identifying and monitoring neurodevelopmental and medical subspecialty needs and treatment.

Care Coordination

It is essential for children living with HIV infection, particularly when pediatric neuro-AIDS is present, that an experienced interdisciplinary team provide coordinated services for the child and family. This is best accomplished with a case manager or service coordinator who is familiar with the needs of children with HIV infection and who is able to marshal the resources necessary to support the child and family during this chronic illness. Regular communication between all treating disciplines and agencies is essential to avoid service gaps and/or conflicts in treatment programs. This case manager must also deal with practical issues, such as health insurance, transportation to appointments, and supporting uninfected family members, all of which may cause significant anxiety in the family.

SUMMARY

The neurodevelopmental manifestations of HIV infection in children are part of a complex chronic illness that affects both the child and the family. It is essential for professionals working with children living with HIV to understand the complex issues that are presented and to marshal the supports necessary to enable the child and family to function maximally given the circumstances of their disease. It is only through coordinated interdisciplinary treatment by experienced clinicians working closely with the family that the best possible outcome can be obtained. As in many complex issues, communication is a pivotal aspect of providing quality of care that leads to an improved quality of life.

REFERENCES

An, S. F., Giometto, B., Scaravilli, T., Tavolato, B., Gray, F., and Scaravilli, F. 1996. Programmed cell death in brains of HIV-1 positive AIDS and pre-AIDS individuals. *Journal of NeuroVirology* 2:24.

Belman, A. L., Diamond, G., Dickson, D., Horoupian, D., Tlera, J., Lartos, G., and Rubinstein, A. 1988. Pediatric acquired immunodeficiency syndrome: Neurological syndromes. *American Journal of Diseases of Children* 142:29–35.

Belman, A. L., Ultman, M. H., Horoupian, D., Novick, B., Spiro, A. J., Rubinstein, A., Kurtzberg, D., and ConeWesson, B. 1985. Neurologic complications in infants and children with acquired immune deficiency syndrome. *Annals of Neurology* 18:560–66.

Browers, P., Moss, H., Wolters, P., DeVeikis, A., Keller, M., O'Rourke, S., and Bryson, Y. J. 1990. Effect of continuous infusion zidovudine therapy in neuropsychologic functioning in children with symptomatic human immunodeficiency infection. *Journal of Pediatrics* 117:980–85.

Connor, E. M., Sperling, R. S., Gelber, R., Kiselev, P., Scott, G., O'Sullivan, M. J., Van Dyke, R., Bey, M., Shearer, W., Jacobson, R. L., Jimenez, E., O'Neill, E., Bazin, B., Delfraissy, J. F., Culnane, M., Coombs, R., Elkins, M., Moye, J., Stratton, P., and Balsley, J. 1994. Reduction of maternal-infant transmission of human immunodeficiency virus type 1 with zidovudine treatment. *New England Journal of Medicine* 331:1173–80.

Da Cunha, D. A., Phil, D., Eiden, L. E., and Sharer, L. R. 1996. A neurochemical and neuroanatomical correlate of HIV-1 encephalopathy. *Journal of NeuroVirology* 2:25.

Eiden, L. E. 1996. Pathogenesis of encephalopathy in SIV monkeys. Presented at Neuroscience of HIV Infection, Basic Research and Clinical Frontiers, March 6–9, Paris, France.

Epstein, L. G. 1996. HIV infection of the nervous system: Pathogenetic mechanisms. *Journal of NeuroVirology* 2:5–6.

European Collaborative Study. 1992. Risk factors for mother to child transmission of HIV-1. *Lancet* 339:1007–12.

Landsman, S. H., Kalish, L. A., Burns, D. N., Minkoff, H., Fox, H. F., Zorrilla, C., Garcia, P., Fowler, M. G., Moferson, L., and Tuomala, R. 1996. Obstetrical factors and the transmission of human immunodeficiency virus type-1 from mother to child. *New England Journal of Medicine* 334:1617–23.

Landsman, S., Minkoff, H., Holman, S., McCalla, S., and Sing, O. 1987. Serosurvey of human immunodeficiency virus in parturients. *Journal of the American Medical Association* 258:2701–3.

Levy, J. A. 1996. Viral and immunological factors involved in HIV neuropathogenesis. *Journal of NeuroVirology* 2:7.

Mellati, P., Lepage, P., Hitimana, D. G. 1993. Neurodevelopmental testing of children born to human immunodeficiency virus type 1 seropositive and seronegative mothers: A prospective cohort study in Kigali, Rwanda. *Pediatrics* 92:843–48.

Oleske, J. M. 1994. The many needs of the HIV-infected child. *Hospital Practice* 63:69.

Oxtoby, M. 1994. Vertically acquired HIV infection in the United States. In *Pediatric AIDS: The Challenge of HIV Infection in Infants, Children, and Adolescents* (2nd ed.), eds. P. Pizzo and C. M. Wilfert. Baltimore: Williams & Wilkins.

Peckham, C., and Gibb, D. 1995. Mother to child transmission of the human immunodeficiency virus. *New England Journal of Medicine* 333:298–302.

Pizzo, P. A., and Wilfert, C. 1994. *Pediatric AIDS: The Challenge of HIV Infection in Infants, Children and Adolescents.* (2nd ed.) Baltimore: Williams & Wilkins.

Power, C., McArthur, J. C., Langelier, T. L., Glass, J. D., Johnson, R. T., and Chesebro, B. 1996. Brain-derived HIV-1 envelope V_1 and V_2 region polymorphism. *Journal of NeuroVirology* 2:19.

Sharer, L. R., Krajewski, S., James, H., Ross, J., Blumberg, J. M., Epstein, L. G., Dewhurst, S., Reed, J. C., and Gelbard, H. A. 1996. Bax is a marker for apoptotic microglia in pediatric patients with HIV-1 encephalitis. *Journal of NeuroVirology* 2:27.

Wachtel, R. C., Tepper, V. J., Houch, D. L., Nair, P., Thompson, C., and Johnson, J. P. 1993. Neurodevelopment in pediatric HIV-1 infection: A prospective study. *Pediatric AIDS and HIV Infection* 4:198–203.

World Health Organization. 1987. Breast-feeding/breast milk and human immunodeficiency virus (HIV). *Weekly Epidemiology Recommendations* 33:245–46.

Subject Index

Author Index